CHINAS

dolls for study and admiration

BY MONA BORGER

Photography
by Judy Reed

Borger
PUBLICATIONS

San Francisco, California

CHINAS

For
Ken,
husband and friend.

FIRST PRINTING

Printed in the United States by A R Lithographers,
Hayward, California.

Copyright 1983, Mona Borger

All rights reserved. No part of this publication
may be reproduced, stored in a retrieval system,
or transmitted, in any form or by any means,
electronic, mechanical, photocopying, recording
or otherwise, without the prior permission of the
copyright owner or the publishers.

Library of Congress Catalog Card Number: 83-91074

ISBN 0-9611838-0-2

THANK YOU / JUDY REED, PHOTOGRAPHY / KEN BORGER, BOOK DESIGN / TERRIFIC GRAPHICS, TYPOGRAPHY

3
CHINAS

CONTENTS

4
PREFACE
STUDY & ADMIRATION

5
INTRODUCTION
CHINAS

7
circa 1840
BROWN-HAIRED CHINAS

23
circa 1840
BLACK-HAIRED CHINAS

45
circa 1850
VARIATIONS & INNOVATIONS

Bald Head Glazed Chinas—46
Frozen Charlottes—55
Glass-Eyed & Painted Brown-Eyed Chinas—59
China Infants—70
China Fashion-Type, French—77

87
circa 1860
ABUNDANT & PLAIN

Men & Boys—96

101
circa 1860
FANCY & DECORATED

127
circa 1860–70
THAT BEAUTIFUL FACE

139
circa 1880
BLONDE & BLACK-HAIRED CHILDREN

155
circa 1890
IN CONCLUSION

160
post-1900
THANK YOU

PREFACE

As a collector of antique dolls, I feel that china head dolls have been ignored long enough. The purpose of this book is to show what is available within the china doll realm, while trying to place the dolls in a framework of time that will help us understand and appreciate them. The dolls are here presented for study and admiration.

My first objective is to show the widest assortment I can muster — each kind that could actually be called a china doll — and to explain the strived-for appearance within each group. What to look at, look for and look out for. What to be informed about and what to be tolerant of. What to expect and what to accept and why. What names, mistakenly or not, have been assigned to certain styles. Any tidbits of information of possible interest that might enhance appreciation of this kind of doll.

My second objective is to share some understanding of what you are seeing, so that you can make sensible decisions if you have the opportunity to obtain dolls of china. This book has been arranged into sections according to period. Each section opens with a large color photograph in which dolls of that time are dressed as they might be for an exhibit or a collector's cabinet. Each color photo is followed by black-and-white photos showing the dolls individually, full length or the complete shoulder head, which has been bared so the entire head and shoulder can be seen. (The shoulder shapes of these dolls slowly changed over the years to reflect the silhouette of fashion; when drop-shoulders were stylish, dolls' shoulders sloped.) In most instances, there are as many as three views of each doll presented. Throughout are detailed descriptions of what you are seeing.

Relative value — that is, price — is another subject in itself. Dolls discussed within these covers range in value, at this writing, from forty dollars to six thousand, five hundred dollars. Prices depend on many elusive circumstances, and the best you can do is to arm yourself with a good knowledge of the doll you are interested in obtaining.

If your interest is caught and you become serious about collecting china head dolls, you may want to use the dolls here as a reference. Many are of Blue Ribbon Award quality. There is not a living, breathing doll collector who would not want a doll in their collection to receive a Blue Ribbon Award at a national convention, admit it or not. Within the china doll realm, there are many candidates so deserving. The trick is to know why.

Whether or not you decide to become a collector, I hope that, through these pages, you will come to share my pleasure in — and affection for — the china head doll.

INTRODUCTION

China dolls have been commercially produced since the 1840s. They are dolls with heads made of glazed porcelain, and are usually — even lovingly — called "chinas." More formally, they are known as china head dolls. Whatever the name, they are made from the same materials as the dishes in your dining room or kitchen, and vary just as much as dishware does, according to the basic substances used.

A really fine old china doll may look much like a portrait painted in the middle 1800s — and it should. That is when these dolls were at their best. It is entirely possible that an early china head doll could have been owned by the equivalent of seven generations. Such a doll would certainly count as a true antique.

The merits of the china head doll were realized by the doll-making industry in Europe during the 1840s; previously, doll heads were made from wood and papier-mâché. The traditional doll-making system already was in place, with different models produced merely by changing the hair style. (That tradition continues to this day.) Consumers must have reacted favorably to the introduction of china as a material for doll heads, considering the great number said to have been produced. The original china head doll styles continued to be manufactured during the 1850s, then, with a new gust of enthusiasm, many variations appeared.

Incredible is the fact that these handmade dolls representing women, children and men of such a long-ago time can still be found. China, of course, is not indestructible; dropping a doll could be disastrous. However, the normal passage of time leaves the dolls unaffected; examples are present now at every doll show and sale, and the selection is good. Perhaps fear of the unfamiliar may have kept you from acquiring one. Information about old chinas is scant; consequently this field of collecting is often overlooked or avoided entirely.

The sections following are divided into time periods of varying lengths and are intended to show as closely as possible when each style of doll was introduced. When a section ends and a new one begins, it doesn't mean that the dolls already pictured were no longer produced; rather, it means that new ones came on the scene, in addition. The production of chinas lasted through the turn of the century and into the first decades of the 1900s. Trying to accurately date the dolls is a futile task. The most anyone can hope to do is acquire enough knowledge to approximate the earliest time a doll was produced. When you work with a good many dolls, a pattern begins to emerge. When you find a doll here comparable to one of your own or one you are studying, you should think of yours as a doll of that same era, though it actually may have been made many years later. The photographs have been arranged chronologically within their sections, after much deliberation. Some of these dolls can step one decade back or one forward and not be too far out of their time.

The dolls shown here have all been studied by me personally, and I've described what I saw. My aim has been to be objective. The book is not intended as a final authority — there can be none — but as the effort of a dedicated student and collector trying to put together a puzzle, many pieces of which may never be found.

circa 1840

BROWN-HAIRED CHINAS

This grouping consists of china doll heads whose molded, painted hair styles are brown; usually the dolls are referred to only as "early," as though everyone would know what that meant. The term as used here indicates that these dolls probably were made at the beginning of commercial china doll making, and no one knows for certain when that was. It is assumed to be in the 1840s.

What need not be assumed, but can readily be seen, is that each of these dolls has its own distinctive and aristocratic appearance. None looks doll-like. None looks figurine-like. Each has the look of a person who lived in the 1840s. The hair styles, though strange to us, were worn by people of that time and reflect the fashion of the time. The doll heads show care, thought and ability in the sculpting; the painting is lifelike — the coloring natural, the features sometimes slightly askew. The shoulder heads all have a definite skin tone, either pink or flesh color, which gives them a warm, soft look not usually associated with china dolls.

These dolls are thought to have been made by craftsmen of established factories in Germany and Denmark whose primary business was producing fine porcelain objects. Doll heads may have been made by them as a special commission or simply as a novel idea, or an experiment. Some china doll heads of this type have no marks; some bear marks of undetermined origin; some have marks of these factories: Meissen, Konigliche Porzellan Manufactur (K.P.M.) and Royal Copenhagen.

Marked or not, these are among the cream of the crop, the ultimate china head doll. They were when made and they are now. They are seldom seen, and when seen may go unrecognized, except by the advanced collector. These are rare dolls that seldom change hands.

Dolls in numbered diagram of color photograph are also shown individually in black and white and fully described on pages indicated as follows:
(1) page 9, (2) page 13, (3) page 14,
(4) page 16, (5) page 18, (6) page 20.

circa 1840

Brown hair china lady doll of uncommon coloring and sculpting. Molded hair is the color of rich chocolate syrup, as are eyebrows; no part in the hair style. Very bright blue eyes are concave; pupils are black, the outline of the eyelids is red-orange (usually that line is black), the same color used for mouth and nostril indications. Her skin tone is pink, a darker value on her cheeks, as well as upper eyelids and tip of chin. Modeling of face shows much attention given to the temple and eye area, molded top and bottom eyelids, the corners of the mouth very deep. Note the length of neck and modeling at base of throat, and the defined bosoms. The profile shows a kinship with the next three dolls. The porcelain was pressed into the mold and entire head was glazed white, as though dipped. She is on an old handstitched cloth body, brown script F. at top; wooden arms nailed on. Shoulder measures 4½", total height is 18½". Inside back shoulder she is marked: 🔔 in red 𝓟𝓼 in brown. Upside down, K.P.M. 71
inside front shoulder the mark: KPM in blue. A twice marked K.P.M. doll.

9
circa 1840

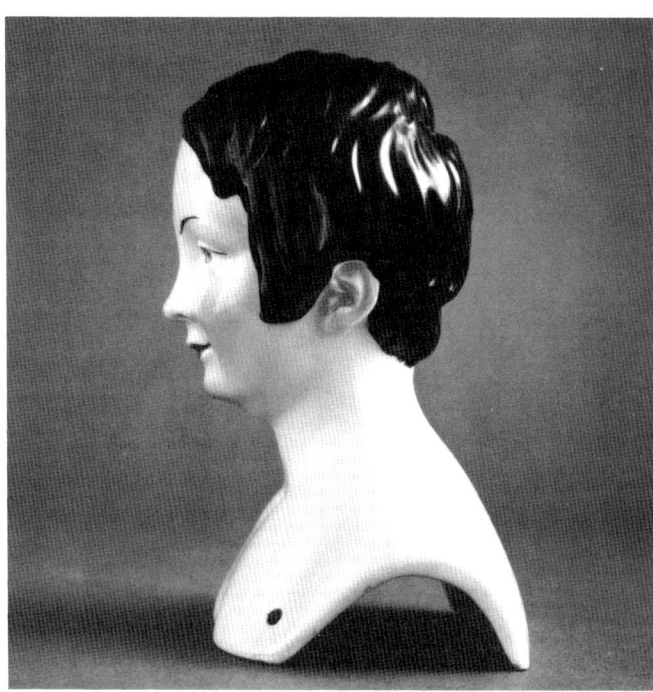

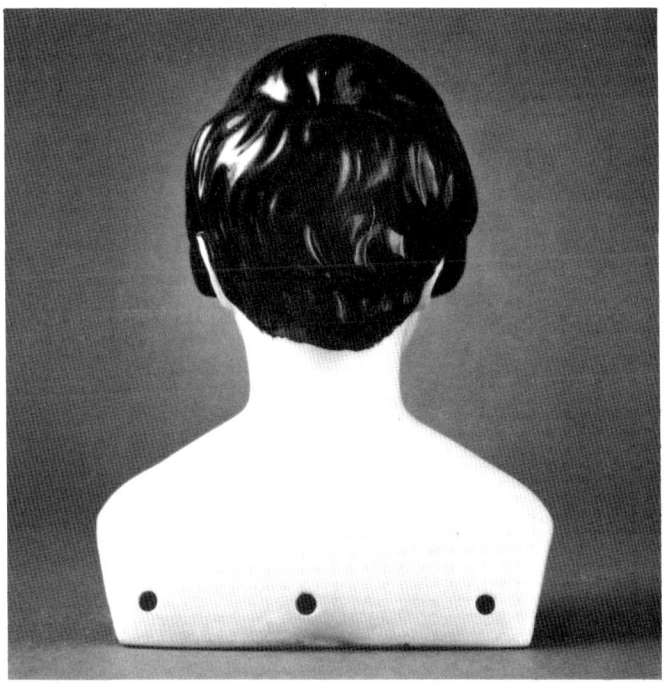

Young man china doll made with the same skill in sculpting and coloring as was the lady doll on the facing page, with a few differences: blue eyes are paler, the skin tone is deep flesh. His face is wider and the neck shorter than that of the lady and he has a double chin; the shoulder is shorter than hers. His hair is deeply modeled, and his detailed, exposed ears are touched with extra flesh color. The detailed sculpting and the color chosen for the painting is this company's style, and though of wonderful color, the actual painting of the features must have been done quickly, almost casually, as eyebrows are not perfectly arched or placed, nor do nostril indications exactly hit the right spot; but all combined give a lifelike and vital appearance. He is on a replacement cloth body, with old china arms. Inside back shoulder at left he is marked: orb in red. Inside front shoulder placed K.P.M. upside down is: the phoenix in grey-blue. He is a marked K.P.M. doll.

Shown in color photograph (1), page 6.

circa 1840

This very special china doll has an overall unique appearance. Her hair style and brilliant coloring are a surprise, even to advanced collectors familiar with the known K.P.M. look. Her painted hair is chocolate brown, swirling at top and about the ears and trailing onto the shoulders. The pink skin tone is obvious, with stronger color on chin and cheeks, but white surrounding the huge concave bright-blue painted eyes. Black pupils. Brown eyebrows. The outline of eyes is bright red-orange, as are the nostrils and full mouth. There is no painted crease line at lids to augment eye expression, and would be unnecessary, as the eye modeling is very deep. Of the four K.P.M. examples shown here, none has the added crease line that we've been told is always part of a good china doll. The shoulder is the shorter type, comparable to the young man K.P.M. doll on page 9, and does not extend to include molded bosoms; thus, she too has a youthful appearance. The leather body has exquisite old pink-toned china arms. The shoulder head measures 4½" and the curl at the top extends it to 4¾". The overall doll height is 18½". Early china dolls with marks can be purchased occasionally when desired and one has sufficient funds; but, regardless of funds, you could wait forever to find a doll of this distinct modeling, coloring and beauty. A very rare shoulder head that has two marks of K.P.M. products: the red orb and the blue phoenix.

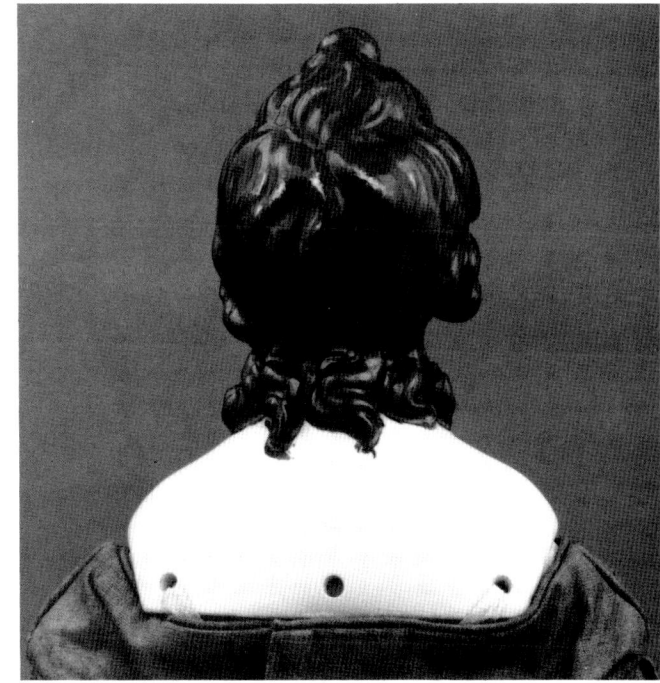

circa 1840

The inside of the shoulder of these dolls is of interest to curious people: look for possible marks of any kind — shown here are photos of marks from doll on page 9, and the scepter mark from doll on page 13 — and look at the porcelain. The porcelain was usually white. To achieve a pink or flesh tone, that color was applied over the white. Actual color can be observed by comparing outside color with the porcelain on the inside of the shoulder. Clear glaze gives the shoulder head its shine; glaze often ran into the shoulder head, and some heads — the early ones — are entirely glazed on the inside. Sometimes the inside porcelain is rather bumpy, indicating that it was pressed into the mold with the fingers, like pie crust into a pan; or it can appear smooth, revealing that it was porcelain poured into the mold in liquid form called "slip." However, these details have little bearing on dating, as one company may have used poured slip — the more sophisticated method — earlier than another. So why look? To observe overall quality and to absorb the idea of how much individual handwork went into the making of the doll.

It is sometimes said that you can tell the date of a china doll by the number of sew holes; note that doll on page 13 has three sew holes in front and two in back; the other examples each have three sew holes in front and back. The shape of the shoulder determined how many holes were needed, and these were then made to suit the purpose, having little to do with date of origin. Dolls on original bodies were often glued on (holes ignored); china shoulder heads on peg-wooden bodies were pegged through the holes to attach them; some shoulder heads were even nailed on through the holes. We now call them sew holes and use them as such.

13
circa 1840

The hair style of this lady china doll makes a difference in her appearance. She too has the same coloring style, and again, she is pink-toned; her hair remains rich brown, styled to show half of each ear, and is brought to center back and a very extended bun. She is slightly larger than the other examples; shoulder head measures 5", and entire doll is nearly 20". She is on a replacement cloth body, but has old pink-toned china arms sewn to the cloth upper arms through two sew holes. This shoulder head has been, at some unknown time, professionally and carefully repaired so that her K.P.M. mark is still evident, inside the right shoulder: ↕ in blue.
      KPM
She remains a marked K.P.M.

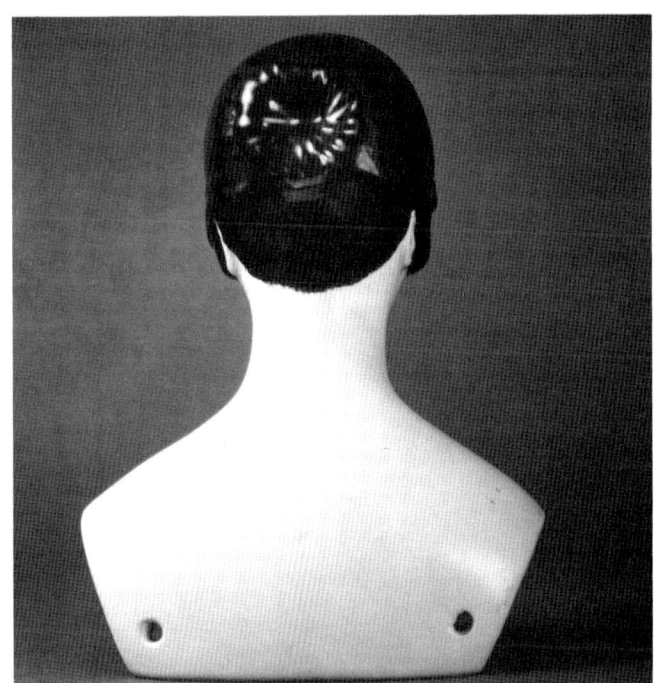

Shown in color photograph (2), page 6.

14
circa 1840

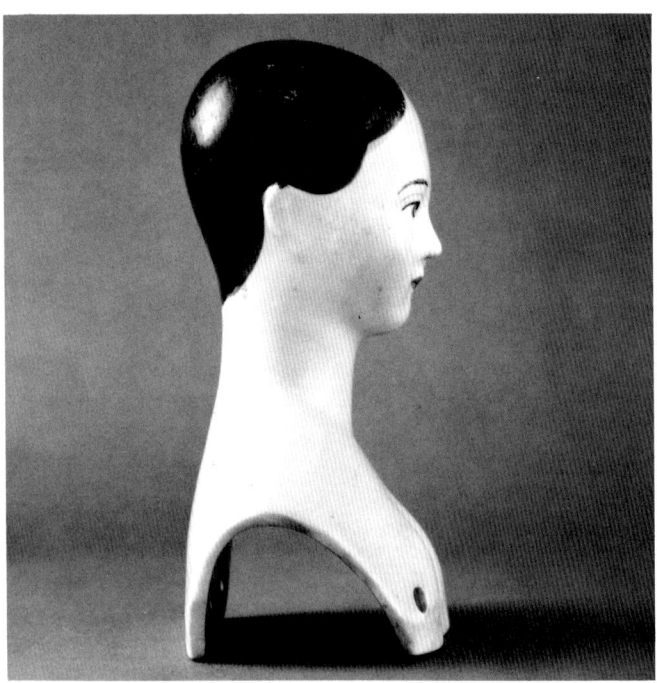

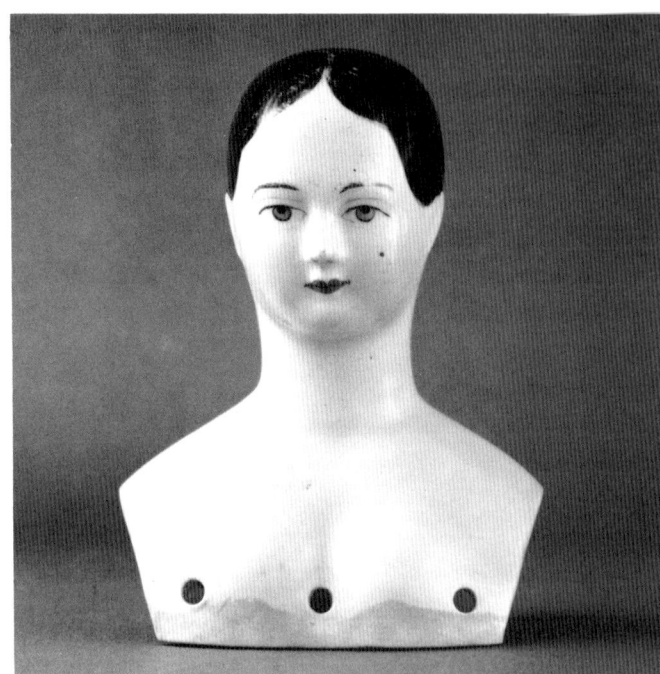

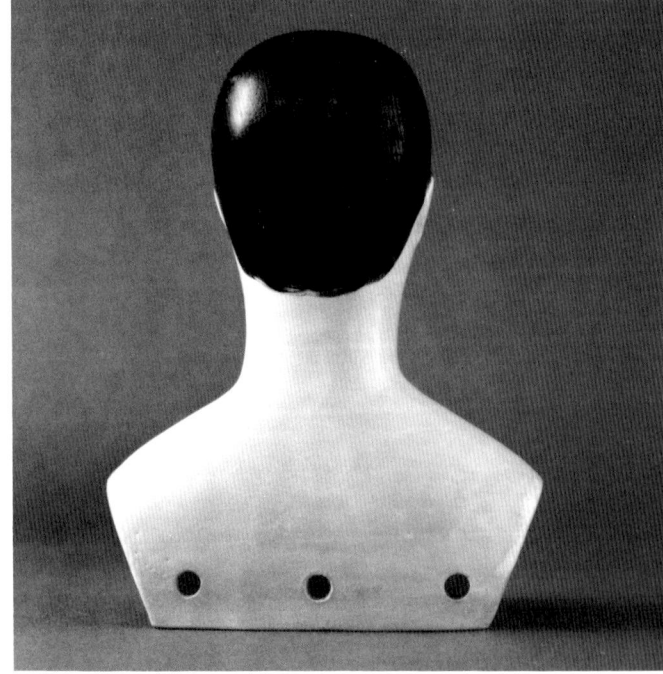

The severe look of this brown-haired lady is of great interest. Her head is smoothly formed with no modeling to suggest hair. It is painted with obvious quick strokes, similar to results of finger painting, though this appears to have been done with a brush. The direction of the painted strokes divides the hair from the forehead to center top, with an additional division, crosswise, down to each ear; her molded ears are not well defined. Her skin tone is flesh, her mouth is red-orange, her cheeks have a light touch of that color. The first eyelid line is brown; her eyebrows are brown, painted with quick, light, brief strokes, called feathered eyebrows. Her eyes are pale blue, irises are outlined with black, and inner eye dots and eyelid crease lines are red-orange. Height is 5¾", and she has a red *G.* under glaze inside back shoulder, unknown as to origin and meaning. There is a china man doll with similar painting style known to exist; his hair modeling is detailed, and the mark inside that shoulder is a black *C.* .

Shown in color photograph (3), page 6.

15
circa 1840

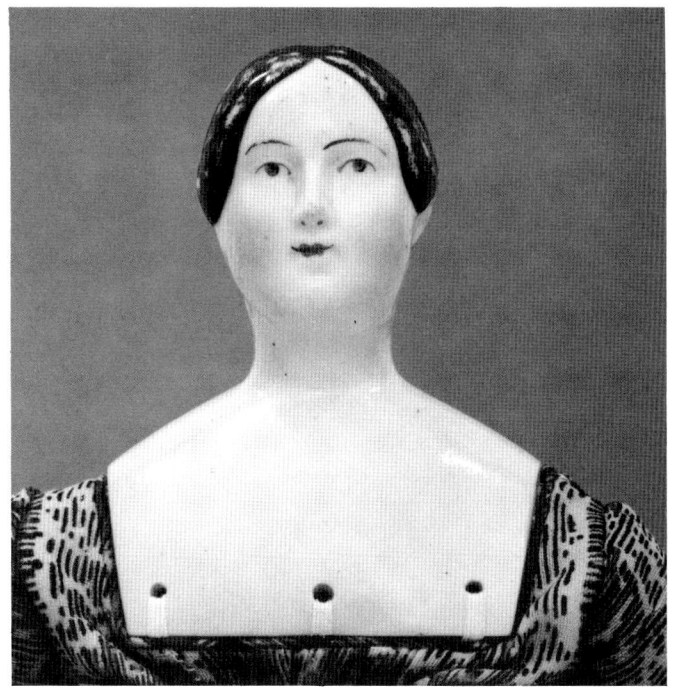

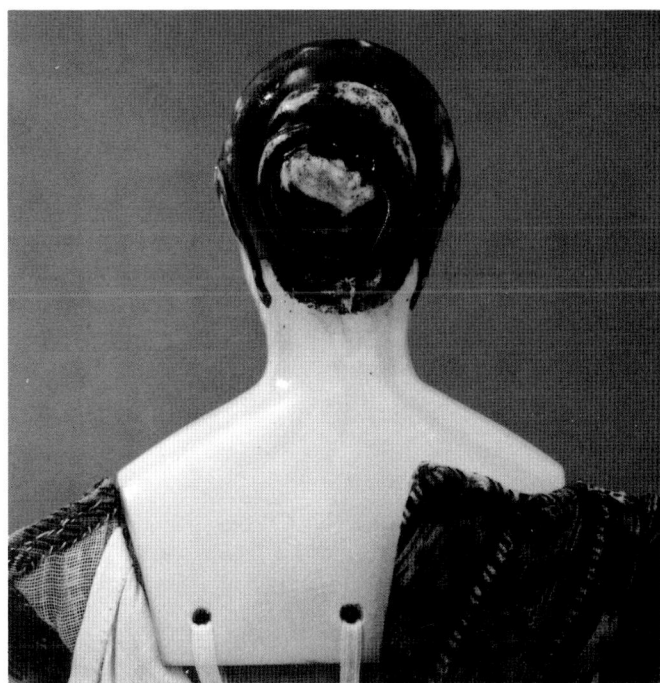

This brown-haired china doll appears to be one of the group made by The Royal Copenhagen Manufactory. Her coloring is the key to what she might be: brown hair and brows, red eyelid outline ending in red inner eye dot, cream-color complexion with additional red-orange tint on cheeks, chin and exposed ears. Her hair style was also a factor: a gracefully draped and wrapped large coil at center back of head, with single curl hanging down behind each ear. The shoulder head measures 3⅝", total doll 14". Due to her small size, some of the molding effect may be lost; she is scuffed, and has had entire shoulder rebuilt. So, why bother? Rarity! If she were to be found in good condition and, especially, in a larger size, she could be magnificent and probably marked. As she is, she is useful for study and the pondering of possibilities yet to be found.

16
circa 1840

A brown-haired, brown-browed, pink-toned china lady of superior quality and great beauty. She has black eyelid lines, with red inner eye half circles (rather than dots) and concave modeling of her very large painted blue eyes. Extremely large features in proportion to face; she is simply and deftly painted, and lifelike in attitude. There is nothing about her that one could think to improve. The shoulder head measures 5⅝" and total doll height is 21½". She is marked IH in green under the shoulder, a 4 incised at center back. The meaning of the marks has not been determined. The doll on the next page may add some light.

Shown in color photograph (4), page 6.

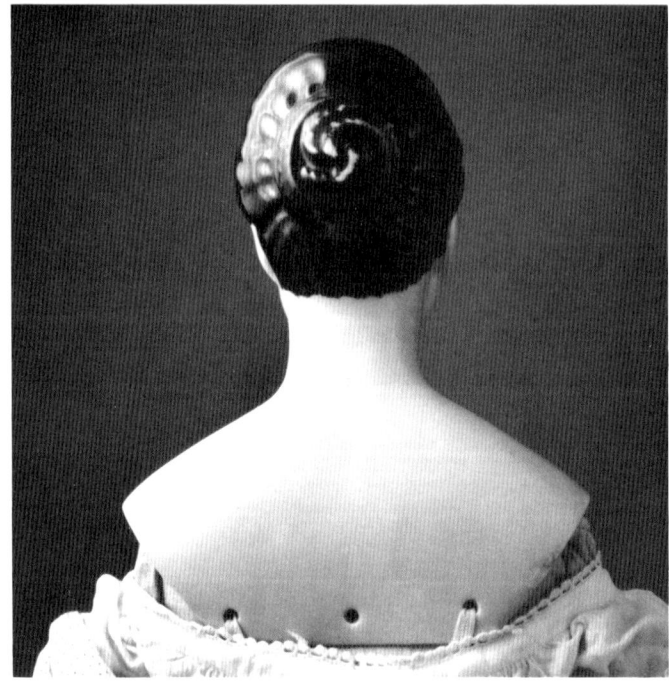

circa 1840

A boy doll of china with brown hair sculpted to indicate a side part, exposing well-modeled ears; pink-toned, but leaving whites of eyes white; shoulder is round at base, an unusual shape. Rounded face, fore-shortened nose, fullness under chin, and short neck all give a childlike impression. The painting style and color same as that of previous lady. Note that features fill a generous portion of the face; eyes are concave and painted blue. He is on an old pink leather body; leather arms and ungusseted legs. Shoulder head measures 4", total height is 15½". Inside back shoulder indications:

$=$ faint, dark 2 impressed with die
                  $/$ in green

The marks here seem to have been of use to the manufacturer, and not an indication of what company made the item; they are symbols of individual workers, or model, or a combination. There is yet another known model with 0 marking and IH in green. Might there be a 1 and 3, and what could they look like?

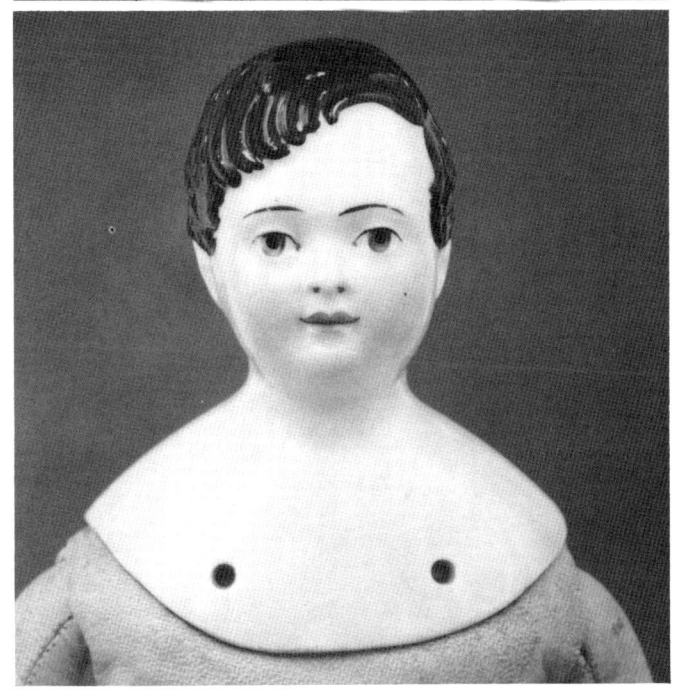

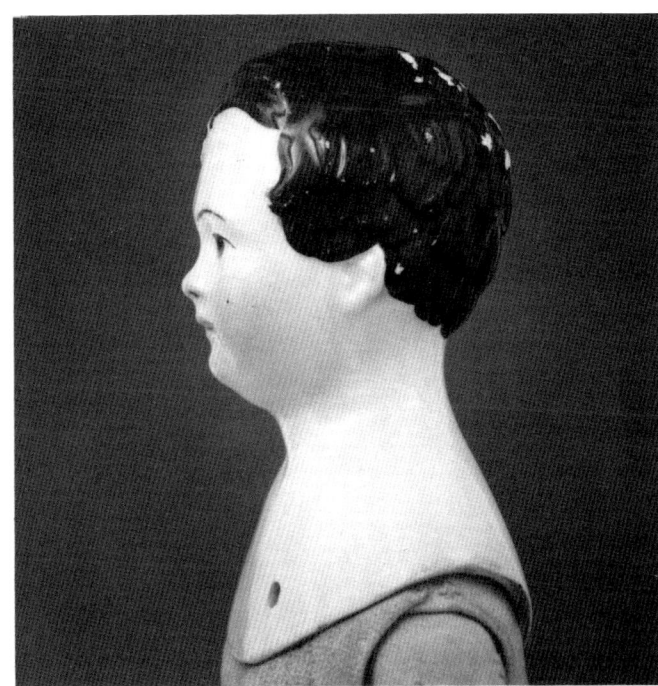

circa 1840

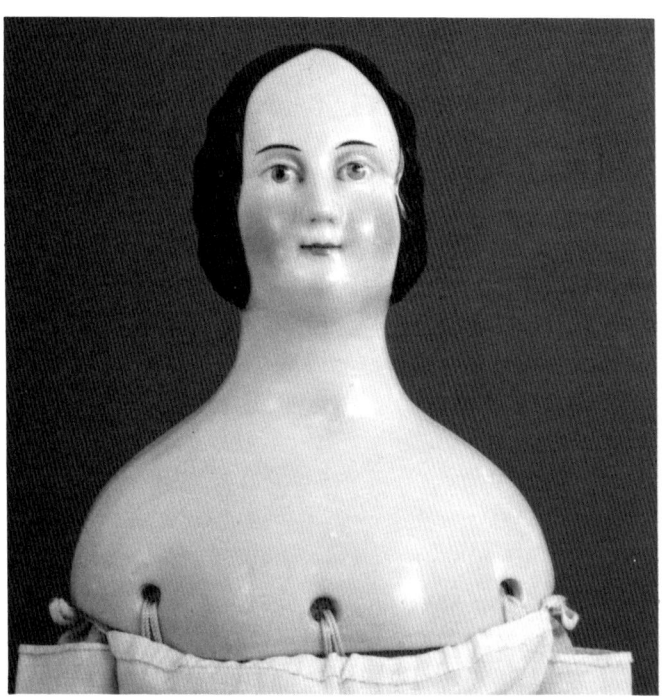

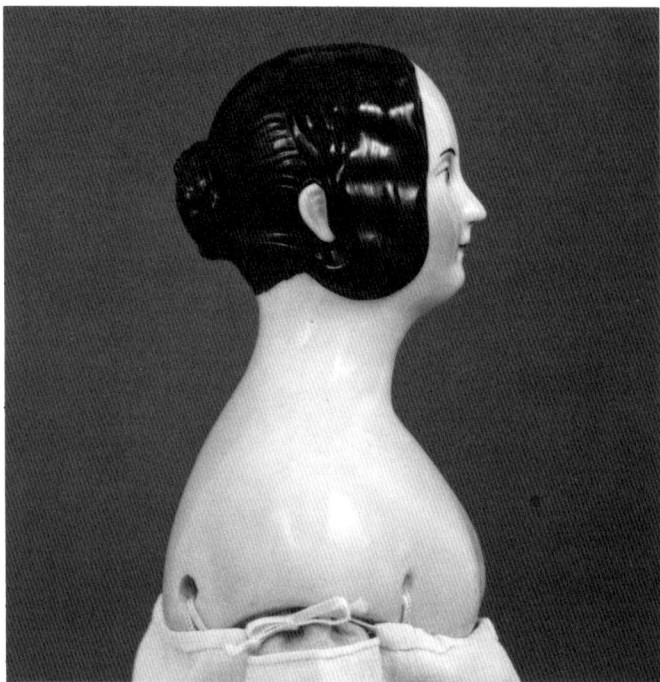

The shaping of the shoulders sets this doll apart from prior examples and places her in a group with the next two dolls; however, a subtle difference in coloring sets her apart even from them. The silhouette shows a long neck; it is broad at the base, not slender; the shoulders are deep enough to include the upper part of the arm and the bosom; indented modeling indicates the difference between torso and arm. The brown hair is very dark, the detail of hair style can be seen in photograph; her skin tone is creamy flesh, accented with pink on cheeks, chin, upper eyelids, hollow of throat and well-modeled ears. Her eyelid lines are pink; the irises are grey-blue, with a small square-shaped void of the iris color, which acts as a highlight; the pupils are black. The highly luminous quality of the eye painting gives eyes a sparkling effect. The paint on this doll was thoughtfully, carefully and lovingly applied. Pressed into mold; three sew holes in front, two in back; measures 4½" and total height is 18½". There are two separate numerals impressed on outside of back shoulder: at left a 6, at right a 5.

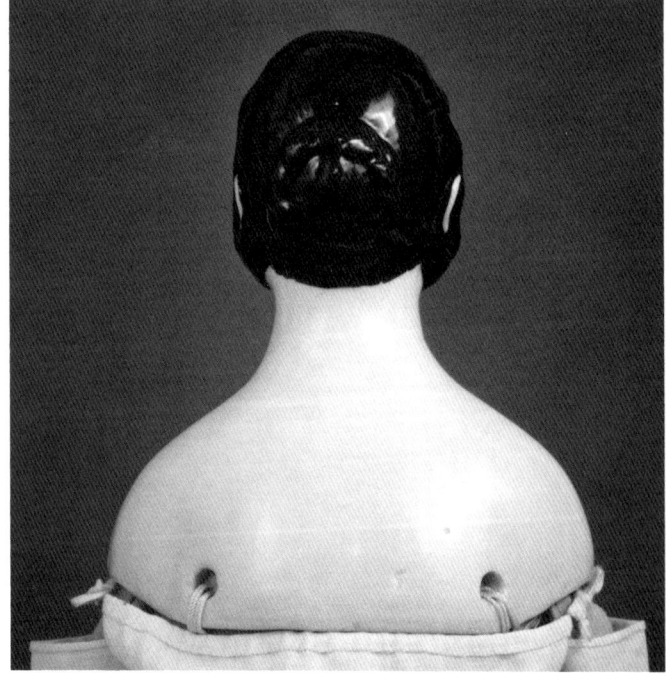

Shown in color photograph (5), page 6.

19
circa 1840

This brown-haired doll was made from same model as preceding example; differences may not be apparent in photographs, as they have to do with color. Her skin tone is pink, accented with deeper pink only on cheeks, chin and ears. Her eyebrows are brown, as are her lid lines, ending with dark pink inner eye dots. The irises are definitely blue, with same highlight treatment. The brown hair is back to rich chocolate color. Her overall height — 4½" — is slightly less than that of the preceding doll, and she appears to be wider. It is possible that in the kiln firing one group may have shrunk more than another, or that a new mold was made at another time, as this lady lacks the depth of modeling around eye and mouth, and hair detail. There is not enough difference to consider them two distinct sizes. She has the number 6 impressed on back shoulder at right.

At some time, the doll met with an accident, but no broken parts were lost. Her beauty is unscathed down to the base of her neck; her shoulder has been carefully glued together. I find this an acceptable condition in a doll of this beauty, vintage and rarity, but would expect to pay considerably less than if she were undamaged. In groups of china dolls more easily obtainable, I would reject this condition in favor of a perfect one. This is a personal attitude, controversial to some, disputed by many.

20
circa 1840

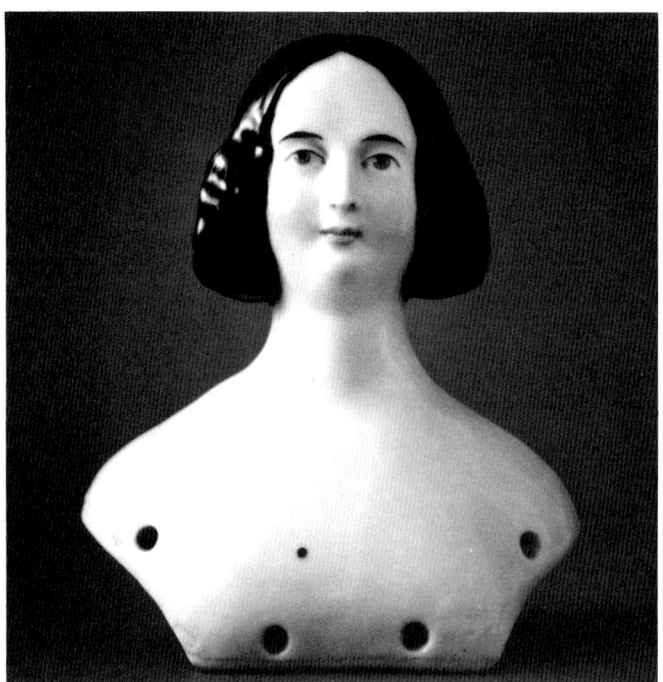

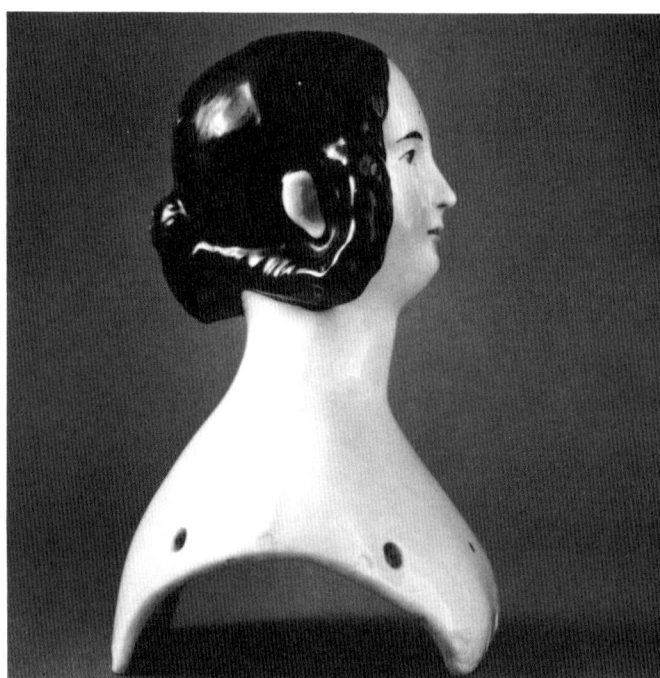

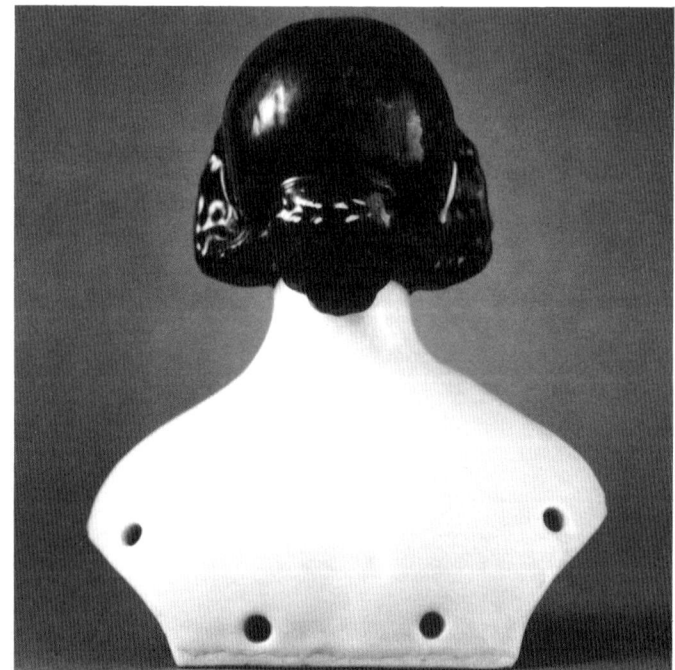

The last in this cluster of three has a most unique hair style and unusual shoulder shape. Note four sew holes in front and back and their placement. Her eyes are grey-blue, and skin tone is creamy flesh (like example, page 18), with added pink on cheeks, chin and ears; eyebrows and eyelid lines are brown (like example, page 19). Her very dark brown hair is arranged close to cheeks, with broad, wavy swags draped in front and under exposed ears, then brought to low center back and ending with five neatly placed curls under a heavy cross braid. Certainly this is remote from our present-day concept of beauty. All three ladies have their chins held high; dolls and portraits of this time often have heads tilting down. This shoulder head measures 5", total height is 19", on a cloth body with well-detailed old china arms. There is a depression on right center back of shoulder suggesting the intent of a numeral, not well formed, thus illegible.

Shown in color photograph (6), page 6.

21
circa 1840

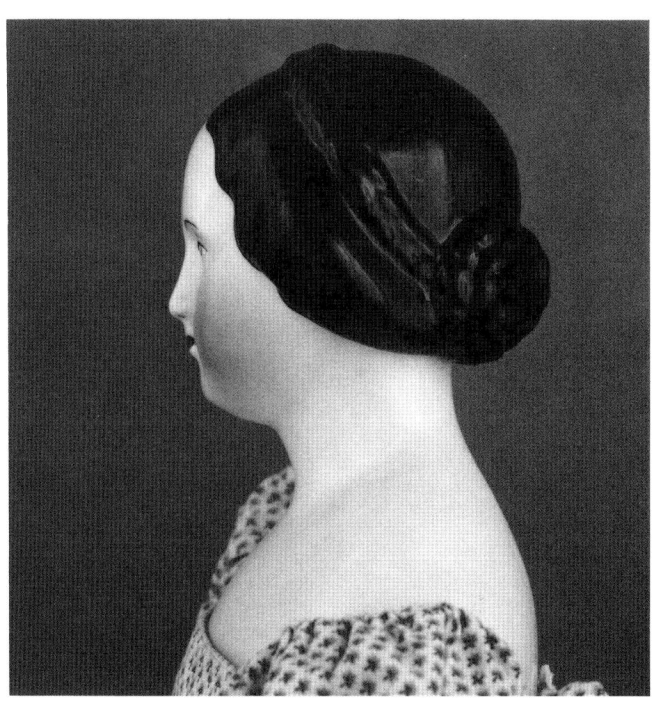

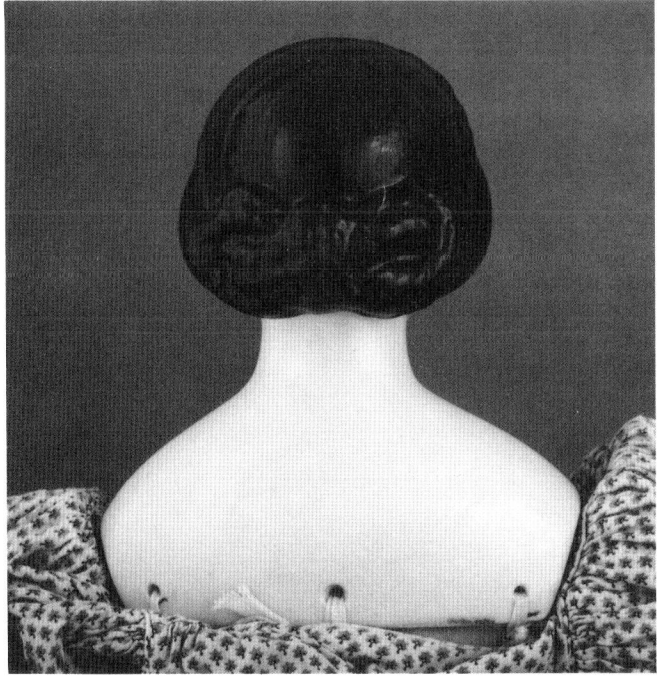

Lady china doll with painted rich brown hair: braid circling head, crossing center part, ending at nape of neck wrapped around bun in a figure eight. An upright, smaller braid is located at center of bun arrangement. The shoulder head is of poured china, but heavy, thick and white, with clear glaze running to inside, while the pink tone was carefully kept only on outside of shoulder. She has black eyebrows and black outline at top of eye, blue outline beneath; irises are two shades of blue; pupils are black with white highlight picked out of paint in a dot shape. The eyelid crease line and the mouth are painted brick-red. The painted lines are smooth, sharp and deftly placed. This doll may be the product of a doll manufacturer, rather than of the luxury porcelain makers, but is placed with this group because of her coloring and simplicity. There are no marks of any kind. The shoulder head is 6¼" high, and the whole doll, on old, stuffed cloth body with hand-sewn leather arms with separated fingers, is 24¼" tall.

circa 1840

BLACK-HAIRED CHINAS

Doll manufacturers in Germany and Denmark produced china head dolls during, and long beyond, this decade, as verified by reprints of pages from doll and toy catalogues. Chinas took their place by the side of papier-mâché dolls, established interest, and became a thoroughly commercial, staple product.

Understand that these doll heads were made from molds. Once a model for making a mold was created, resulting doll heads could be produced for as many years as that design was popular enough to sell. The time assigned here to a doll should be thought of only as the beginning of the period in which that doll could have been made.

Some chinas made in this period are lady dolls with long graceful necks and well-molded bosoms. Their black painted hair styles cover the ears and sweep up in back into buns or braided coronets — plain, simple and typical of this time. Skin tones are often pink, sometimes quite deep in value, or flesh-colored.

Children are represented by a stockier silhouette, with shorter facial features and shorter necks. They may also have pink or flesh-toned complexions, as well as various hair styles often thought of as a lady's: short, windblown; or smooth on top, center-parted with ringlets — either curved or hanging straight. Occasionally there is a side part, thought to indicate a man or boy.

The modeling shows skill and concern with establishing a firm difference between ladies and children. The painting is well done, detailed, often highly exact, and warm in color, as though high standards were carefully maintained to reach a fine finished product. Marks that signify known companies are not apt to be found in these dolls; but old-style script initials sometimes appear, painted inside the shoulder, as well as incised numbers, which may pertain to the model's style or size.

Dolls in numbered diagram of color photograph are also shown individually in black and white and fully described on pages indicated as follows:
(1) page 31, (2) page 36, (3) page 38, (4) page 40, (5) page 95.

circa 1840

A china lady shoulder head, painted hair like black satin, contrasted with deep pink toned complexion; a fine example of "Damenkoph" — lady heads, as seen in old catalogue reprints — complete with obvious bust modeling. She could be used as a reference guide for looking at china lady dolls of this period:

hair, black
eyebrows, black
eyelid line, black
pupils, black, with white highlight
iris outline, black
iris, blue
eyeball area, left white when pink tone was applied
crease line, in upper lid, red-orange
inner eye dots, C-shaped, red-orange
nostril indications, open oval in red-orange line
mouth, lips separated, red-orange
cheeks, additional color over glaze
eyelids, molded, can be seen and can be felt with finger
long neck
molded bust line
complexion, deep pink tone
part in hair, white line follows V-shape modeling
inside shoulder, white, all glazed, pressed in mold
body, none, few could actually retain originals
size, shoulder head measures 5"
dark spots, present, most are pinpoint holes in glaze that accumulated dirt; indicative of old heads; if annoying, can often be soaked away
any marks? painted script *F.* in black incised *10.*

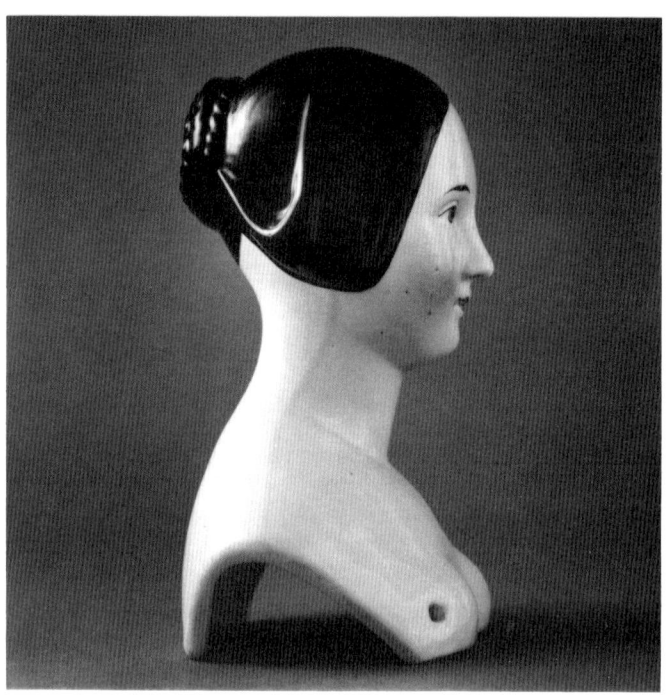

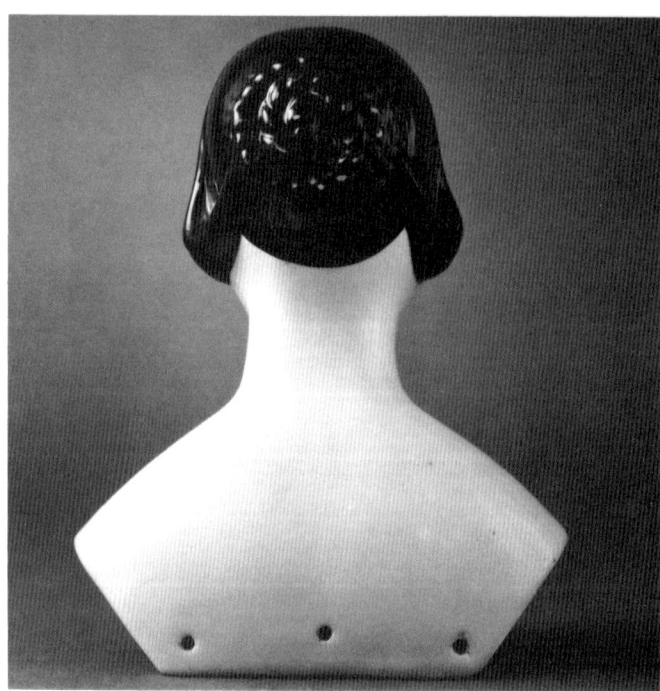

circa 1840

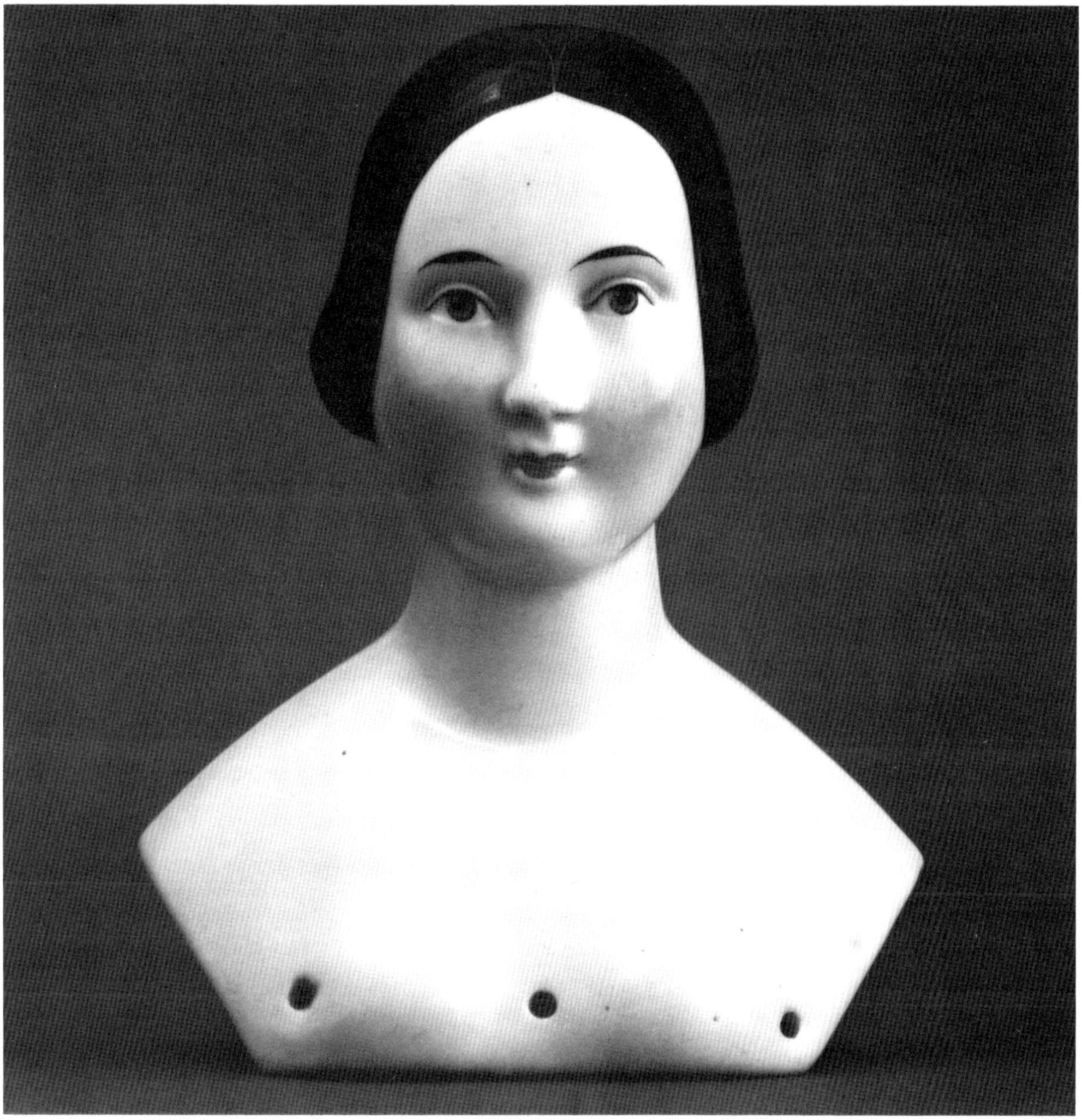

A shoulder head of this caliber is sometimes obtainable as head only; there is no body. Some collectors object to a purchase of this type, and it is their privilege to set rules for themselves. But do not let anyone dissuade **you** from obtaining a beautiful china head just because there is no body. If making the body yourself is within your abilities, and you maintain the right proportions for the era, and dress the doll to your satisfaction, you may truly enjoy your purchase more than another that needed no help. Traditionally, chinas often were sold as separate heads for use with homemade bodies; if you realize that, you will have little trouble with this idea. My experience has been that the most desirable china heads are the least likely to still have their original bodies. As it is now 140 years since some of these dolls were produced, it is reasonable that frail cloth bodies might not have endured and may have been replaced long ago.

26
circa 1840

This era appears to be the beginning of this kind of china doll, called "Kinderkoph" — child head — in old catalogues. This one has wavy, windblown-styled black hair; brushmarks surround face. Highlighted eyes are brown; eyelids outlined in black; crease lines above are red-orange, as are parted lips and cheeks. Lightly pink-toned over all except eyeball area; that remains white. Old cloth body; leather arms with long, individually separated fingers, handstitched. Shoulder head measures 6⅜", total doll 24½". Inside shoulder is an *H* painted black.

Brushmarks are the result of lifting the brush lightly at the end of a stroke so that the paint tapers to many fine individual hairlike lines; often used with dolls to soften hard edges and give hair a wispy look. Sometimes called stippling, an incorrect term.

This child style, meant to serve as either boy or girl, in accordance with apparel customs at that time, still often leaves you with the impression of a definite boyish or girlish look; though this doll is dressed in an ankle-length lady's garment, you can't help but call it him.

27
circa 1840

This windblown-styled, black-haired china shoulder head may have been manufactured to represent a child, but in this instance depicts a very different sort. The 4½"-tall shoulder head is on an early stiff-legged leather body with leather arms; the costume, representing a regional area, was not researched to my satisfaction. However, it had particular meaning to someone, as it is all handstitched, hand-embroidered, fits the body with perfection, and is complete down to petticoats, leg and feet coverings — no drawers. The shoulder head has all the features and details of the early child style, except there is no complexion tone. Looking for marks under this doll's shoulder was out of the question because of the beautifully made and close-fitting costume; I left it undisturbed. Total height is 20½".

28
circa 1840

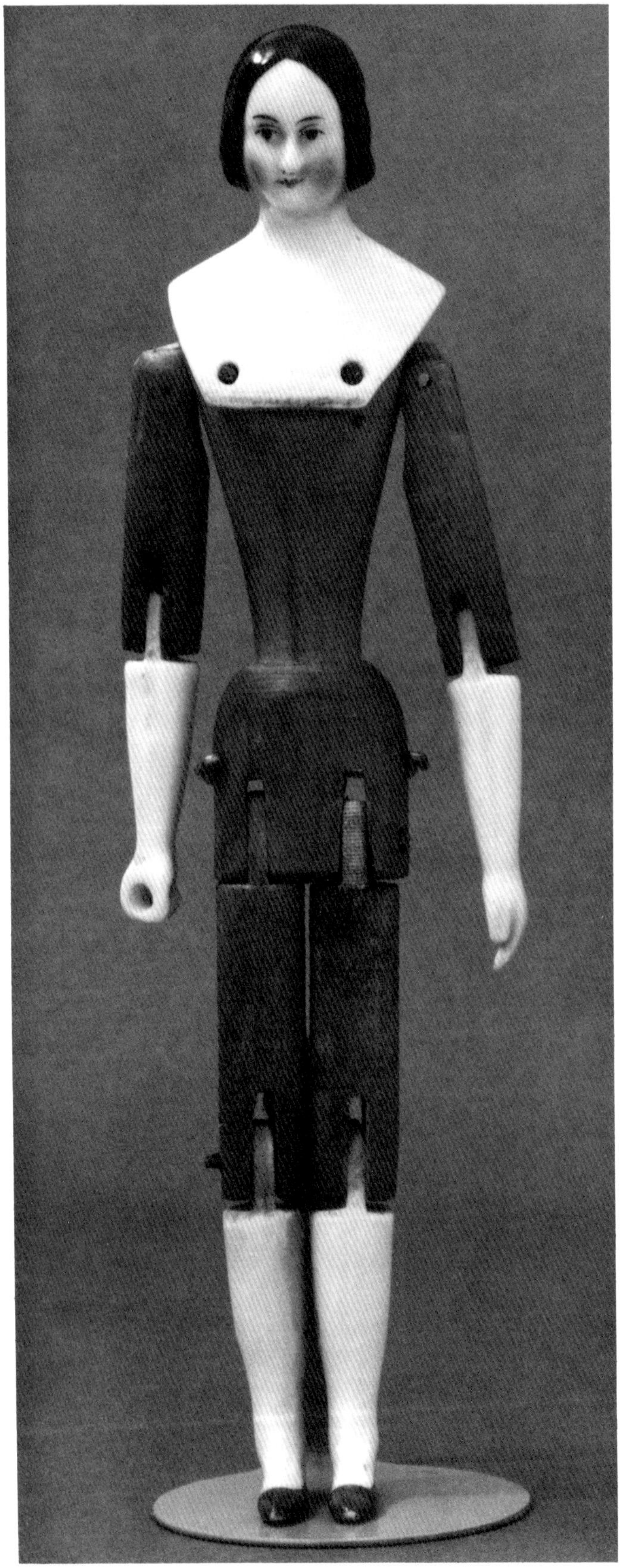

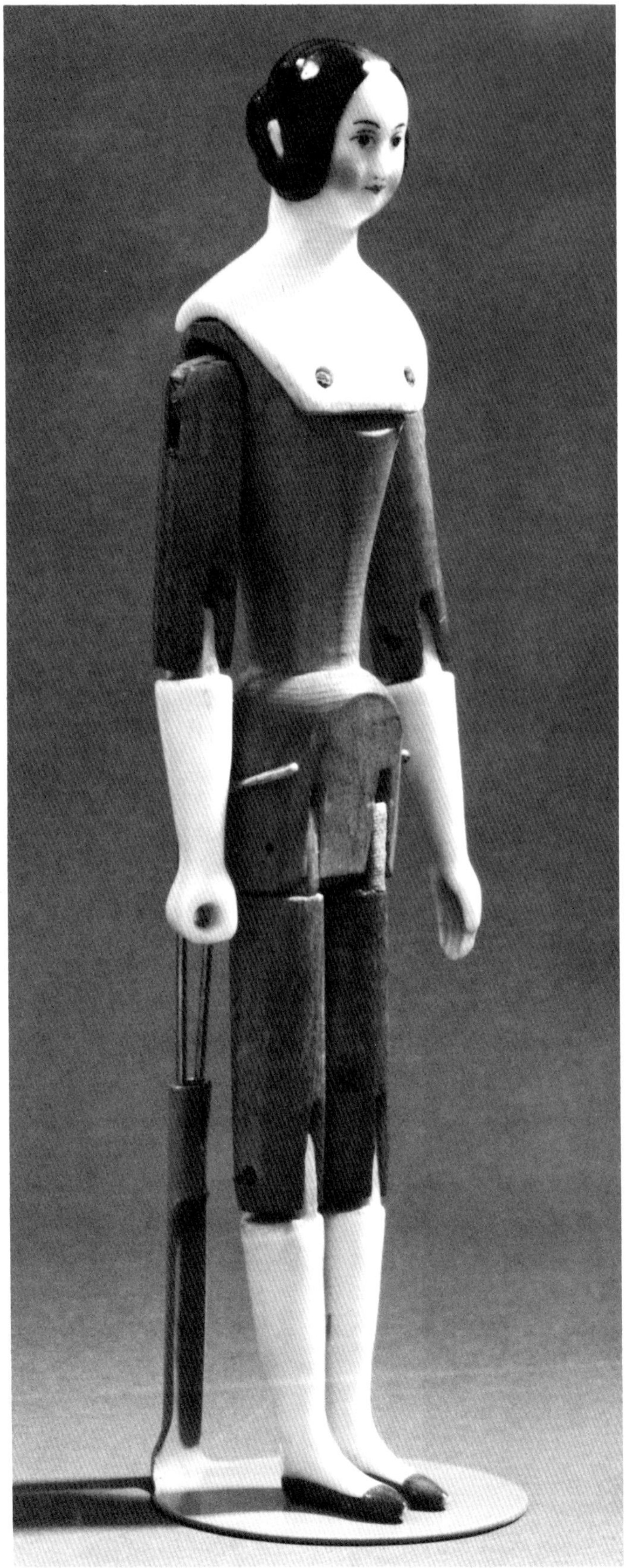

circa 1840

China Head Doll,
articulated peg-wooden body

Usually a doll is called china head, if, indeed, her head is made of china; or bisque doll, if her head is made of bisque, regardless of her body material. This doll, whose head, arms and legs are china, should properly be called a china head doll. However, her body is so seldom found that it is hard not to call her peg-wooden with china head. In other words, the most distinctive feature of a given type is usually placed first in the title. Call her what you will, but realize that for a doll only 6½" tall this china doll has remarkable attributes. She has a well-molded 1840s hair style with exposed ears and bun in back; her facial painting has every desirable detail, and along with that, she has brown eyes and a pink tone on head and arms; her shoes are orange. The hand of her right arm is shaped in a circle, like a doughnut — enabling her to hold something, possibly a walking staff or accessory. Her left hand is in a relaxed position, the usual hand style. The china arms and legs are fashioned with extended tabs in which there is one small hole. The tabs fit into a slot in the wooden upper arms and legs. A small wooden peg slips through the matching holes, joining the parts. The shoulder joint allows the arms to be twisted, as well as lifted or lowered; the elbow and knee joints allow for bending; the the hip joint allows for sitting.

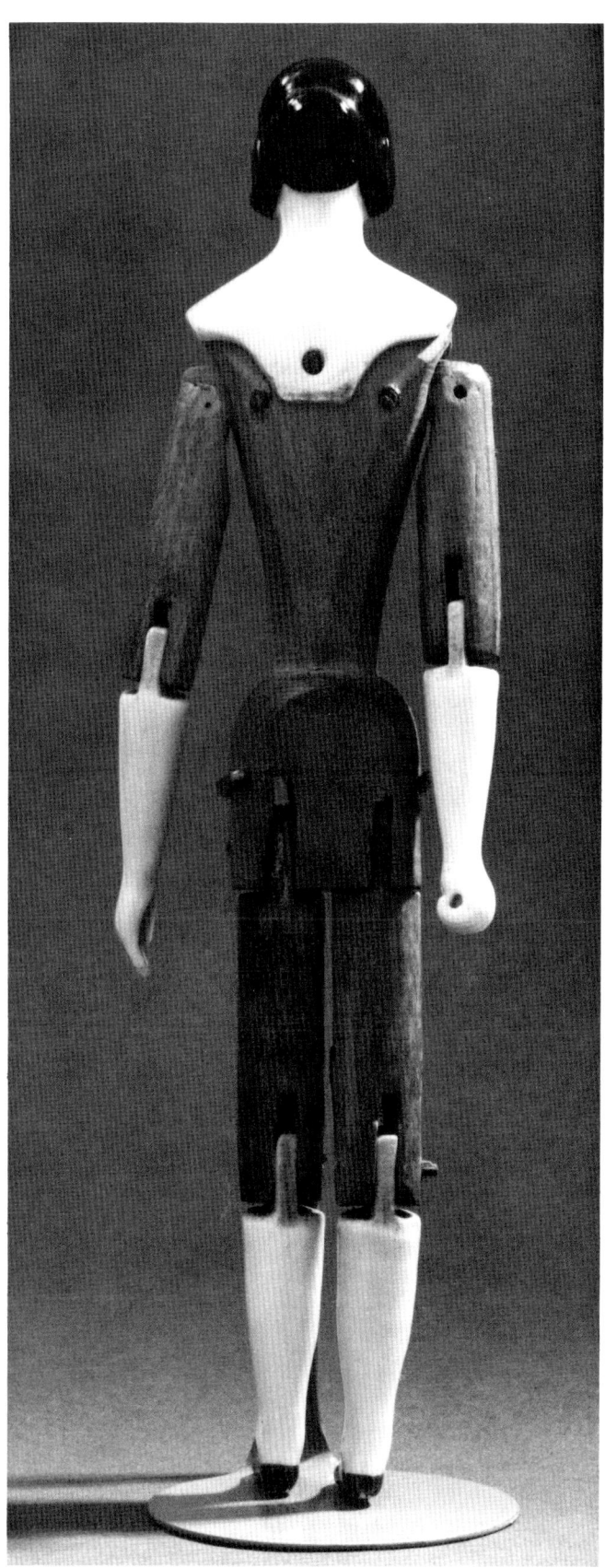

30
circa 1840

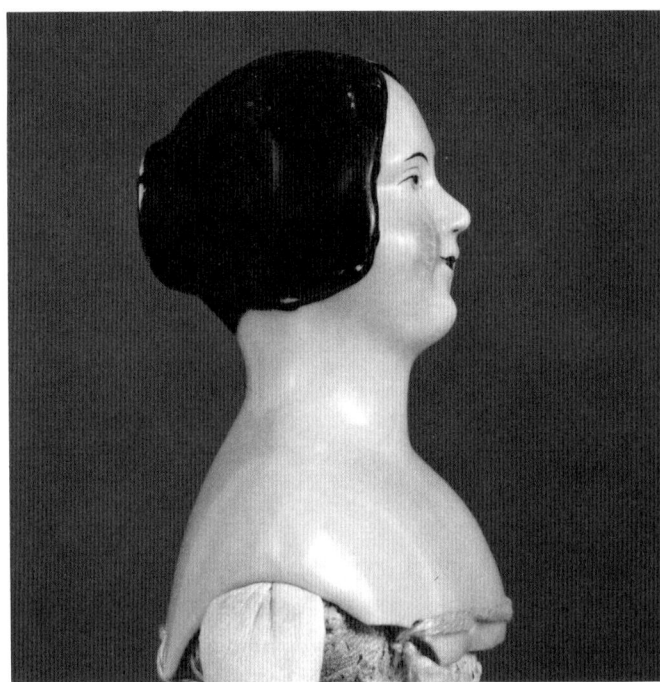

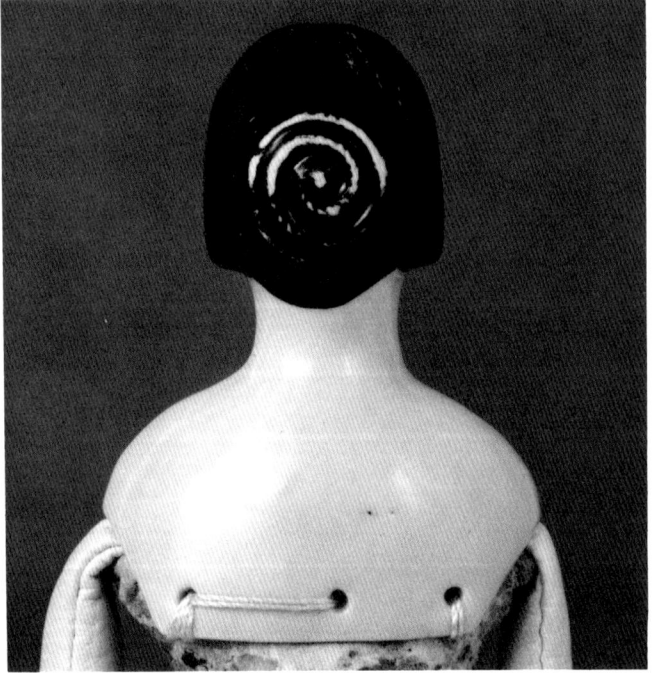

This doll's fat cheeks and narrow forehead give her a different look from that of the other braided coronet ladies. However, her black hair and covered ears, light pink tone, and facial features all are in keeping with the period. She came on a worn leather body with stiff legs, no gusseting, shaped feet, all handstitched; arms were missing. Though she is worn and scuffed, the unusual shaping of her face and that very old leather body make her of interest. Shoulder head is 4½" and total doll is 18½".

circa 1840

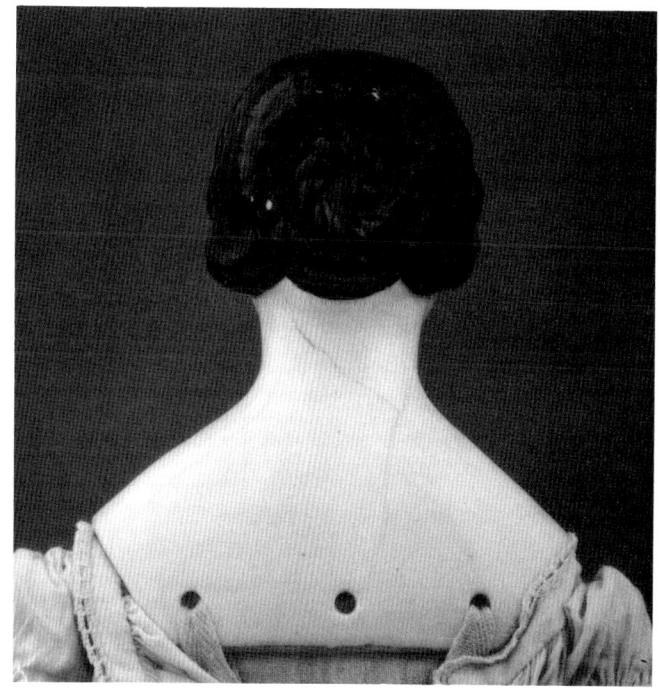

Black hair is waved down from V-shaped modeling at center forehead to enclose ears and brought to back of head where braid is wound into coil. The V-shaped modeling acts as the part, no white line; modeling is distinct. Her well-painted eye detail includes large blue eyes, black and red-orange outlines. She is lightly pink-toned, and has an old commercial cloth body, marked #3; leather arms. Shoulder head measures 4¼" and total height is 17". Inside shoulder is incised 8.

Shown in color photograph (1), page 22.

circa 1840

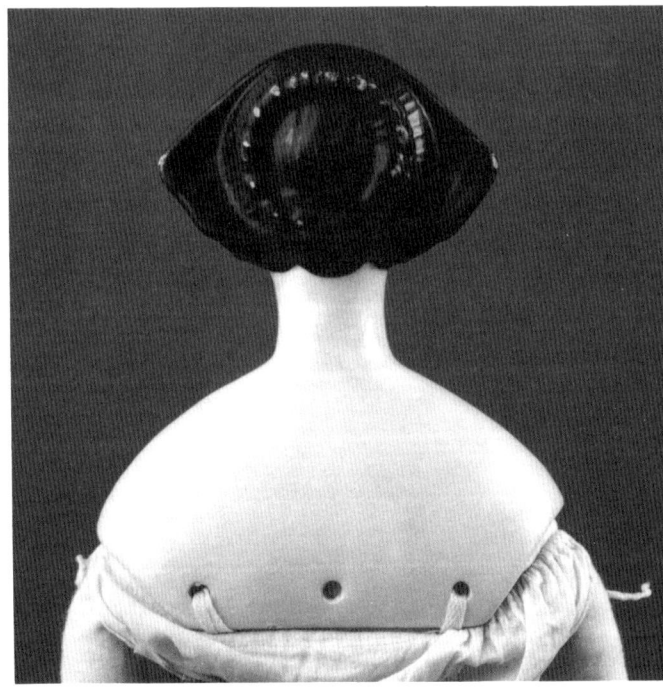

The expected braided coronet hair style waved down to cover ears with additional unexpected feature: a smoothly molded extension on each side and across top of head — a cap — similar to a nurse's cap. It is open at the crown so the hair detail shows, but is painted black, like the hair. Finely detailed highlighted blue eyes; fine thick and thin black strokes outline molded lids, even finer red crease line above. Her neck is extremely long, shoulder is very wide and deep, with contoured bust. Cloth body with old china arms. Her condition lacks merit, her interest and rarity outweigh that. Her unmarked shoulder head has three sew holes, front and back, is 4⅞" high; entire doll is 18½".

circa 1840

A black-haired, blue-eyed smaller doll with a complete old leather body. The wavy hair covering ears is flared out at the bottom, in a style sometimes called "spaniel ears." As she is small, some expected details are lacking; no painted crease line in lids, no complexion tone, no hair part. She has defined bust line and three sew holes, front and back. Her body is probably original, judging by perfect fit of body to shoulder; pink leather, three-seam seat, small waist; shapely ungusseted legs end in tiny feet, and arms end with mitten hands, separated thumbs. Handstitched; faded and worn, but an example of one kind of complete body that was used with this type doll. Shoulder head measures 2¾", complete doll is 10⅝". She wore a homemade cotton dress, laced for closure, full skirt applied to bodice with gauging, and one petticoat.

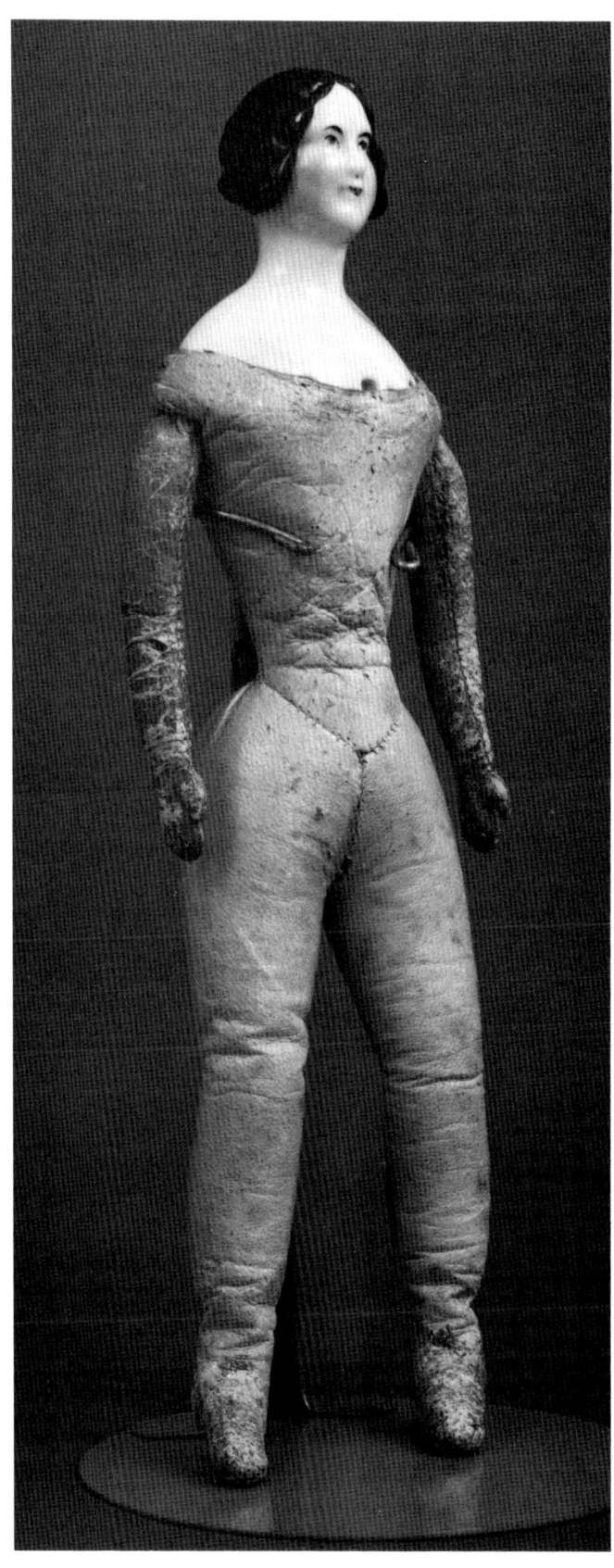

circa 1840

A large comb, painted to look like tortoise shell, is located high in center of coronet arranged with braids wrapped four to five times around the back of the head; the black hair is also close to the cheeks and encloses the ears. Her complexion is flesh-toned, eyeball area left white, with added pink on cheeks. Highlights in blue irises of eyes, small black pupils, single black eye outline; her mouth is red-orange. A dark red color is used for inner eye dots, nostril dots and single stroke dividing lips; a most distinctive color selection was used here. Her body is old cloth, commercial, with leather arms; her costume depicts Russian festival attire for quality lady. Shoulder head is 6" high and whole doll is 24½". Inside shoulder shows: poured into mold, and a 36 in red paint; outside center back, a small 1 is impressed. Her long neck, wide shoulders and erect bearing add to her formidable quality — she commands the cabinet.

36
circa 1840

A child doll, often used as a lady doll. The hair style was worn by girls, boys and ladies, as seen in 19th century fashion prints; doll collectors sometimes call it "covered-wagon" style. This molded version is black, combed from center top to form thirteen curls that curve following the shape of the head and end at chin level. A detail to note is the eyebrow painting style called **two-toned** — a grey margin surrounds the heavy black stroke of the brow. This doll is a fine example: well-molded and painted, and very pink in tone. Broad, deep shoulder, short neck and no bust definition. Old cloth commercial body with old pink-toned arms and legs. Her shoulder head measures 5¼"; entire height is 20¾".

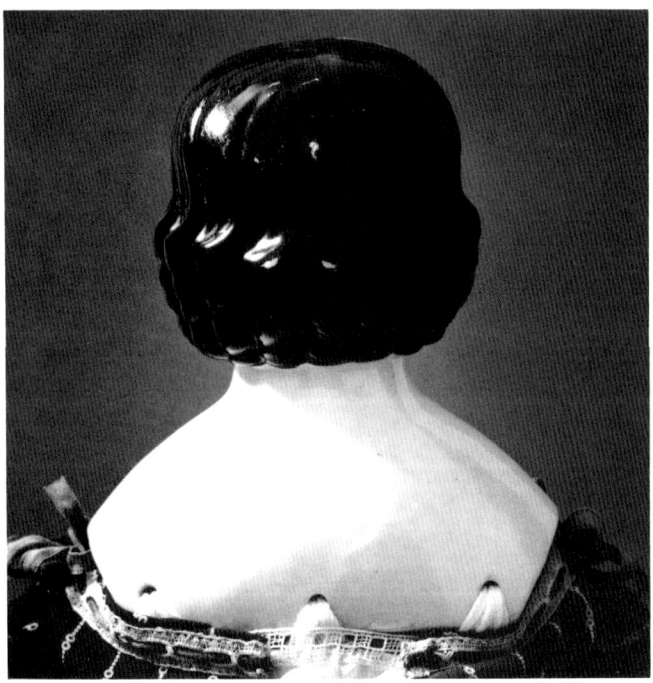

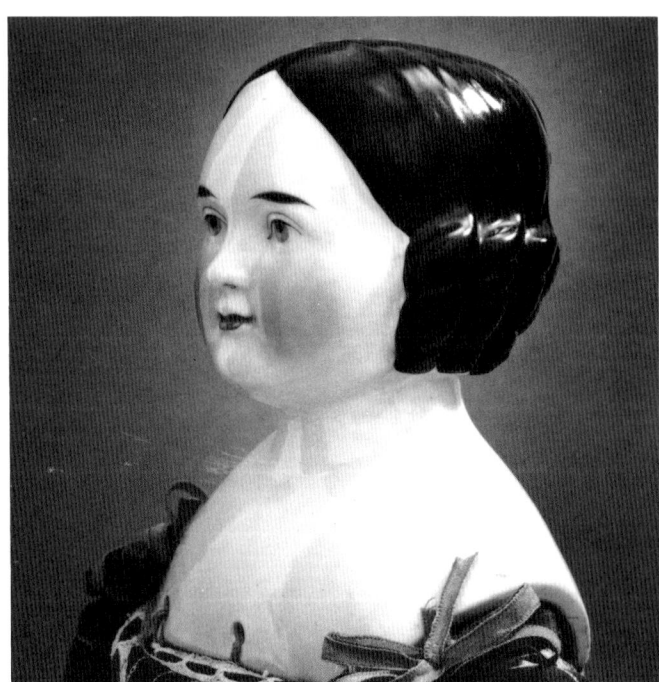

Shown in color photograph (2), page 22.

37
circa 1840

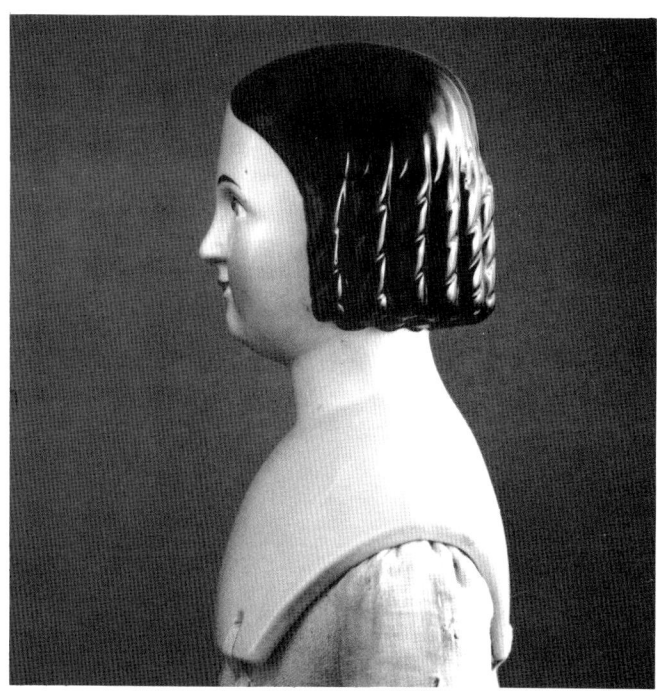

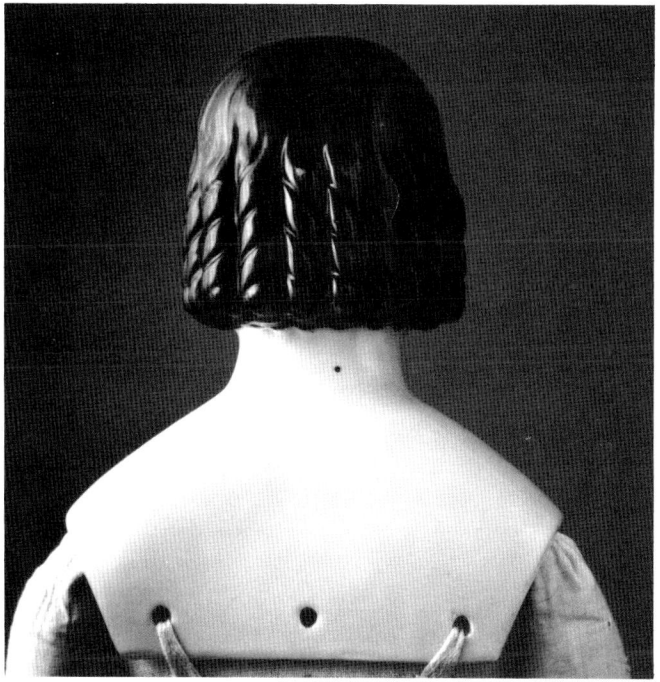

There are thirteen sausage curls on this black-haired doll; however, they hang straight down, and end in ledge at chin level; center-parted with fine white line. Her coloring is very pleasing — deeply pink-toned, eyeball area left white — and eye painting is skillfully done. Her parted lips, crease lines in eyes, inner eye dots made in half circle and nostril ovals all are red-orange. Old cloth body, machine-sewn, but partly hand-embroidered in red to indicate corset lacing; old leather arms, handsewn separated fingers. Shoulder head measures 6"; entire doll is 24." Inside shoulder shows: pressed in mold, heavy and thick; in back a painted red *F.* and an incised *13*. Doll on page 24 has same F; the two show equal quality in skilled workmanship.

Amelia Bloomer is pictured in a Currier and Ives print, circa 1850, with a hair style like this, showing that it was worn by women as well as children.

38
circa 1840

Braided coil placed in usual location, but rest of hair rolled over and under, then fastened lower on the nape. Short white part. Pink-toned, and in eyeball area, as well. Other detailing is very good, including two-toned eyebrows. She is black-haired and blue-eyed. Cloth body with slim old china arms. The shoulder, only, has been professionally repaired, but area beneath was entirely painted, impairing investigation. Deep inside the head, one can see that the china was pressed into the mold. The shoulder head measures 4¼" and total doll is 19".

Shown in color photograph (3), page 22.

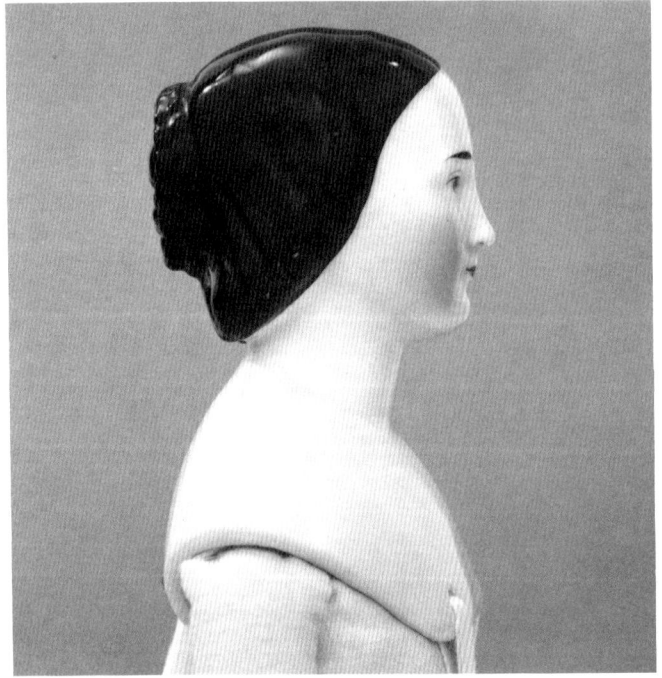

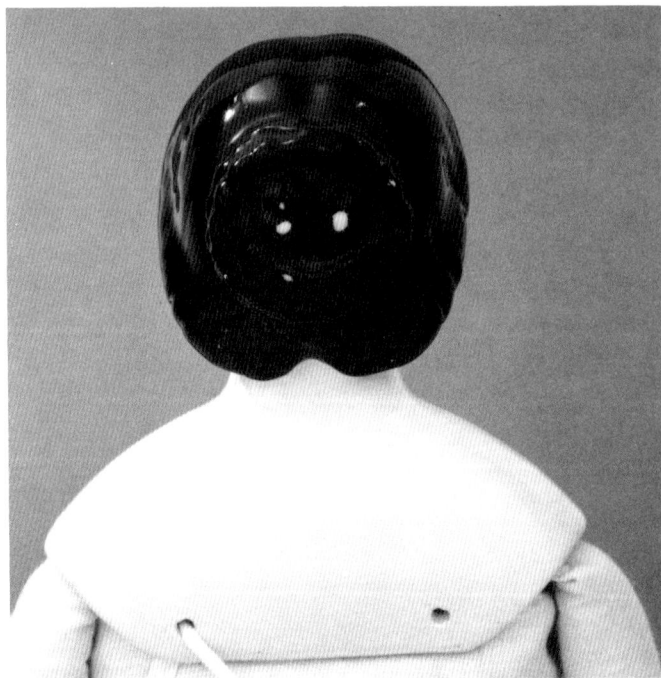

39
circa 1840

Black-haired china lady with center part line in hair; orderly waves down over ears only to level of nose-tip; hair brought to back, where it ends in a wide braided coronet. Her features are painted with fine lines. Pale blue eyes, highlight in blue of iris. Open oval nostril indications, parted lips, crease lines in eyelids all are red-orange; remainder of eye detail is black. Her body is old cloth, commercial. Inside shoulder: poured into mold, and an incised *12*. Shoulder head measures 5¾", entire doll, 22".

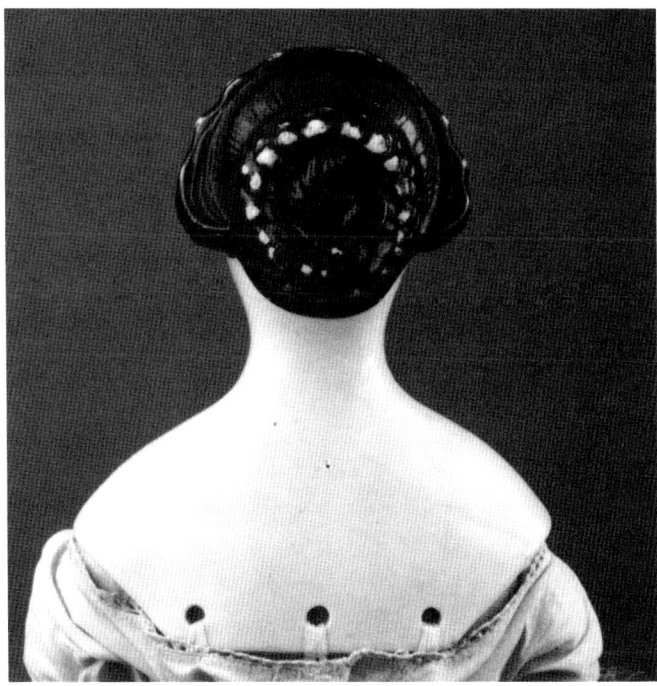

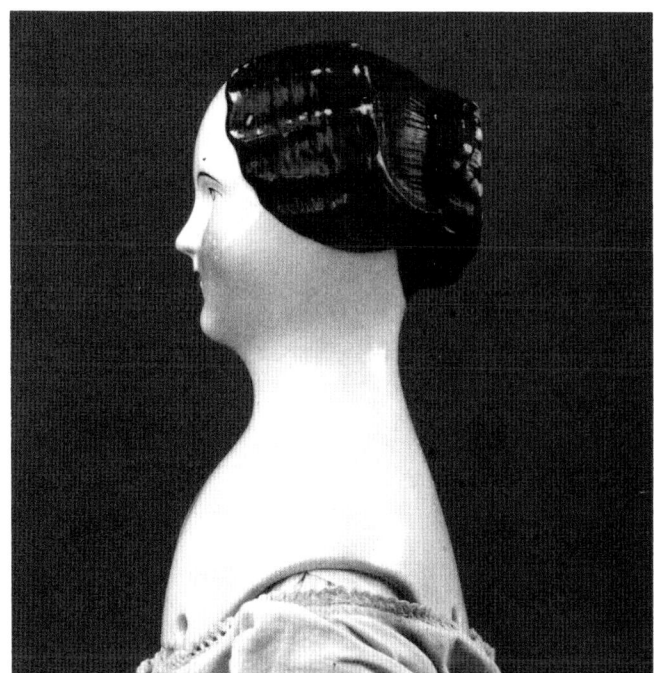

40
circa 1840

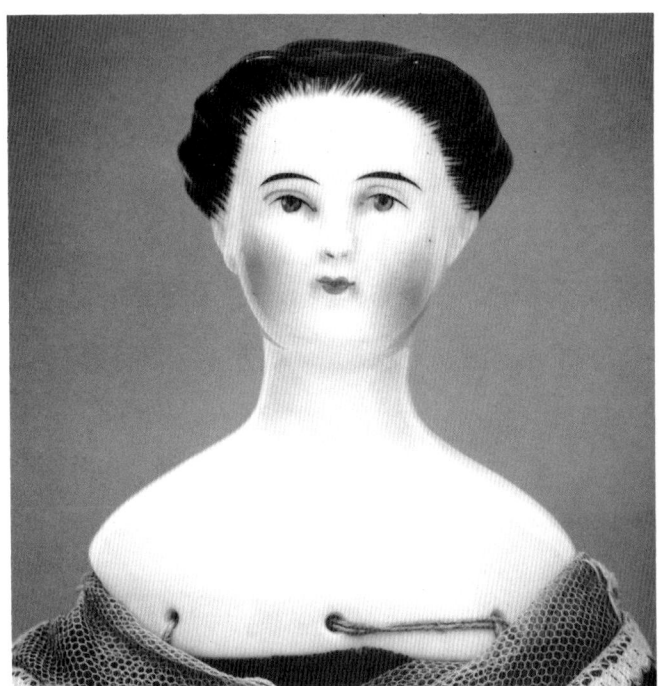

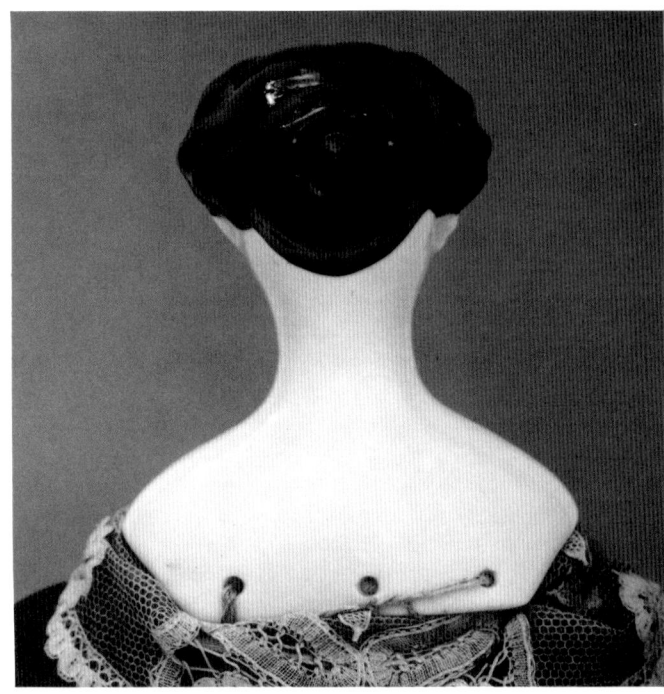

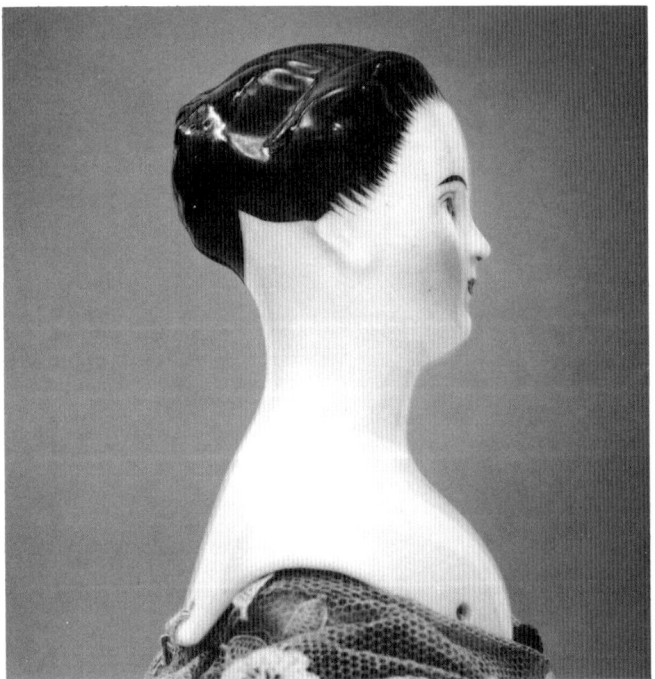

This black-haired lady has all desired painted details, except lacks complexion tone. She too has a braided coronet at center back of head, with this variation: the ears are exposed, and the hair is painted very high at the nape, which could have been the painter's fancy. Observe generous use of brushmarks around the face. She is on an old cloth body, china arms and legs. The porcelain is poured, and glazed inside to top of neck. A red 5 is inside back of shoulder, probably the painter's identification. Shoulder head measures 3¼", whole doll is 13".

Shown in color photograph (4), page 22.

41
circa 1840

Hair style in black also has waves, close to the cheeks, brought down over the ears, but has increased height and width, with additional rolled-under hair across the top and brought out wide to the sides and back. With doll wigs, or in real life, one would accomplish this width by rolls or pads fastened under the hair. The braid is coiled into an oval and dropped low at the back of the head. She has a slight pink tone, fine painting lines and turquoise eye color, and a slightly molded bosom. Inside her 4"-high shoulder head are an incised 6 and a red painted *6.* in fine line; pressed in mold, considerably black-specked.

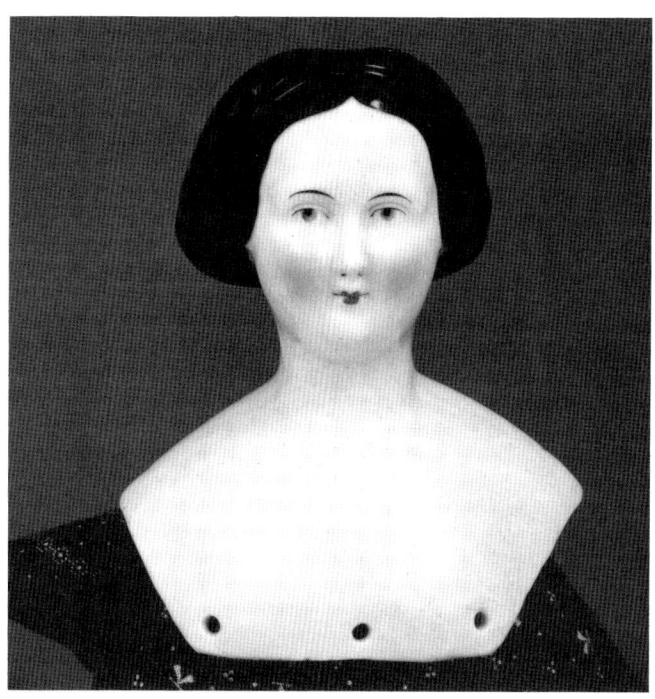

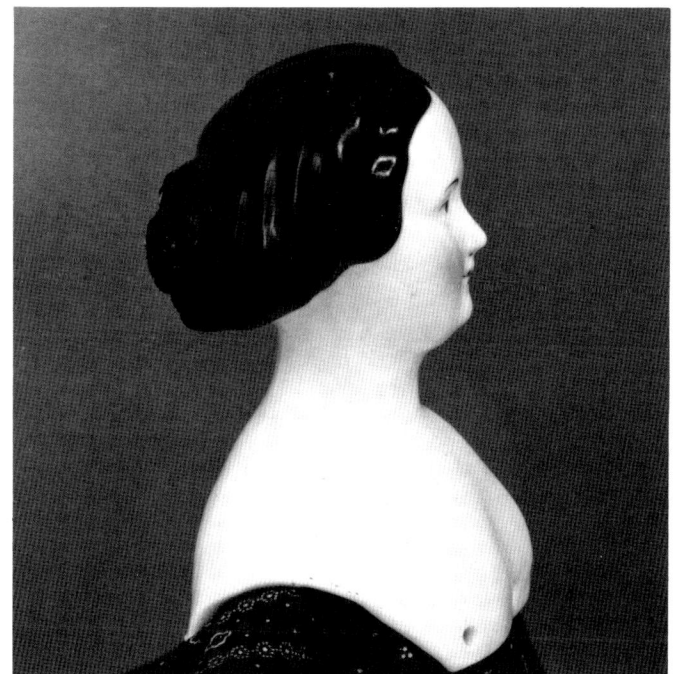

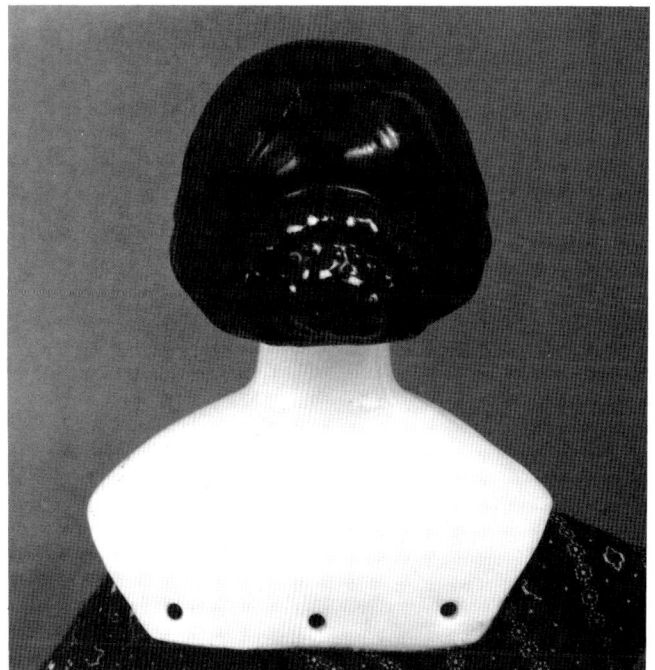

42
circa 1840

Windblown hair style (kinderkoph) in black; brushmarks surround face, not behind exposed ears. Deep pink tone, highlighted bright blue eyes; all proper painted details, including oval nostril lines. Old cloth body, good detailed china arms; legs have black shoes, painted to above ankle height, V opening with lacing inside foot, slight heels. Shoulder head is 3", whole doll is 11¼". Inside shoulder, an incised .4 and 𝓗 in black paint.

Two curls hang from center of back bun; hair is swept from temples with brushmarks. Hair, black; complexion, white; eyes, blue. Old cloth body, china arms and legs. Height is 10".

This shoulder head is quite unusual: the painted black hair curves down from extremely high center forehead, dips slightly at ears, is brought behind them and rolled under across back. Facial detail all present, but is placed below level of ear-top; unusual positioning of features makes that extreme forehead. Slight pink tone. Old cloth body, pink-toned china arms, and clothing too fragile for under-shoulder inspection. Shoulder head is 2⅝" and whole doll is 10".

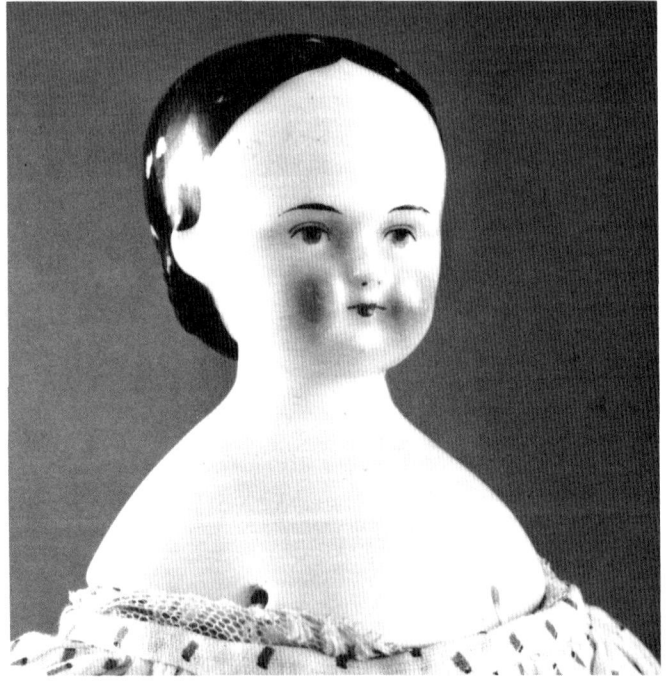

China head dolls of this time were sold on various types of bodies made of wood, leather or cloth. The wood-bodied doll was not news, but placing a china head and china limbs on that body was new.

Leather bodies had been made in many shapes prior to this time; they too were used with china heads. Similar to what collectors think of as fashion-type, these bodies do not have gussets in the arms or legs. Leather bodies were also made in the style of the cloth ones, where the hips and knees are flexible, because of simple, sewn joining.

Cloth bodies are found too; all-cloth, right down to the toes; cloth with leather arms; cloth with china arms; and cloth with china arms and legs, shown on this page for shape and length of types used in this era. When a cloth body was commercially made, proportions resembled those of papier-mâché dolls — slender-waisted and long-limbed. When a body was homemade, the maker's skill determined the result — crude or ingenious, and often surprising.

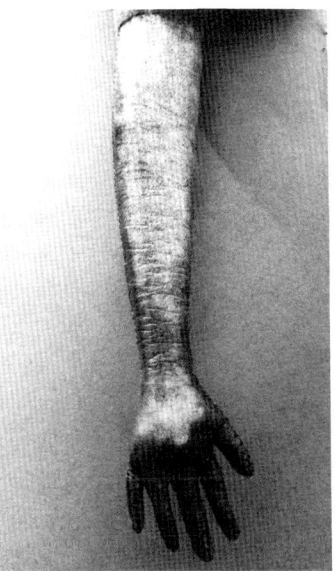
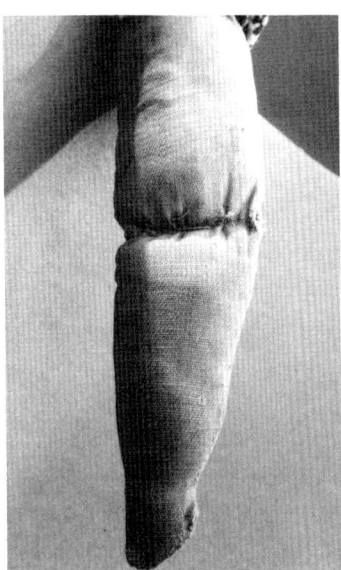

circa 1850

VARIATIONS & INNOVATIONS

You say, "Serious, these dolls look so serious, solemn, so cold." Of course. It was a serious time to be a child and especially to be a female child. There was much to be learned — many skills to acquire before one could attain the expected and ultimate goal of marriage. Dolls were an important part of this learning process.

As a homemaking educational device, those china head dolls must have been revolutionary. Their faces could be washed without fear of erasing the features. And if you got one of the little ones that was all china, it might have come with a cloth or sponge and a bit of soap, and you could plunge the whole thing into a bath and nothing would be spoiled. Sewing for the china dolls was easier and more gratifying for the beginner. Misdirected pins and needles couldn't damage them, and because the limbs were flexible, the garments could be put on or taken off with ease.

These new dolls had other advantages. Versatility. The head could be joined onto cloth, leather or wood bodies, either when purchased or later at home. If the body was made at home, it could be fashioned short, tall, thin — take your pick and change it later. Durability. Critters could not nibble at the precious head, and if they did damage the body, it could be replaced. And no worries about heat from the hearth melting the features. Convenience. If you got one of the "new" dolls that had china legs too, you couldn't even lose the shoes — they were painted on. Could anyone pass by a doll with all these qualities?

There is nothing like success in the marketplace to generate interest by other manufacturers, and that kind of success may have been responsible for the many innovations in china dolls known to have occurred around this time. During the 1850s, the basic traditional style of ladies and children continued (like those of the 1840s), but variations appeared: bald head chinas with intricate wigs, glass-eyed chinas, frozen Charlottes, and an infant with a squeaker in its tummy. The products showed varying degrees of skill in craftsmanship, but they were all inventive. The French saw the possibilities, and they too used china shoulder heads with their progressively more intricate bodies.

This era brought forth an assortment of types, each interesting enough in itself to become a new avenue to explore, if not a specialty for a collector. It was an exuberant and highly competitive time in doll-making, when many innovations were tried, some with long-lived results.

Dolls in numbered diagram of color photograph are also shown individually in black and white and fully described on pages indicated as follows:
(1) page 46, (2) page 60, (3) page 62,
(4) page 67, (5) page 103, (6) page 114.

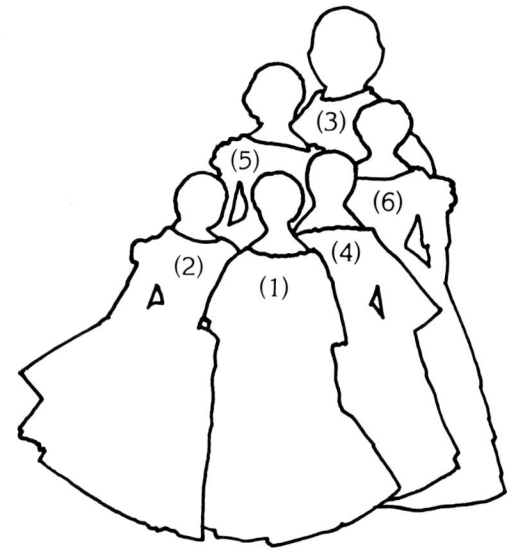

Bald Head Glazed Chinas

This type of china doll appears in reprinted catalogue pages dated 1845–60 — next to wigged and glass-eyed papier-mâché ladies — and was made over a long period thereafter. The dolls could be used to represent any type of lady; merely by changing wig or headdress, the manufacturers added variety to their wares. The dolls are often found in regional costumes, if in original attire. The meaning of the black spot painted on the head is not known, but wooden dolls with religious significance from a century before sometimes had such a spot beneath their wigs, as did the wigged papier-mâchés made before and after the introduction of china dolls. Queen Anne woodens also sometimes have a removable black cap under their wigs. Not all dolls of this sort date from this period; silhouette and painted features may denote a later time. The dolls have been called "black spots," and "Beidermeirs," and most recently we collectors have been asked to call them **bald head glazed chinas**.

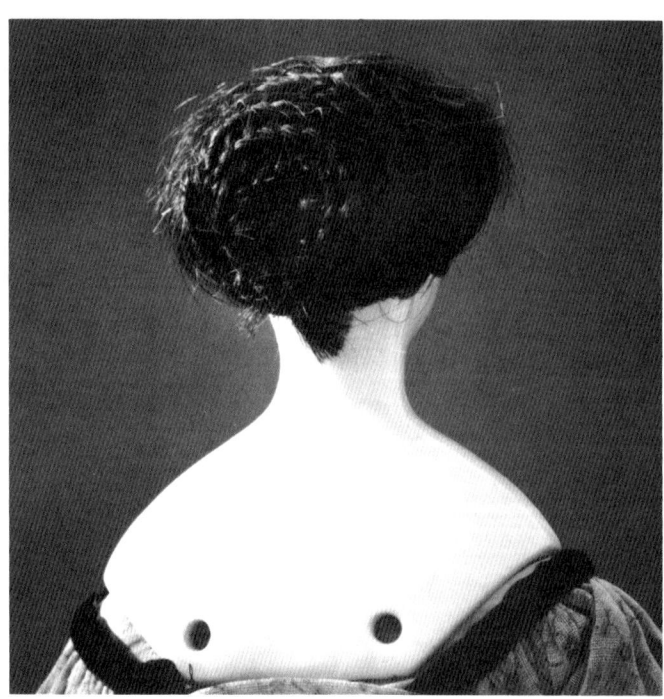

Bald head glazed china lady doll with intricate hair wig, molded ears and graceful long neck. She has a deep shoulder with slight bust modeling. Under her ventilated wig, she has a large painted black spot. She has no complexion tone, but has fine-lined feature painting in all the expected colors — black, blue and red-orange — in all the appropriate places. She is on an old cloth body with old slender white china arms. The shoulder head is 4⅛" tall; the entire doll is 16¼".

Shown in color photograph (1), page 44.

circa 1850

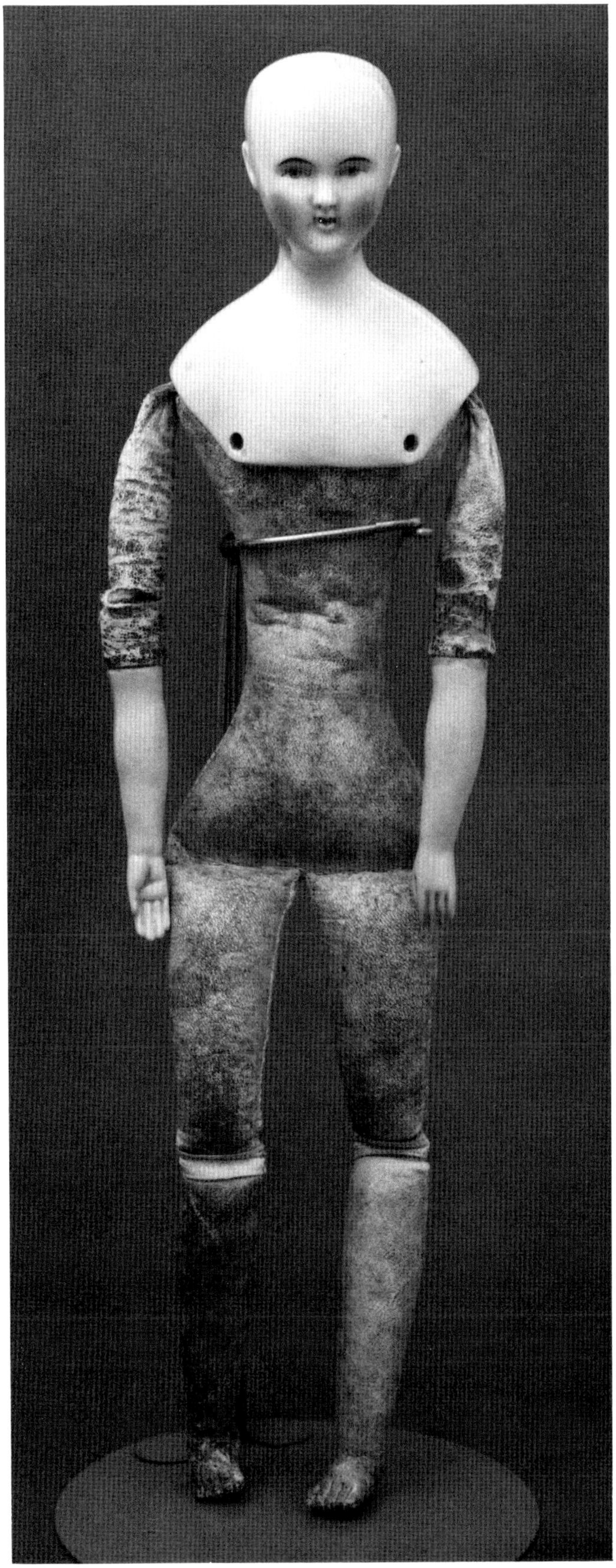

This bald head china has a brown hair wig similar to prior doll: center part formed by wefted hair strands placed edge to edge, divided again crosswise at back; each section becomes a braid and all three are wound around entire head. There is padding beneath hair above ears. Her handstitched once-white leather body is of much interest, appearing to be original. Note: the long, slender shape of torso and limbs; the tiny feet, seamed at ankle and clear around sole, with stitching to indicate toes; and the flexible knee joints. A former caretaker made certain that the frail leather arms did not lose the well-modeled arms and hands. Thank you to that person, as a complete commercial body of this design is seldom found. The doll has skillfully applied facial features in expected colors of black, blue and red-orange on glazed, very white china; her shoulder head measures $4\frac{3}{8}$", overall height is 17". No visible marks.

48
circa 1850

The impressive stature of this lady leaves little to point out. She has every desirable attribute in a bald head glazed china; the most obvious are the slender face and extreme length of her neck. Her hair wig is original and has not been removed; the painted black spot can be seen beneath the edges. Pressed into the mold, the china is thick, white and heavy; three sew holes; molded bosoms are quite defined. The painting is accurate and skillful, with blue eyes (no highlights), dark tan eyebrows that match her wig and the rest red-orange. Cloth body with leather arms. The shoulder head is 7", total height is 30". Impressed inside right shoulder are these indications: 8 59 000

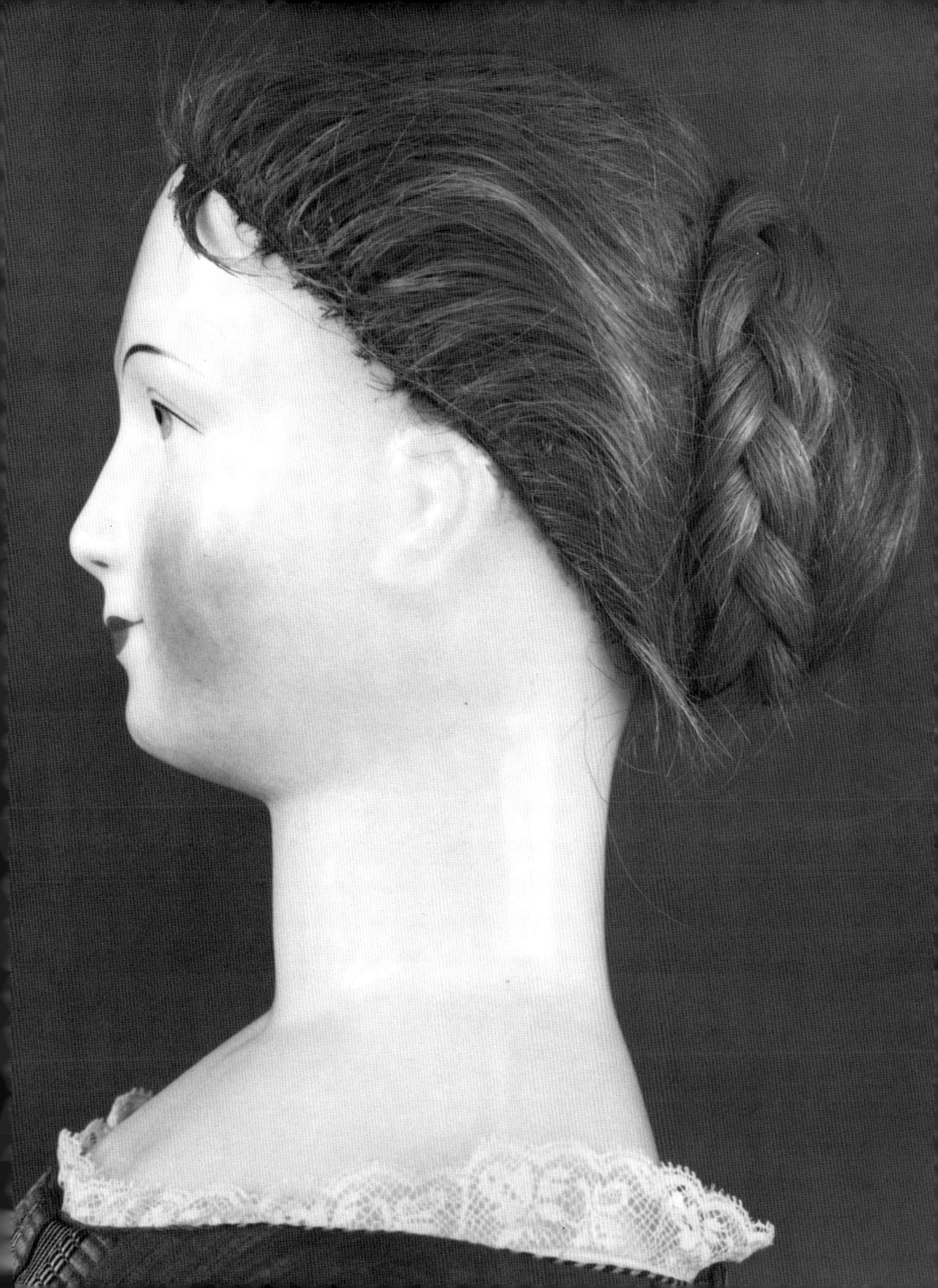

50
circa 1850

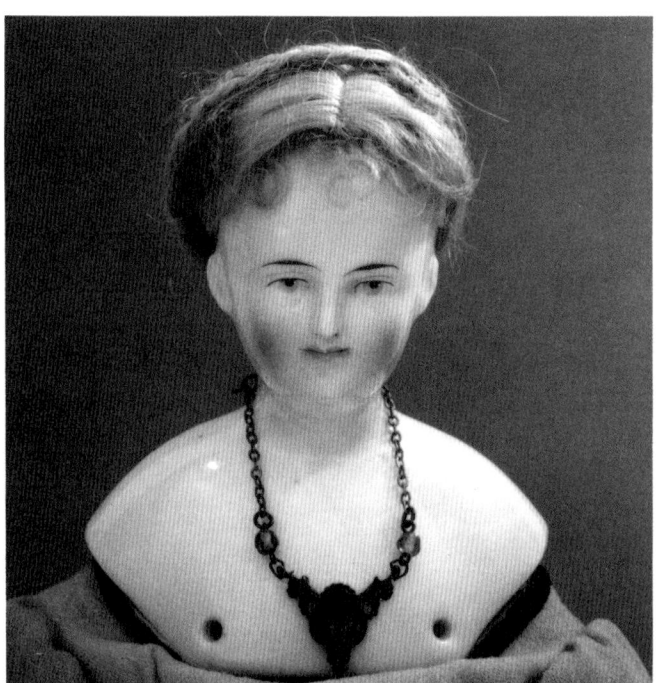

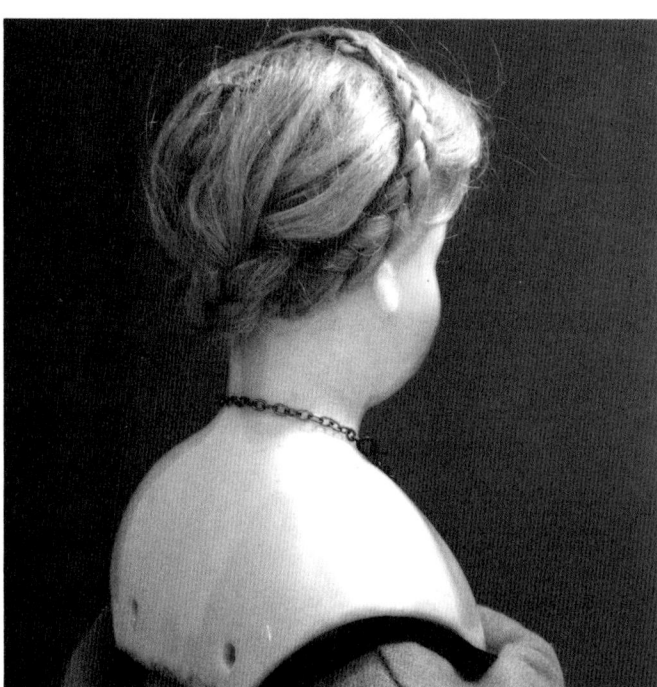

At first glance, this doll appears different from the others in her group because of her blonde mohair wig; there are other differences as well. Her shoulder head is not slender, but rounded and shaped with shorter neck; her facial features take up more than the usual space; unseen, but present, is a smaller than usual black spot; but mainly there is a difference in color. Red-orange is expected on facial features; here, it is replaced with a pale rose-pink. The color gives a soft, feminine, sweet look; the painting is delicate and fine; she has pale blue eyes, and the dark details are black. I feel this doll and some others with the same painting style to be of a later vintage, but have placed her here because she is a bald head glazed china. Her shoulder head is 4¼", and total doll, on old cloth body with china arms and legs, is 14¾". No visible marks.

51
circa 1850

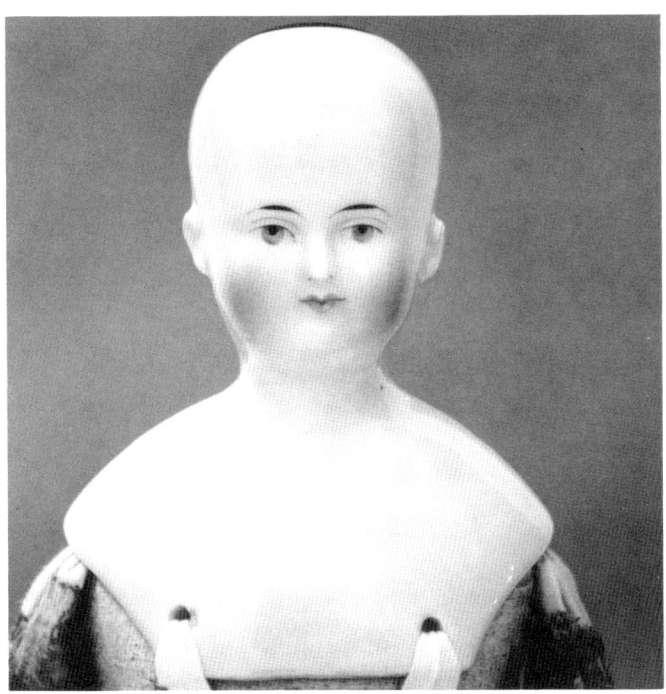

Bald head china doll that was found on old cloth commercial body with china arms and legs. The painted-on shoes are flat-soled, ankle-high, orange with tan soles. The china arms are slender and in relaxed position. She has all the fine line painting one wishes and a black spot on head, and is shown here for shoulder head shape for comparison with others in group. She lacks wig; her total height is 15½". No marks.

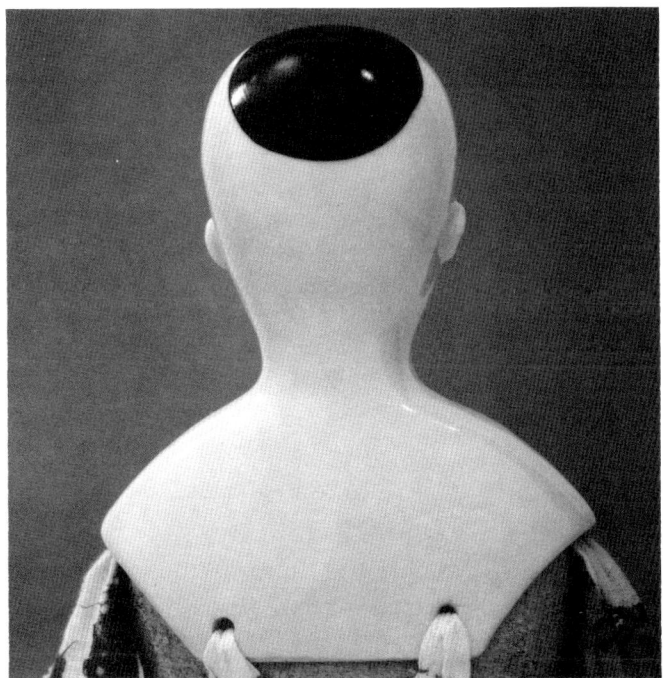

Small bald head china doll, replacement wig; no black spot on head. Note the short neck and the ball shape of head. Very nice painting for this size; her eyebrows are brown. When wearing wig, she has a youthful, cute look. She is 11" tall; cloth body, china arms and legs.

Bald Head Glazed China Child

She is not a lady; she is clearly intended to be a child. Certainly not "pretty," but she is extremely interesting and she is unusual. Her shoulder head is modeled with exaggerated childlike chubbiness at upper shoulders; indentations show separation of arms and chest; no bust line, a deep hollow at throat, detailed ears and mouth, broad chubby face and double chin. There is no painted spot, as far as can be seen; there are four sew holes in the head — center top, above ears, at nape — and the brown cloth wig base is sewn to head through the holes. The hair is brown mohair, parted at center. The shoulder has six sew holes — two in front, two in back, and one at top of each arm. The china was thickly poured; the inside of head is smooth, white and highly glazed. All the china parts have same flesh tone, and facial features are brightly colored. The irises, in which there is a rectangular shape void of color — the highlight — are dark blue. Pupils are dark; the whites of the eyes are left white. The eyelid outline and eyebrows are brown. The crease line in lid, eye dots, nostril half circles, mouth and cheeks are brick-red, with the mouth having a darker line of the same color dividing lips. The full, rounded arms are shaped to show bend of elbow; depressions surround tip of elbow. Chubby folds at wrist, hands dimpled at back, and fingernails defined. The legs show bend at dimpled knee, inner and outer ankle bone, short chubby foot, and chubby roll at base of toes. All toes molded to show bend at joints, and toenails; the natural shaping extends underneath the foot and toes, and big toes are separated from others; one even sticks up. The arms and legs each have four sew holes, by which they are attached to body. The body is lightweight cloth stuffed with fluffy cotton; the torso and upper legs are cut in one piece; a single seam at center back torso, and side-front darts from front of each arm to hipbone level; inner leg seam forms

circa 1850

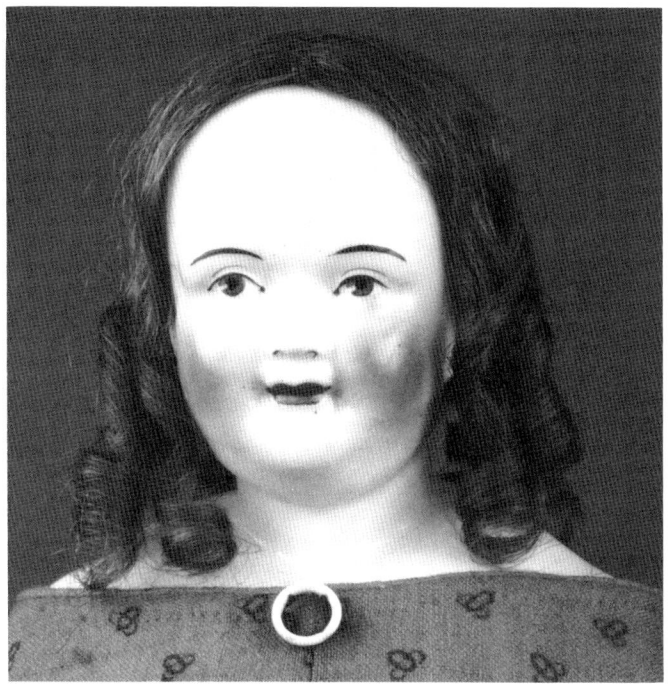
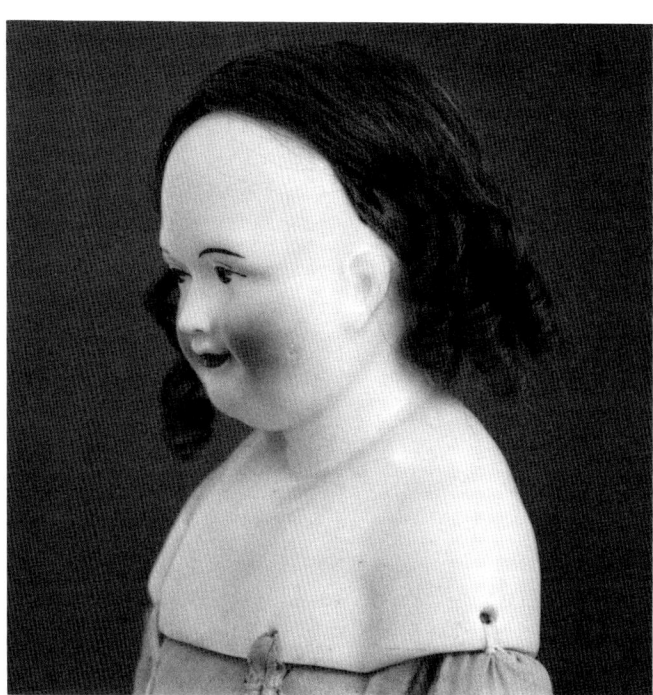

the crotch, and then body is flat-stitched, front through back, dividing the upper legs from torso. The cloth lower leg is formed of a single piece, stitched at an inner leg seam, then joined to upper leg. A single piece of fabric forms the cloth upper arm also. All is hand-stitched in a simple manner. The body is long for a child's, yet it is thought to be original. Shoulder head measures 5¼", arms and legs, 4"; total doll is 21". Inside right shoulder is a painted brown ∕ ; left leg and right arm marked 7.

A similar china child doll was in the doll exhibit at The Museum of The City of New York, in a show mounted in the summer of 1979; she was placed among the earliest of French china fashion-types — not exactly with them, but at their feet.

There are several known examples that appear to be by the same manufacturer — one with painted blue eyes and one with brown — but they are modeled as ladies.

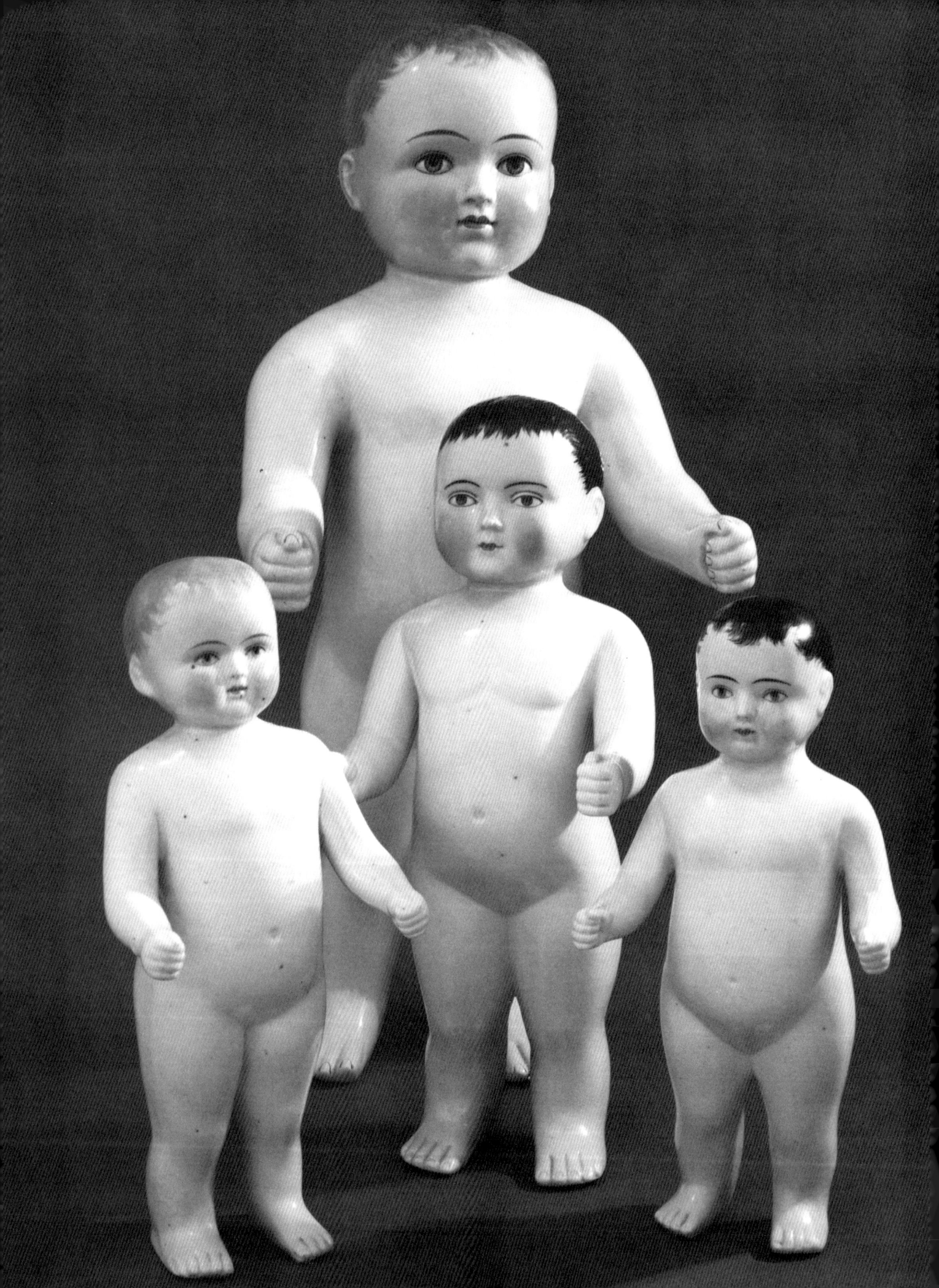

circa 1850

Frozen Charlottes

Frozen Charlottes, as they are most recently called, arrived on the doll market early in 1850 and remained through 1914. They were called **Badekinder** — bathing child — in early catalogues, and later, pillar doll, solid china and now frozen Charlotte and/or Charley. They are all-china, with molded hair in various styles; sometimes with a wig instead, and infrequently with a molded-on bonnet, or a single molded item of apparel, such as chemise or shorts. They were made in white or pink-toned china, or a combination of the two, and also in black china. An 1850s catalogue advertised them with clenched fists, bent elbows, lying in a bathtub, sized one to eight inches. An 1878 catalogue showed a seated version, dressed and in a fancifully painted pewter eight-inch baby chair.

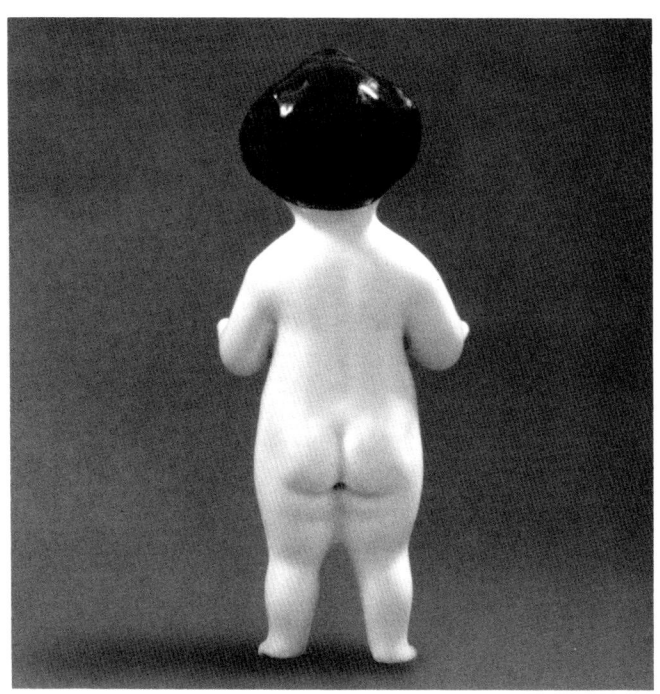

These dolls can be found stark naked or sometimes clothed in garments ranging from simple childlike "let's pretend" items, through anguished first sewing attempts, to skillfully sewn beaded, beribboned crocheted garments that appear to be made by adults. As with other chinas, the dolls should be observed keeping in mind molded and painted details, while looking for the best or the one that is least often seen. Realize that they were usually unmarked, and that reproductions have recently appeared — generally reproductions are made only if it is worthwhile financially. If you have become acquainted with older china dolls, you will probably be prepared to tell the difference.

Frozen Charlottes shown opposite all have pink-toned heads; blue, brown or grey painted eyes; blonde or black hair; and they are 8⅝" to 16¼" tall.

Color photographs overleaf, show dolls that are 1⅛" to 7¾" in height.

circa 1850

Complete with original cloth body and china arms and legs, this shoulder head, though it has two sew holes, front and back, was glued onto body. Nearly eleven inches tall. Entire face can be obscured by a quarter, but she has desired facial features in molding and painting; lightly pink-toned with big bright blue eyes. Black painted hair has deep comb-like modeling in loose waves from center-part to ten sausage curls behind semi-exposed ears. The modeling of arms shows wrist indentions; finely shaped tiny fingers are creased to indicate joints; her china legs extend above knees, and her painted black high-top, flat shoes have wrinkles at ankles — all highly realistic.

Factory-dressed, handstitched with minimum of swiftly placed stitches. Clothing includes: partial drawers sewn on at hips; two petticoats of glazed cotton; a once-white gauze double skirt with fancy edging; separate piped, pleated upper waist, inset three-quarter sleeves, crisscrossed ribbon replacing original pink silk, pinned straight through clothes into body. Home-sewn later additions are: a sheer fabric wrap, pink, silk-edged; a four-tucked lace-edged petticoat; and a fragment of a plaid silk cape or wide collar. A happy-faced doll holding lots of information as to how "they" — whoever they were — made dolls over a century ago for the delight of children.

The style of the shoulder head of this doll was in general use during this era; it is like those in the following group, but there is no way to tell whether it was made by the same manufacturer. My guess is that it was not.

Glass-Eyed & Painted Brown-Eyed Chinas

This is a distinct group of china dolls, with attributes unlike any other, a group that can be set apart by style of sculpting, style of painting and colors used. The glass-eyed chinas among them are perhaps the earliest chinas produced with this feature. The dolls pictured here could have been manufactured as early as 1855-57; most certainly all are by the same manufacturer.

The basic characteristic of this line of dolls is that the faces are all modeled alike. Variations were achieved by adding a few simple hair styles (five are shown here) and by varying size, coloring, method of painting the eyebrows and amount of detail in the eyelashes. Add to all that the use of glass eyes and you have quite an assortment of dolls.

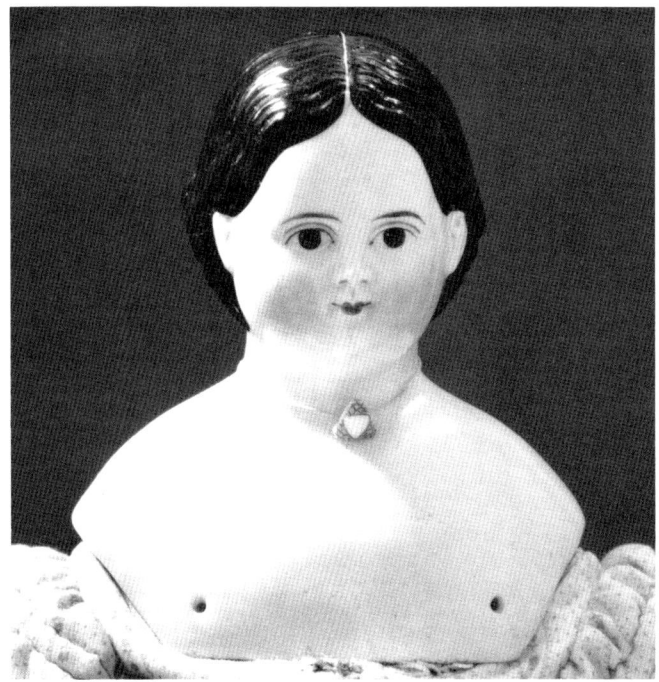

Both the painted brown-eyes and the glass-eyes can be found with each hair style and in several sizes. The insides of the shoulders are incised with numbers from eight to sixteen, referring to size. There may be smaller or larger sizes also. An additional numbering system — described later with the examples — is used with the glass-eyed dolls. No initials or marks are present to suggest a particular manufacturer or place of origin. Researchers have pointed out that Aîné Blampoix, Père, may have been associated with this style of doll. Several in the group have been found on a distinctive cloth body, which may have been original, or was available as a separate item, possibly later. The porcelain is thin and delicate, and the dolls often are found with fractured shoulders. Fortune has indeed smiled on you if you obtain one of these dolls in perfect condition. Their simple charm gives them great appeal.

60
circa 1850

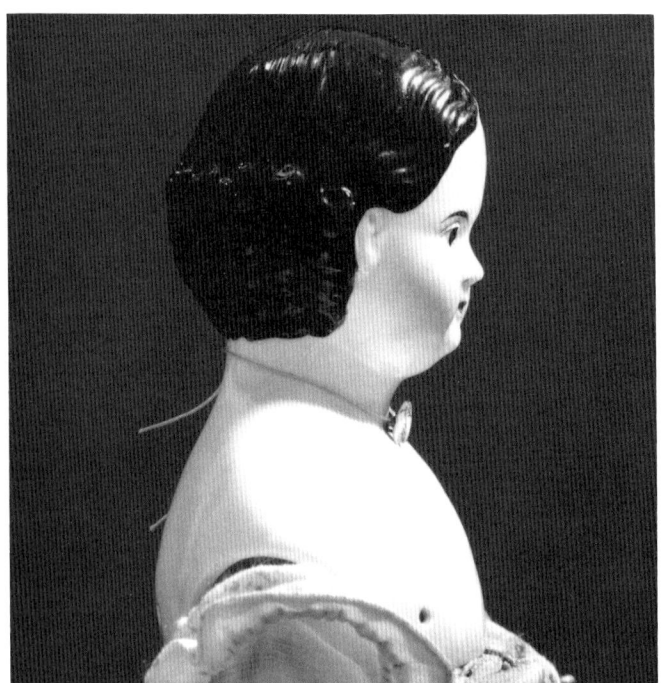
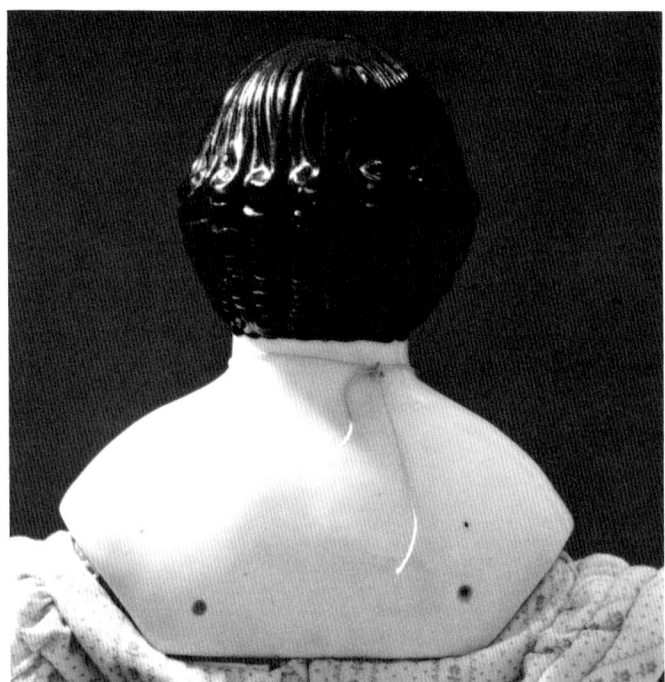

Painted brown-eyed, round-faced china doll; grey eyebrows and no lashes. Black molded hair, deep comb-like detail, waved from center white part exposing ears; twelve sausage curls around back. Brick-red best describes color used on mouth and cheeks, eyelid crease lines, single straight line at nostrils (larger dolls have open ovals at nostrils). Brick-red facial detail found in all dolls described within this group. Cream-tone complexion. Old cloth commercial body, small waist, slender china arms and legs. Inside back shoulder an *8* in black paint. Viewed quickly could easily be mistaken for a script-style G; that has happened in the past. She has 4¼" shoulder head; whole doll is 17". Hair style is that most frequently found within this group; this particular doll has extremely appealing coloring and molded detail.

Shown in color photograph (2), page 44.

61
circa 1850

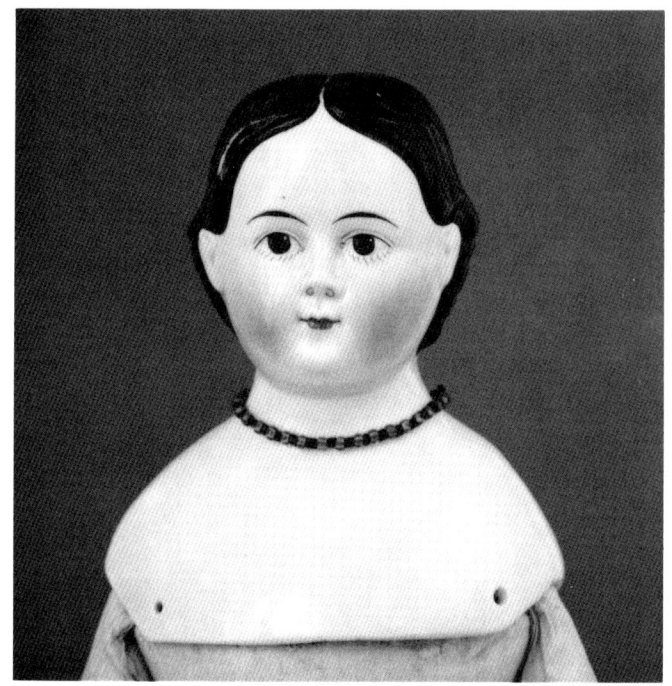

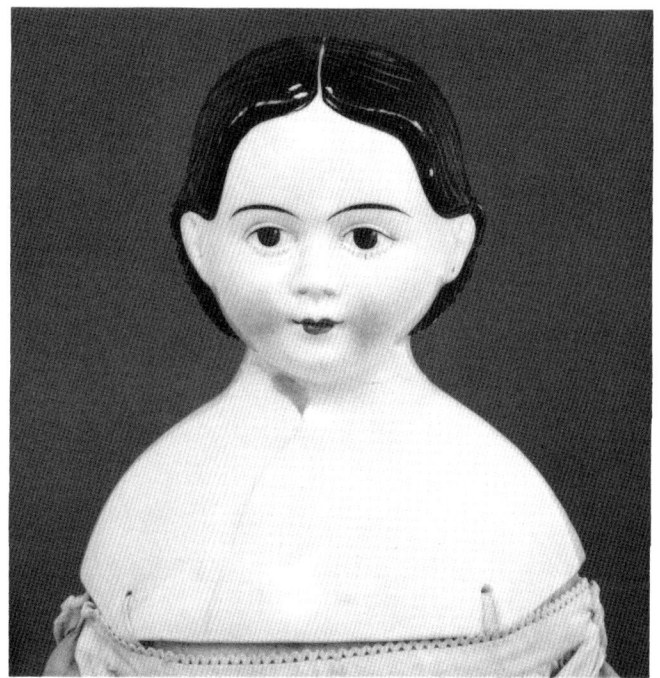

Brown painted eyes with lower lashes; irises highlighted with small round void spot and outlined in black, pupils are black; eyelid outline and eyebrows of black. Expected brick-red detail; typical black hair style with good comb-like texture. Deep pink tone. On old cloth body. She is presented because of her eyelashes, appealing pink color and charming good looks, though her shoulder is rebuilt and no inside marks are visible. Shoulder head is 5½" and whole doll is 22".

A still larger painted brown-eyed china with lower lashes and solid black eyebrows. No pink tone. Has typical black hair style and brick-red facial detail, on nice old comfy cloth body. Glazed inside and out, no incised numbers. Inside back shoulder: *15* in black paint. Shoulder head is 7"; entire doll, 25½".

circa 1850

This large doll has dark brown glass eyes called **pupilless** — a collector's word meaning the iris color is all that can be seen, there is no separate pupil color. Her eyebrows are separated black strokes over a grey base; black upper and lower lashes. Brick-red facial detail. Deep cream-toned complexion. Molded black hair in style most typical of this group. Inside top of head reveals a triangular section had been removed before kiln firing, incised *11*, matching an incised *11* inside front shoulder. It is thought the section was removed while head was in the greenware (before firing) stage, for easier access in making the eye cuts; then triangle was replaced in matching numbered head. Inside back shoulder, a *16* painted in black (the size, I believe). Her old cloth blody is stuffed with straw and cotton; marked on top *Oe*, and *10* above back waist. Shoulder head is 7½" and entire doll is 26½". She is warm-colored, utterly charming and most informative.

Shown in color photograph (3), page 44.

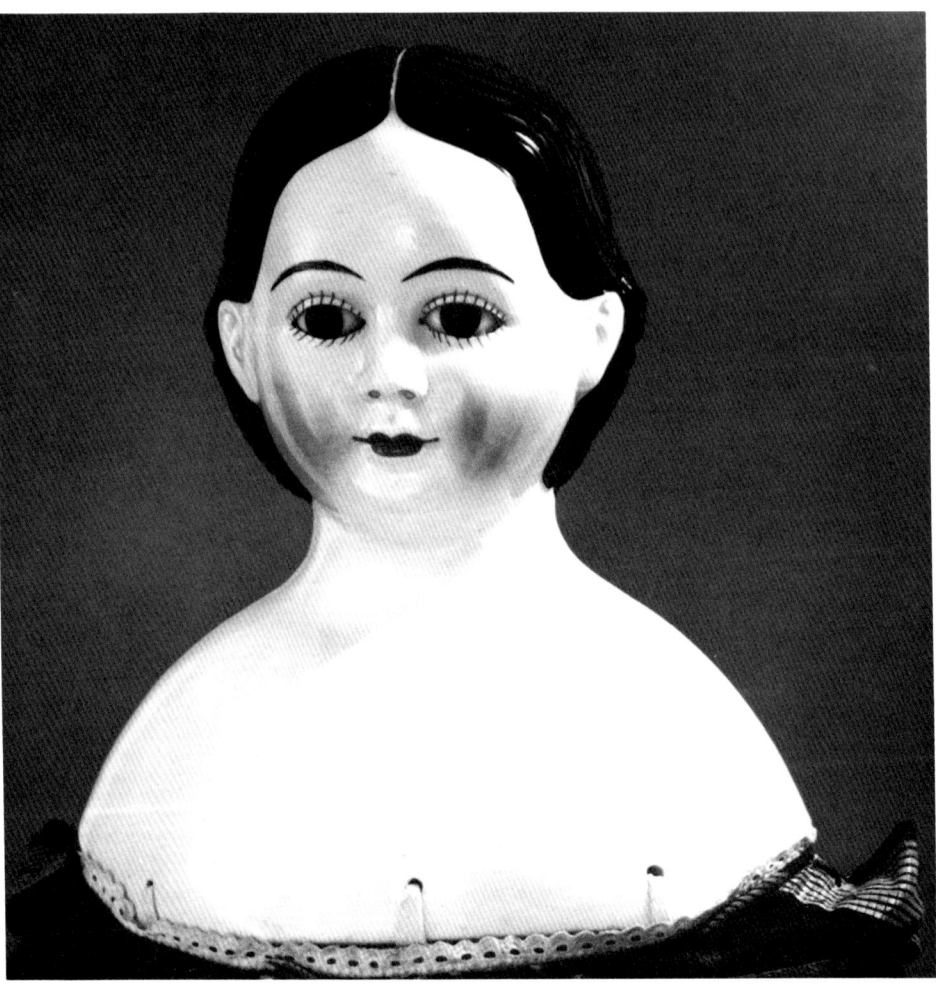

63
circa 1850

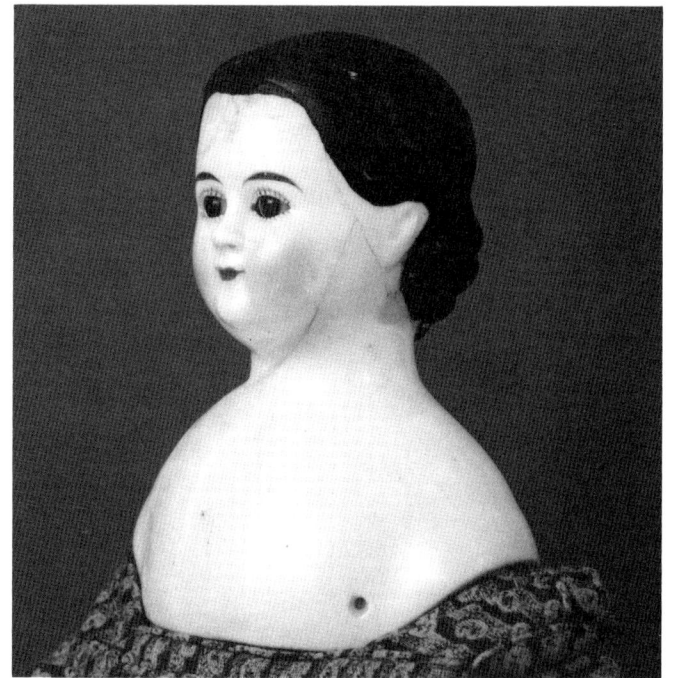

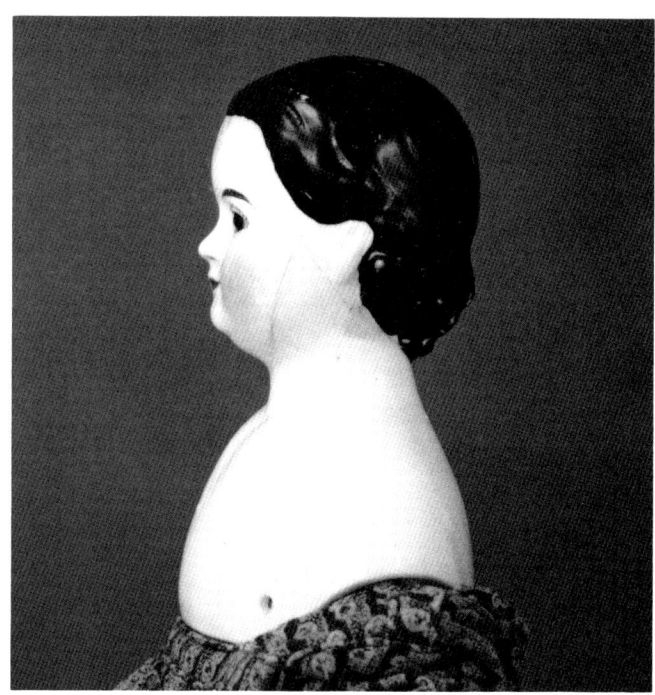

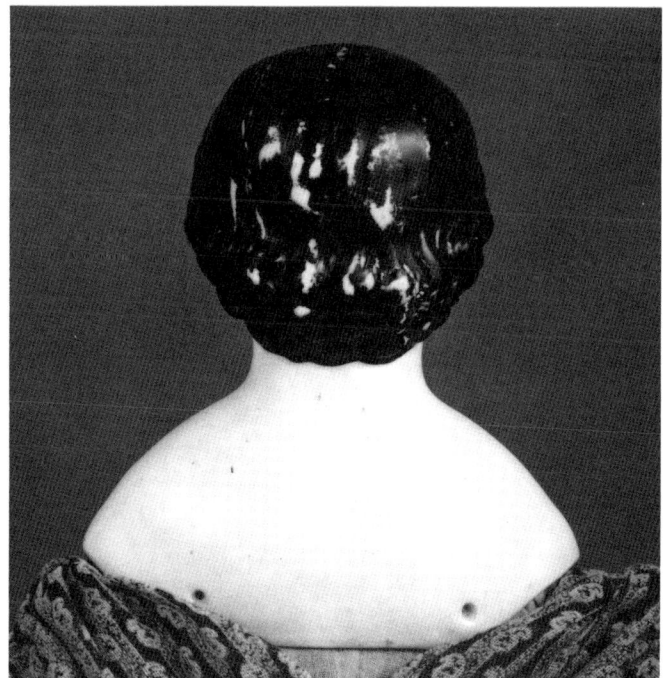

Brown glass eyes, dark pupils; brown eyebrows and top and bottom lashes. Slight cream tone, mostly evident on face. Brick-red details. This molded style has hair brought back from rounded forehead (comb marks suggest no intention of center part) to three rows of ringlets at back and semi-exposed ears. This version has a throat hollow and gently curved shoulders. Incised 8 inside back shoulder; these 8's may have been misinterpreted as script G's in the past. An incised 3 inside crown. Old cloth body; shoulder head is 4½" and whole doll is 17". If other numbers existed, they have been obscured by repair; acceptable to me at a moderate price, as variety was the aim — rarity outweighed condition. If you have the choice between a perfect example or a repaired one, the perfect one is always the one to pick, if finances allow. One seldom has that choice in pursuit of unusual dolls.

circa 1850

From the front, this hair style repeats that of preceding doll, except that this one has added molded hair band across back. Brown painted eyes, well-modeled throughout with deep eyelids; nice sharp nose; dimple above and below mouth. Brick-red details; lashes and complexion tone omitted. The mold used for this style has the same throat hollow and gently curved shoulders as preceding doll. Also incised *8*, but painted *gm.14* inside back shoulder. Her shoulder head measures 4½", and on old commercial cloth body with waist seam and gathered hips, whole doll is 17".

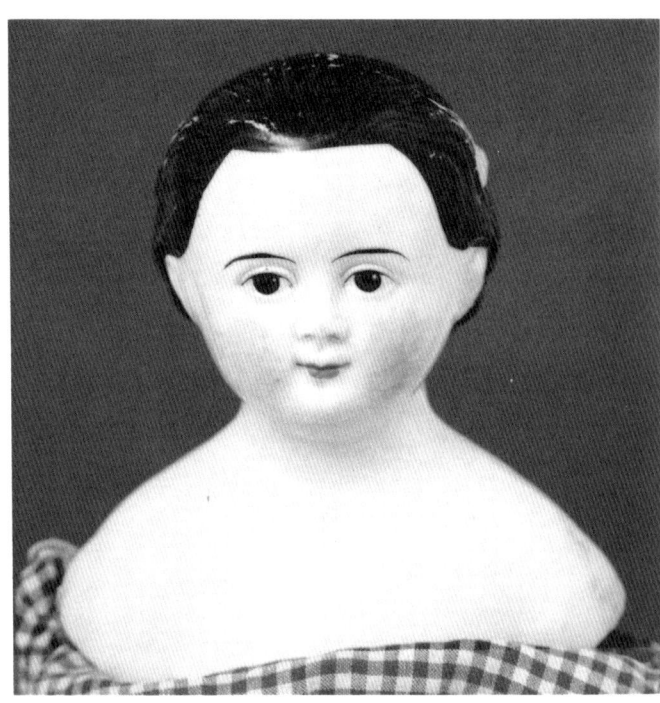

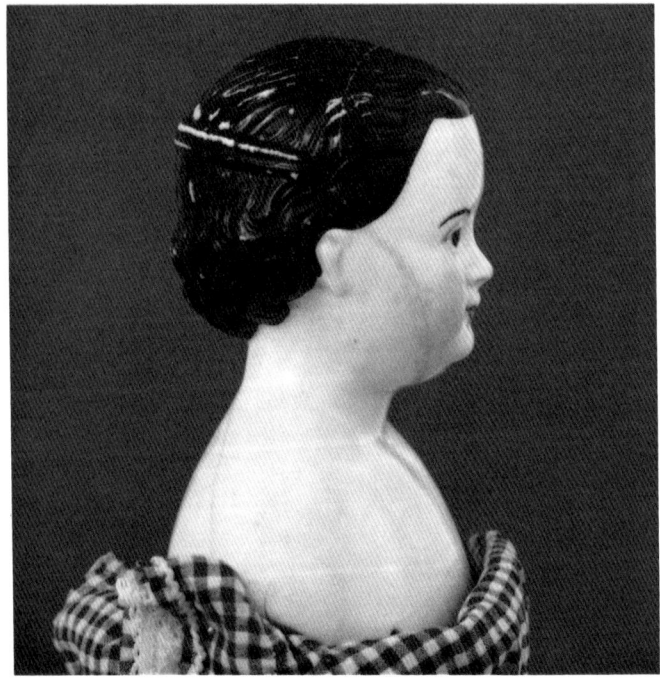

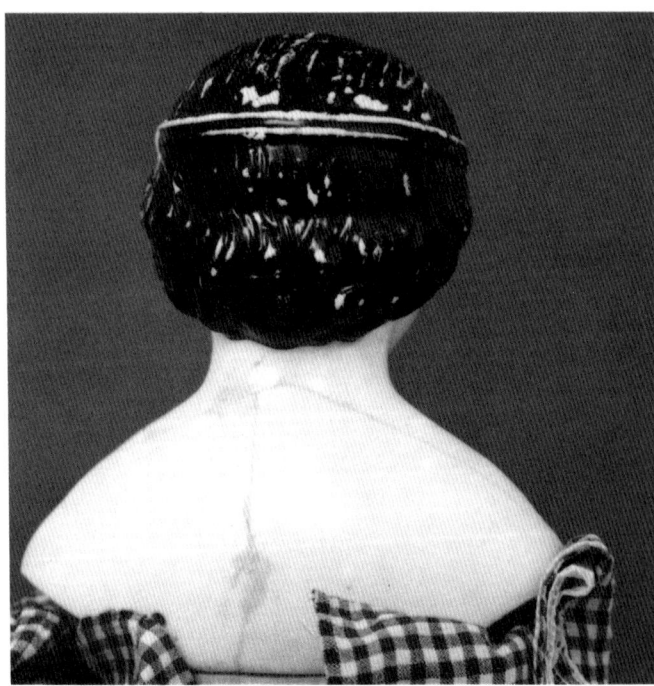

65
circa 1850

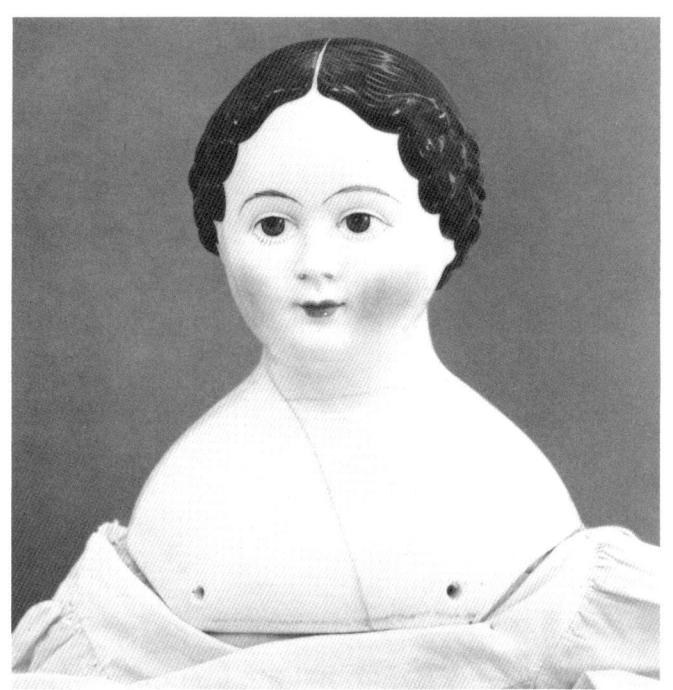

Though it may be difficult to perceive at first glance, this is a slightly different hair style; double wave from center white part to temple, then small curls becoming five casually arranged rows at back, all black, only lower tips of ears show. This painted brown-eyed version has eyebrows of fine black strokes over grey, lower lashes only. Upper and lower eyelids are deeply modeled, as well as area around nose and mouth, including dimple under mouth. All brick-red details present. Poured into mold. No pink tone. Inside back shoulder, a *13* in black paint. The shoulder head is 6½", and on her old cloth body she comes to 24".

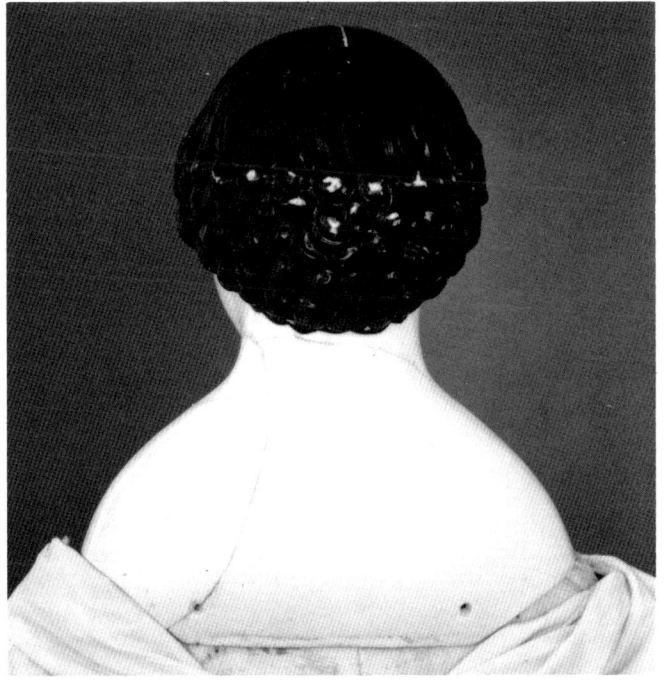

66
circa 1850

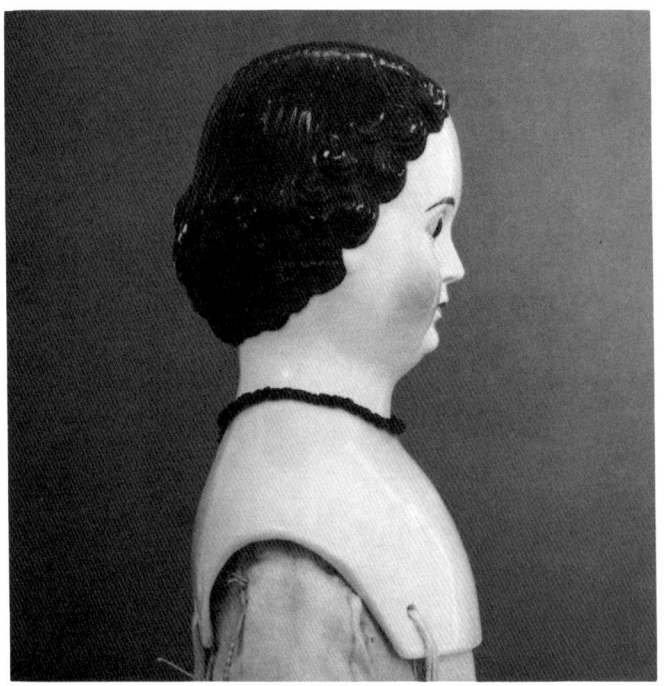

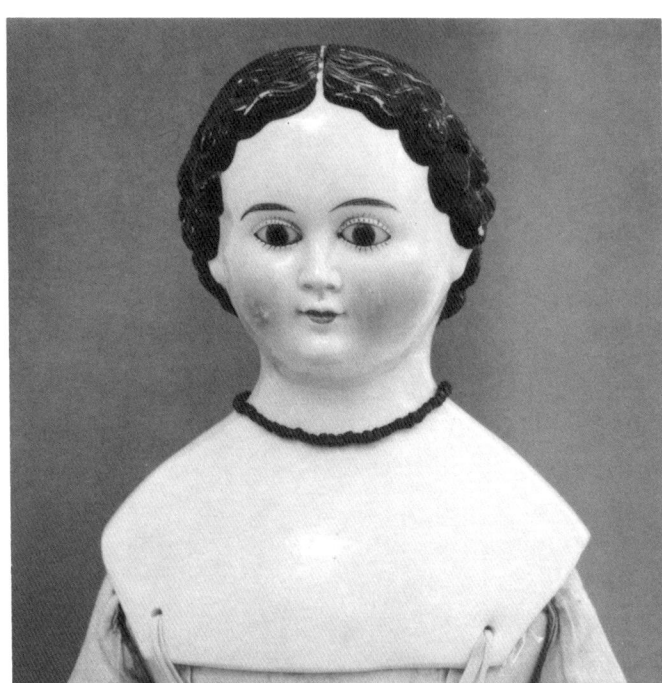

Glass eyes, brown with pupils; eyebrows are two-toned, fine black lines cover a tan undercoat. Black eyelashes, top and bottom; all brick-red details present, but no complexion tone. Her black hair style is the same as preceding doll. Inside back shoulder, a *10* is incised on left side, an *11* incised and painted on right, and an *11* incised inside the crown of head, marking the section that had been temporarily set aside before firing. Her shoulder head is 5⅝" high; on her old cloth body, she measures 21".

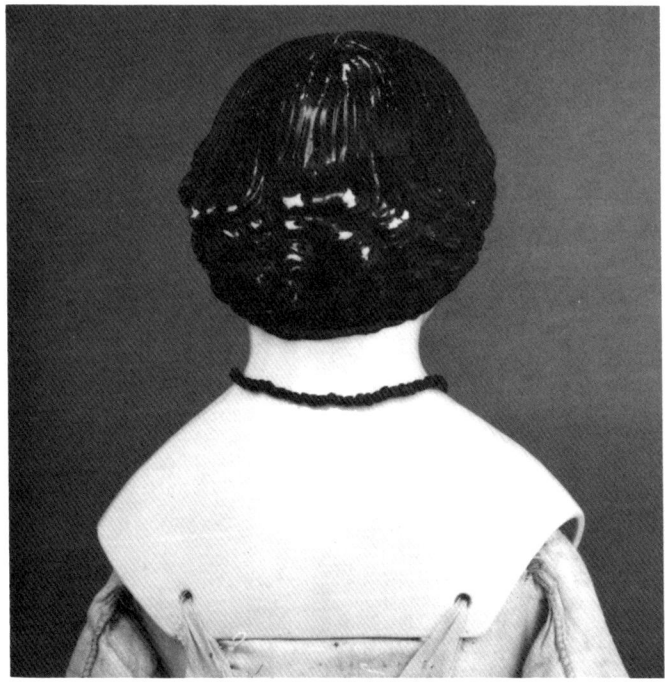

circa 1850

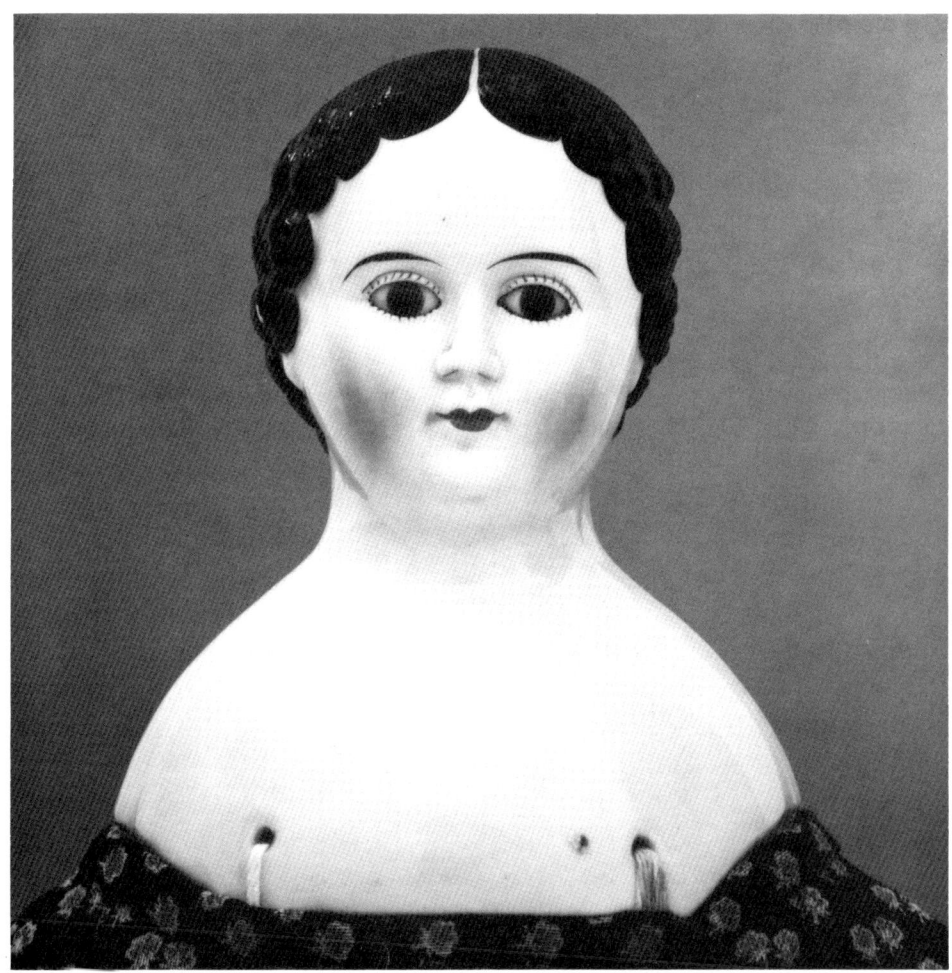

Glass-eyed china doll, brown eyes with pupils; solid black eyebrows, upper and lower eyelashes. The brick-red details are all present. From white center part, black hair is styled in individual curls framing face, ending at back in five rows of casually arranged curls; only lower tips of ears show. She is glazed inside and out. The inside top of head reveals that a triangular section was removed from head before firing, incised 135, and rejoined, matching an incised 135 inside front shoulder. There is also an incised *8* inside front; and a *15* in black, at back. She is on a cloth body with a waistline seam and gathered hips, often found on this type of doll. Shoulder head is 4½" and whole doll is 18".

Shown in color photograph (4), page 44.

69
circa 1850

A bald head glazed china with slot in head for inserting wig and brown glass eyes: three desired features in one doll in this innovative manufacturer's group — signs of the experimental time. Her eyebrows are black feathered lines over grey; black upper and lower eyelashes; eyelid crease lines, nostril ovals, mouth and cheeks are brick-red. The triangular crown section has been removed and replaced. The pate was encircled with an incised line, and within that area, the surface is matte, or bisque — left unglazed for applying hair; outside incised line, surface is lightly pink-toned and glazed. She is on an old made-at-home cotton body with leather hands. Inside back shoulder: a *10* in black paint. Shoulder head is 4⅞" high; whole doll is 21".

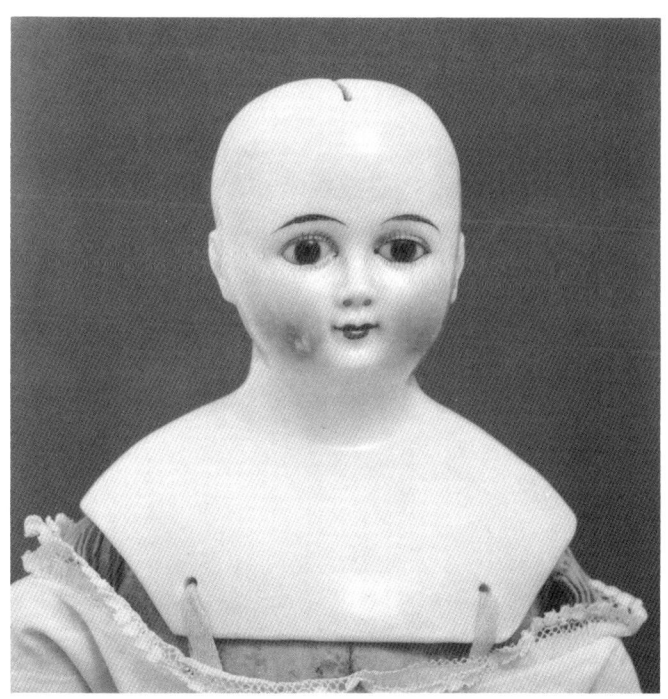
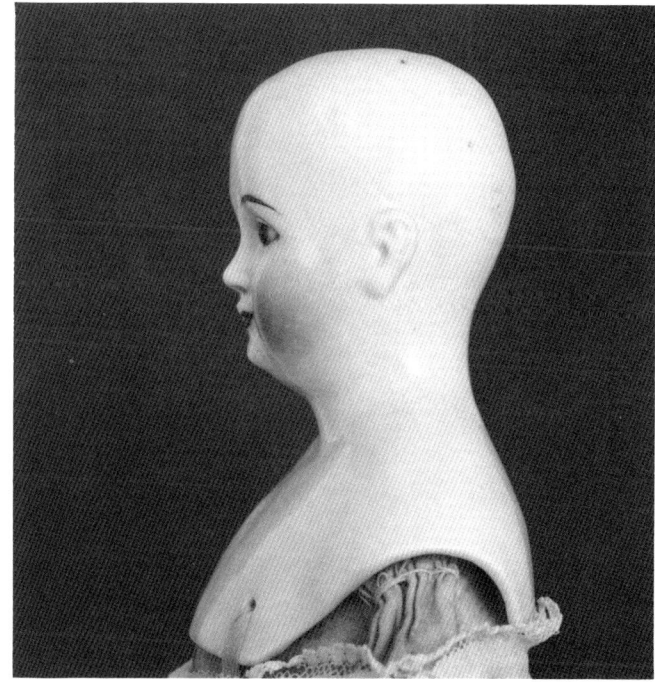

China Infant

Another innovation of this era was the china infant or baby, a simplified and hopefully apt name. This type was probably the first commercial effort to produce a porcelain doll portraying an infant; these of pink-toned or white china have neck joints enabling their heads to be turned from side to side; or have head and upper torso — that term replaces "shoulder," due to shape — molded as one piece. They had crying devices placed in their tummies, and china arms and legs with bare feet whose little toes are shaped beneath as well as on top. In addition, there can be an upper torso and lower torso of china with the remainder of body made of lightweight twill. This style is called a Motschmann-type body. There is also a china infant, again with swivel head and a tummy squeaker, made on a plain cloth body with china arms and legs. Some of the head styles appear to represent a child slightly older than an infant. Of the examples shown here, none is exactly the same shape; those with china torsos have the same twill fabric. A most unusual, curious and interesting type of doll, and so few remain that each one should be appreciated.

China infant doll with bald head, swivel neck, squeaker in tummy — activated by pushing upper and lower torso together, no longer works. There is no painting to indicate hair; blue painted eyes outlined in black, black eyebrows; crease in eyelids, inner eye dots, nostril indications, mouth and cheeks are all red-orange. Baby's neck fits into receiving hole in shoulder like a short hollow stopper in a bottle, and can be turned from side to side. Carefully, please! The arm style is long enough to include the bend of the elbow; leg style includes the knee. Baby measures 11½" long.

72
circa 1850

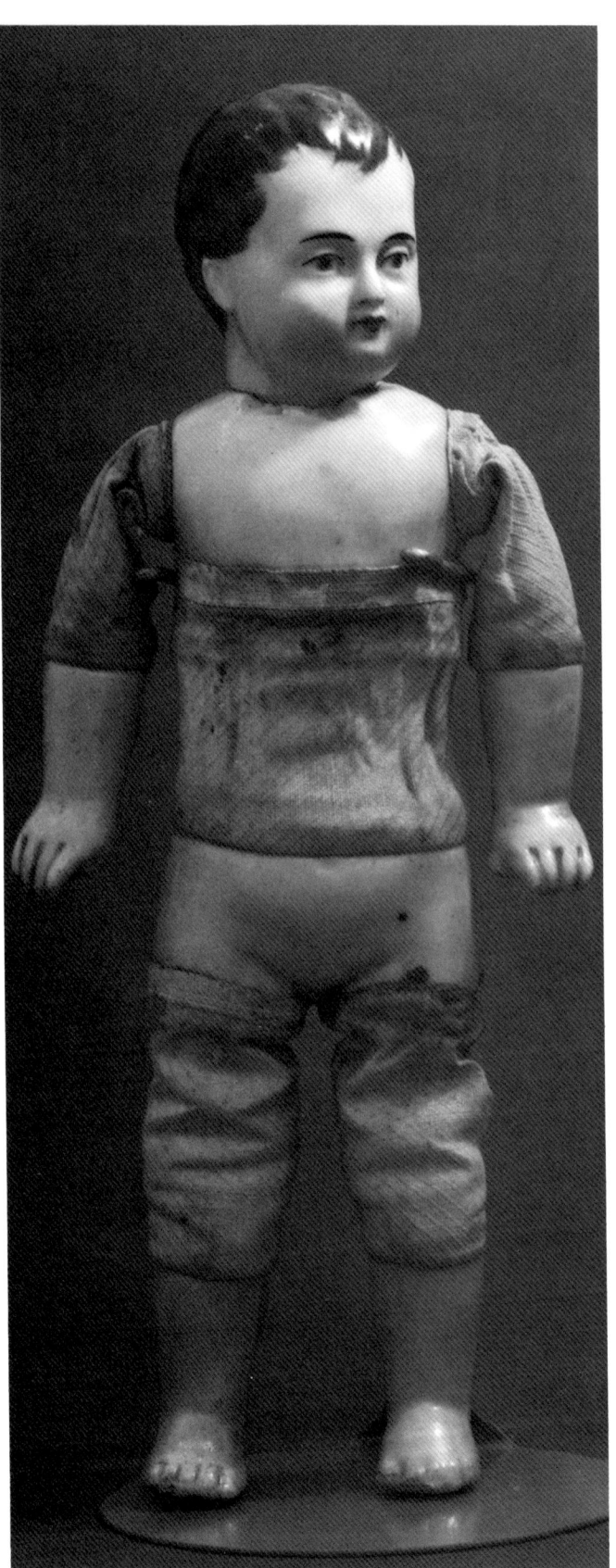

Golden brown describes this china infant's brushmarked hair; has swivel neck and crying device; Motschmann-type body with all pink-toned china parts. Blue painted eyes, black eyebrows and eyelid line; inner eye dots, nostrils, mouth and cheeks of red-orange; no crease line in lid. Has the appearance of a toddler and is 7⅜" tall. No marks.

A similar body, sans head, has arms and legs incised with a *4* and measures 8½" from neck to toe.

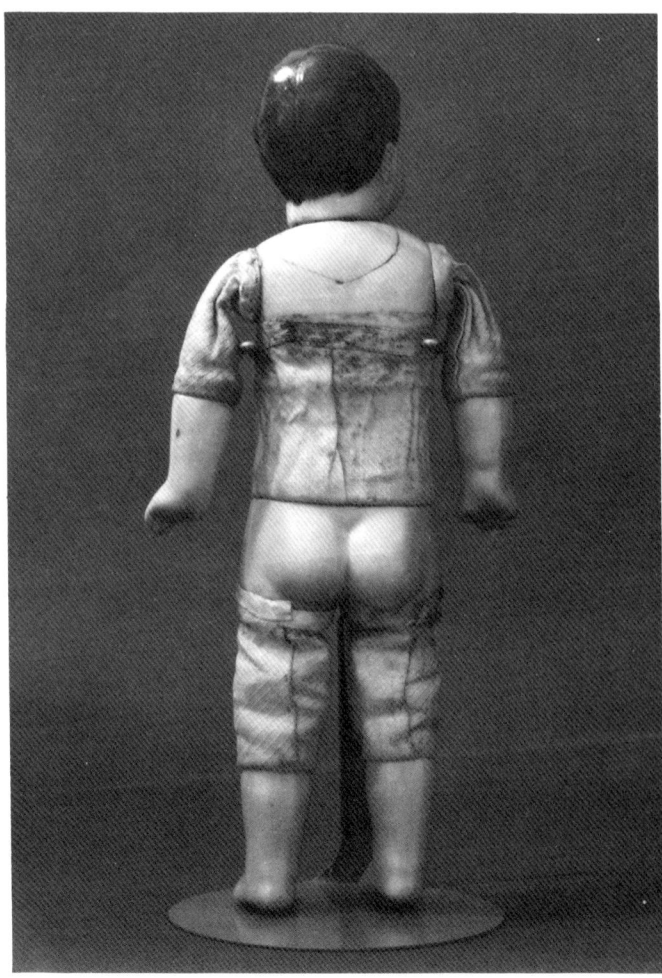

circa 1850

Blonde painted hair, china infant; head has flange at neck attached to wooden shoulder piece inside cloth body, enabling it to be turned from side to side; tummy squeaker, operational. Well-modeled white china parts, nicely glazed; notice shaping of legs and detail of toes. Blue painted eyes, black pupils and eyelid line; the crease of eyelid, inner eye dots, nostril dots, mouth and cheeks are light red-orange. Eyebrows are painted to match hair; has a baby look and is $9\frac{3}{8}$" tall.

A significant point to recognize about these unusual dolls is that they were being made more than a half-century before bisque baby dolls became popular.

74
circa 1850

Black-haired china infant, boy style with swivel neck; hair is brushstroked at face only, plain in back; eyes are blue; expected line painting is present and correct, but small in scale. Upper and lower torsos are quite pink-toned; arms and legs with bare feet are various shades of pink. The torsos are glazed inside and out — probably by dipping; the inside is amazingly white, glassy and slick; the pink tone was not allowed on the inside. His handstitched cloth parts are twill-type diagonal weave cotton, once bright white; the arm and leg sections are stuffed with a mixture of fibrous material and wood slivers. The mid-section houses a 1⅛"x3" squeaker, or bellows, composed of wood, wire, fine white leather (still flexible) and dark grey heavy paper. The wire rectangle at the top serves to hold the bellows in proper position inside shoulder. Above bellows is a wooden rod wedged in arm holes and running crosswise through shoulder; it anchors the head to the shoulder. It is amazing that any of these dolls survived, as they have such play appeal, with a head you could twist about and all those dangling parts. He is 9¾" tall. The bellows is pictured.

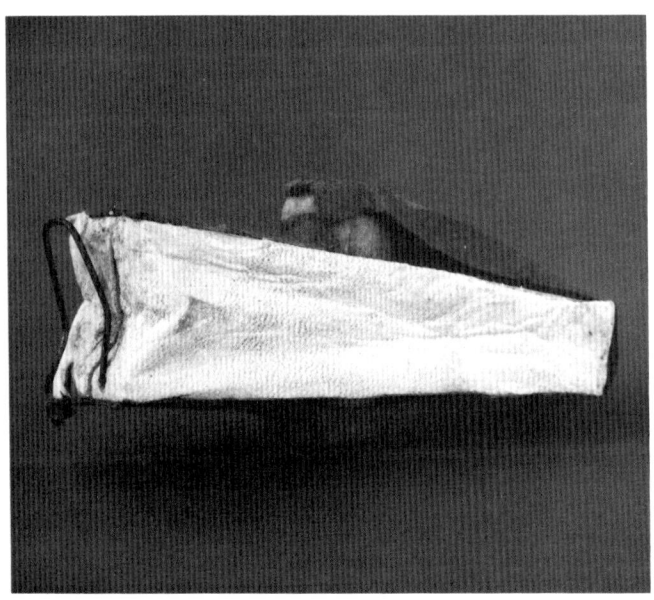

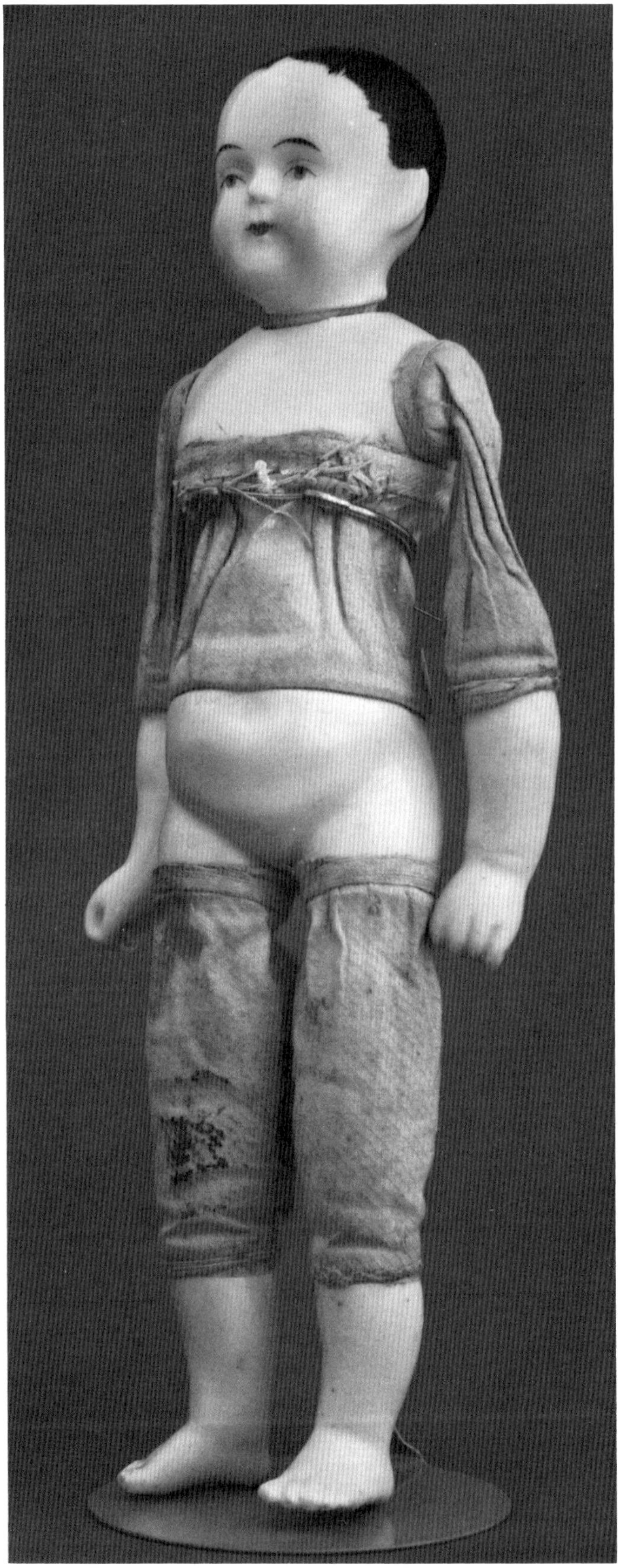

circa 1850

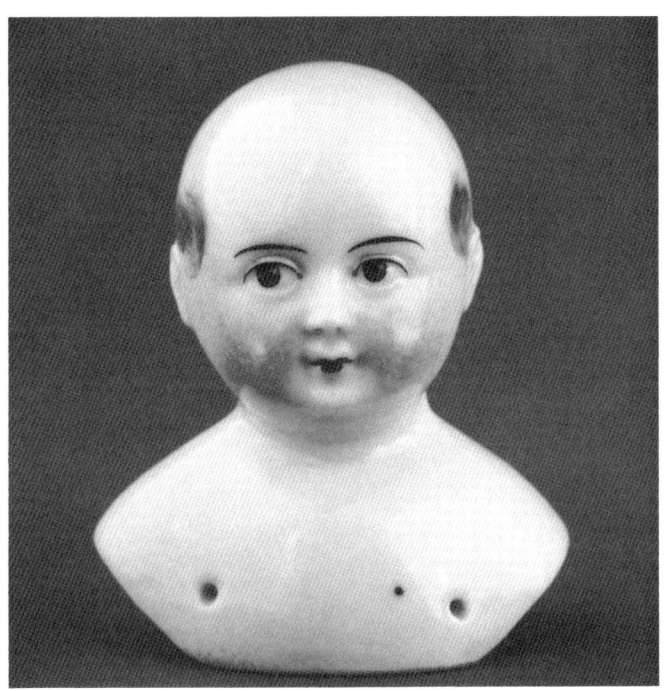

A china infant shoulder head with brushstroked wisps of tan painted hair above ears. Large dark blue eyes with highlights, black pupils and molded eyelids. All proper line work and red-orange cheeks and mouth. His ears are quite detailed. Heads with wisps of painted hair are sometimes present on the Motschmann-style arrangement. This shoulder head would be appropriate on a cloth body of simple design with arms and legs styled like the others in this group — little bare feet and curved, chubby hands. It is glazed inside and has a small O. in black paint; measures 2¾".

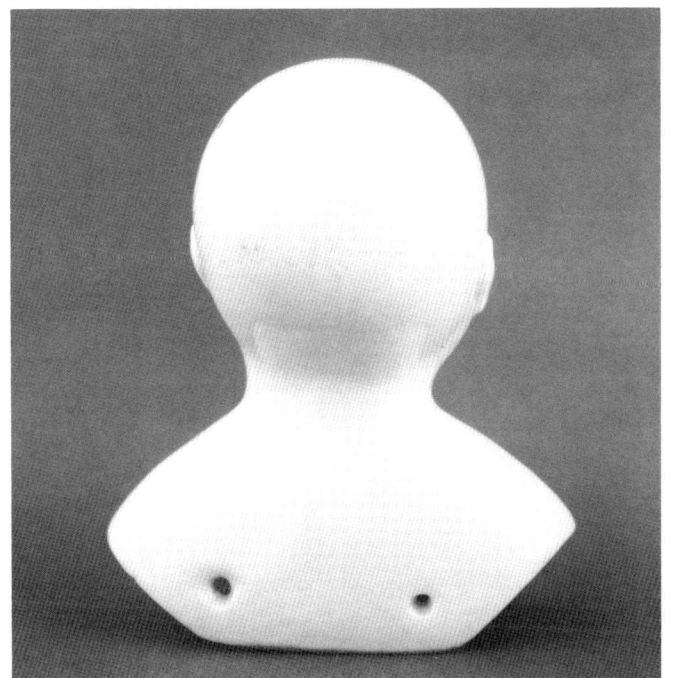
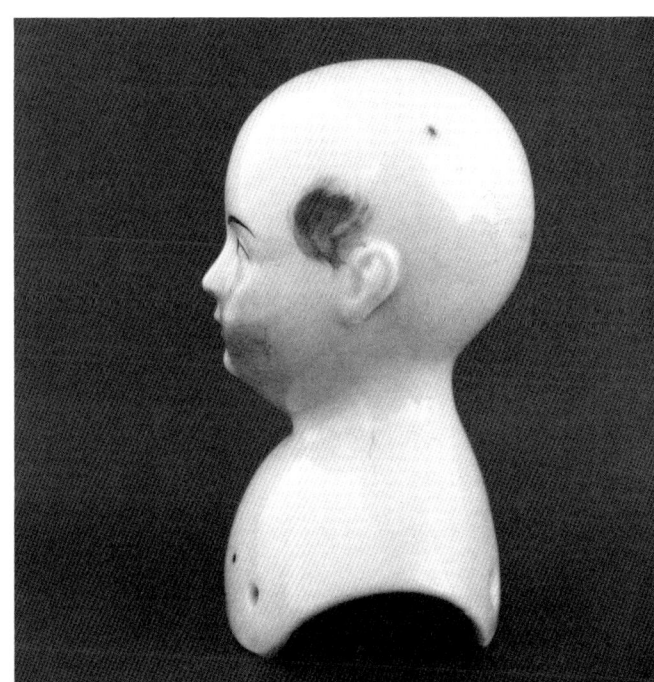

circa 1850

China Fashion-Type, French

These dolls stimulate interest and lively discussion among knowledgeable collectors, while novices may not know they exist. They're glazed china shoulder heads of an entirely different design, with cut-off pates, a cork inserted in the hole, and a wig attached to the cork by nails or glue; they are the forerunners of the luxury fashion doll era. This construction was an innovation. It allowed access to the inside of the head so that glass eyes could be set in, and the cork made attaching a wig a simple process. The painting style differs too from that of other china heads, both in color and delicacy. Though these dolls sometimes have glass eyes, the painted-eyed versions are treated vibrantly, and both are desirable. As with all things made by hand, the face of one doll may be more expressive than that of another.

The bodies of these dolls were made of various materials: leather, leather and wood, gutta percha — the most fragile — and even tin. Some will have china arms with separated fingers; some, china legs. Some may have the doll-maker's stamp on the body, or the stamp of the shop where they were purchased.

Verification exists that the bodies were made in France. French patents dating as early as 1850, and into the 1860s, were applied for by French doll-makers such as Mlle. Huret, Mlle. Rohmer, M. D'Autremont and M. Barrois — all consumed with inspiration and competitive spirit. Rohmer patent drawings — some published in doll books now hard to obtain — were explicit as to body details, describing increasingly complex arm, leg and, finally, turnable head-and-shoulder arrangements. The information notes the heads may be porcelain, but neglects to specify origin or appearance; the manner is so casual it seems there was no concern about the heads. Perhaps the doll-makers were using heads furnished by another source? If so, surely the heads were made by specific instruction, for, as a group, they are unlike any china shoulder heads previously made.

The Rohmers and Hurets of the fashion-type may be found in bisque as well as glazed china, and so may the others. But the distinctive appearance of the dolls by these two makers would make searching for a matching bisque doll somewhat easier, though not less time-consuming nor less costly.

The dolls in this group come from a highly competitive, creative era in French doll-making and are eagerly sought by highly competitive collectors, each of whom is searching for the most appealing face and the ultimate in material and body style, preferably stamped with a manufacturer's mark. Fortunate indeed is the collector who acquires all that, plus clothing contemporary with doll.

Dolls in numbered diagram of color photograph are also shown individually in black and white and fully described on pages indicated as follows:
(1) page 78, (2) page 79, (3) page 80.

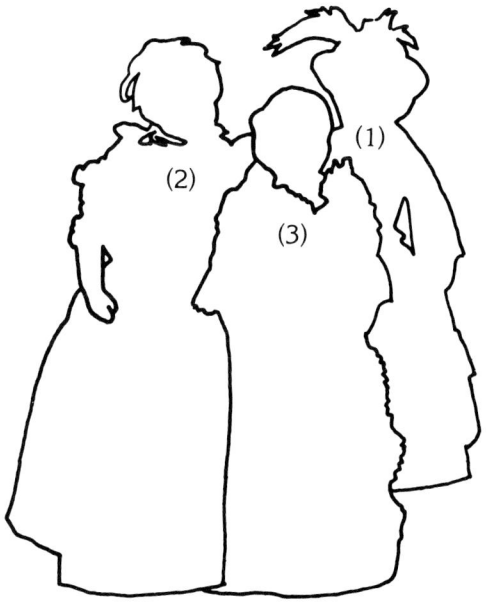

78
circa 1850

The coloring of this china fashion's features is typical of dolls within this group: two blues, grey and black at eyes; pink cheeks, nostrils and mouth; feathered tan eyebrows; white complexion here, some have overall pink tone; she is beautifully painted. Typical too is the bend of the china arms. Plain handstitched, stuffed leather body in good condition — usual gusset fill-up; unlabeled, unstamped. Cork pate; replacement sheepskin wig, remains of original nailed to cork. Shoulder head was nailed to innerlining of torso. She is marked DEPOSE, meaning registered, on front shoulder under leather; 17" tall.

Shown in color photograph (1), page 76.

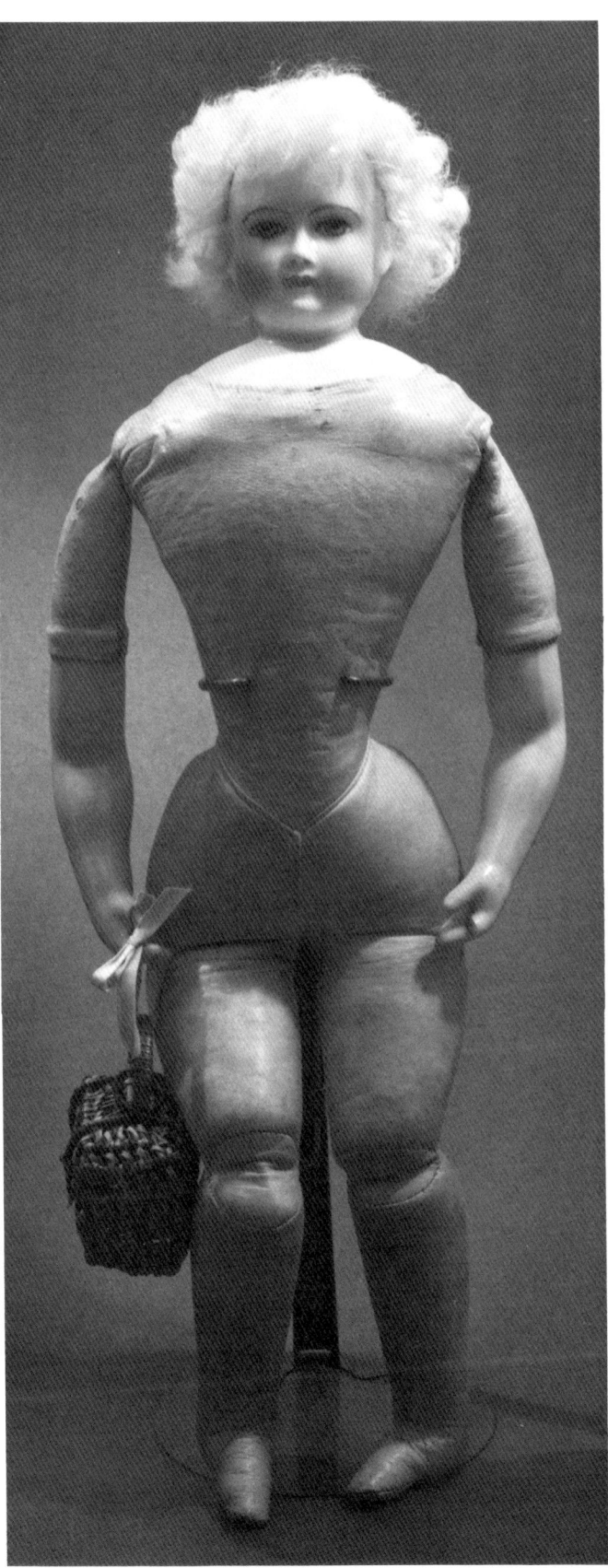

circa 1850

A china fashion doll with doll-maker's stamp in two places on body — a decidedly Rohmer fashion. Her head turns from side to side, from a joint sometimes called "cup and saucer" — flat surfaces are held together by tension of an elastic. The elastic runs through hole near top of pate cut-off, through neck openings of both pieces, then encircles wooden bar beneath shoulder. Arm tops are leather-covered wood, and desired positions can be maintained with this shoulder joint; note length of white china arms, separated fingers, tips tinted pink. Knees are of wood, ball-jointed, fitting firmly into a tubular opening inside thigh. The eyelet holes at waist hold cotton tape — ribbon, if original — with hooks that may latch onto knees, a positioning aid. Despite head damage, a thoroughly innovative, youthful-looking doll from approximately 1858; 18½" tall.

Shown in color photograph (2), page 76.

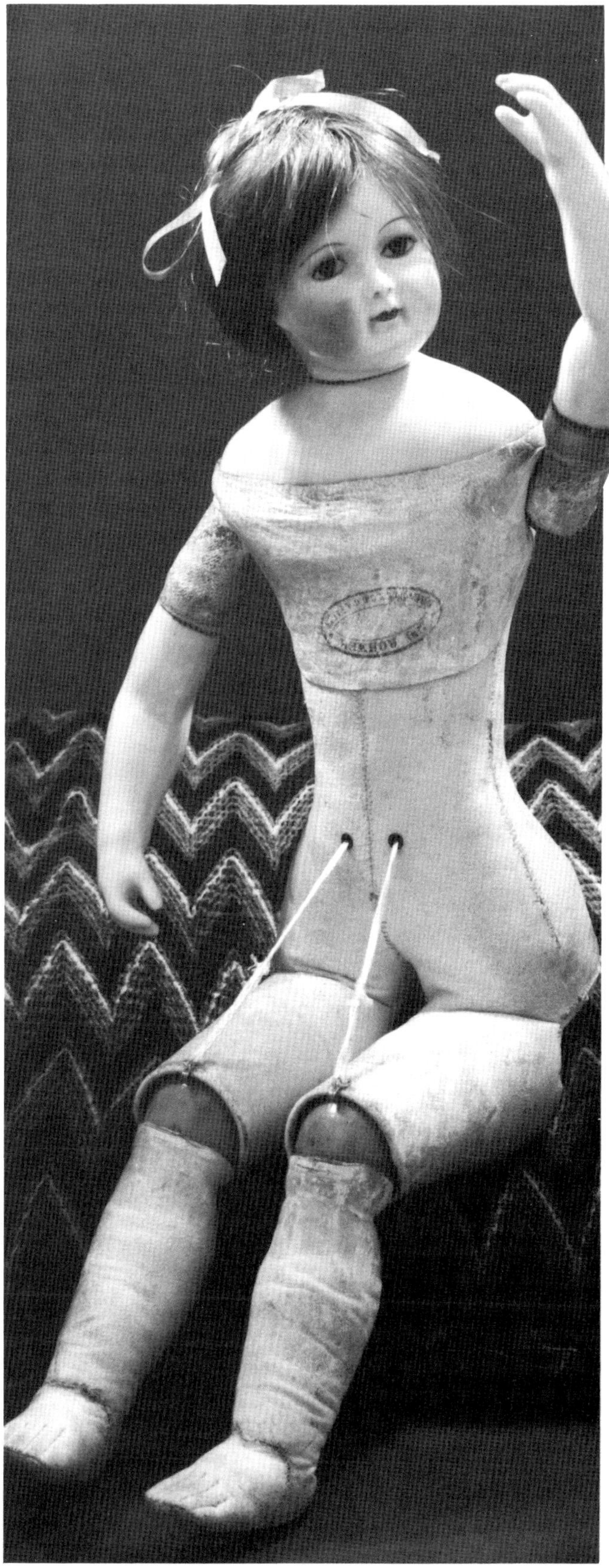

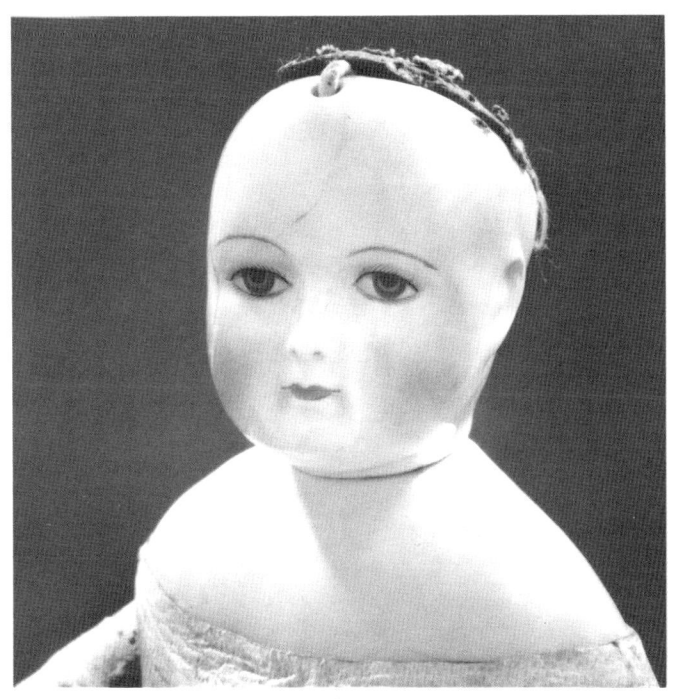

80
circa 1850

My heart and experience tell me that this china fashion-type is an example of Huret; technically, I should not say that, as body marking is absent. She is a straight-necked shoulder head, and her painting is typical of Hurets; she is of superior beauty. In Hurets of china, the glaze sometimes dulls the sharpness and depth of the painting, but this face is particularly expressive and appealing. The eyebrows are light tan, the eye outline and upper and lower lashes are grey, the irises are light blue bordered with brighter blue. No highlights. Pupils are jet black, as are the upper lid outlines — a sharp accent, drawing the viewer's gaze right to the eyes. No overall pink tone, but generously painted pink on plump, rounded cheeks and chin; molded ears. Early fashions often had sheepskin wigs, the skin sometimes cut with a small flap hanging in front of each ear; earrings were affixed to the flaps. The lady's stuffed leather body is gusseted at knees and seat; the sawdust has filled in, due to her lengthy lifespan. As in real life! The leather upper arm contains a wooden post with a slot; fitted into the slot is a bar that passes beneath the shoulder across to the opposite shoulder, enabling the arms to swing independently 360 degrees. The leather hands have separated fingers. The body is entirely handstitched in the tiniest of stitches; remarkably white with only lower arms showing signs of time. She owns flat black leather shoes laced in a V shape on the inside of the ankles and a faded brown and white cotton print dress. The color photograph shows her wearing a borrowed two-piece off-white satin gown. Shoulder head measures 3¾"; overall height is 16".

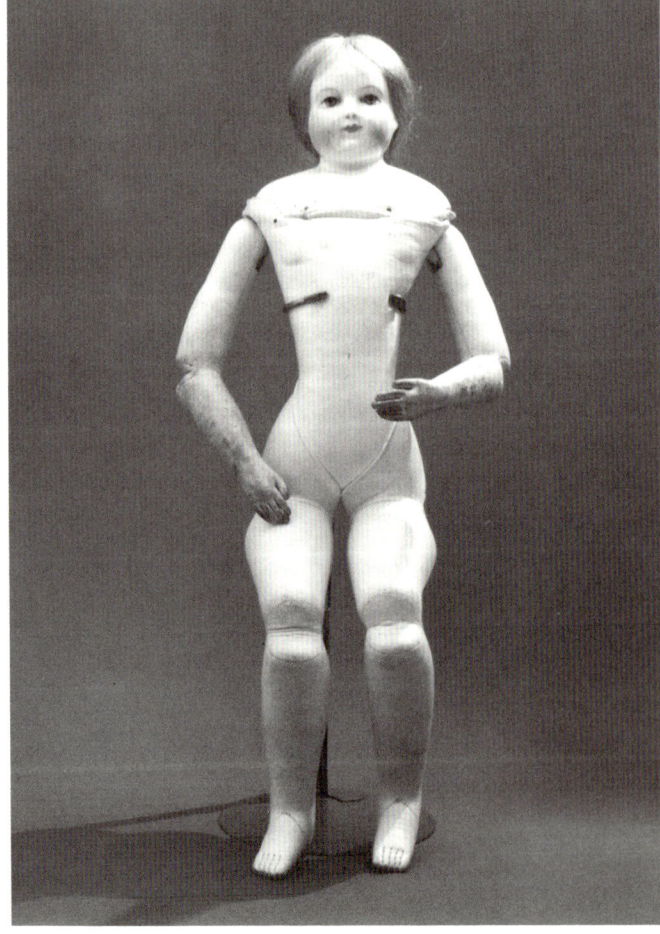

Shown in color photograph (3), page 76.

circa 1850

China fashion with molded hair painted black. Brushstrokes encircle all of black and are abundant at face; a windblown look, thought to depict a child. The facial painting is much like that on page 78; this one, lightly pink-toned overall. Entire body of leather; hand-stitched, separated, wired fingers; gusseted only at seat, stamped in green double oval at chest: BREVETEE S.G.D.G. — meaning, patent, without government guarantee. This style shoulder head, without cut pate and cork, is occasionally found with painted brown hair. 14¾" tall.

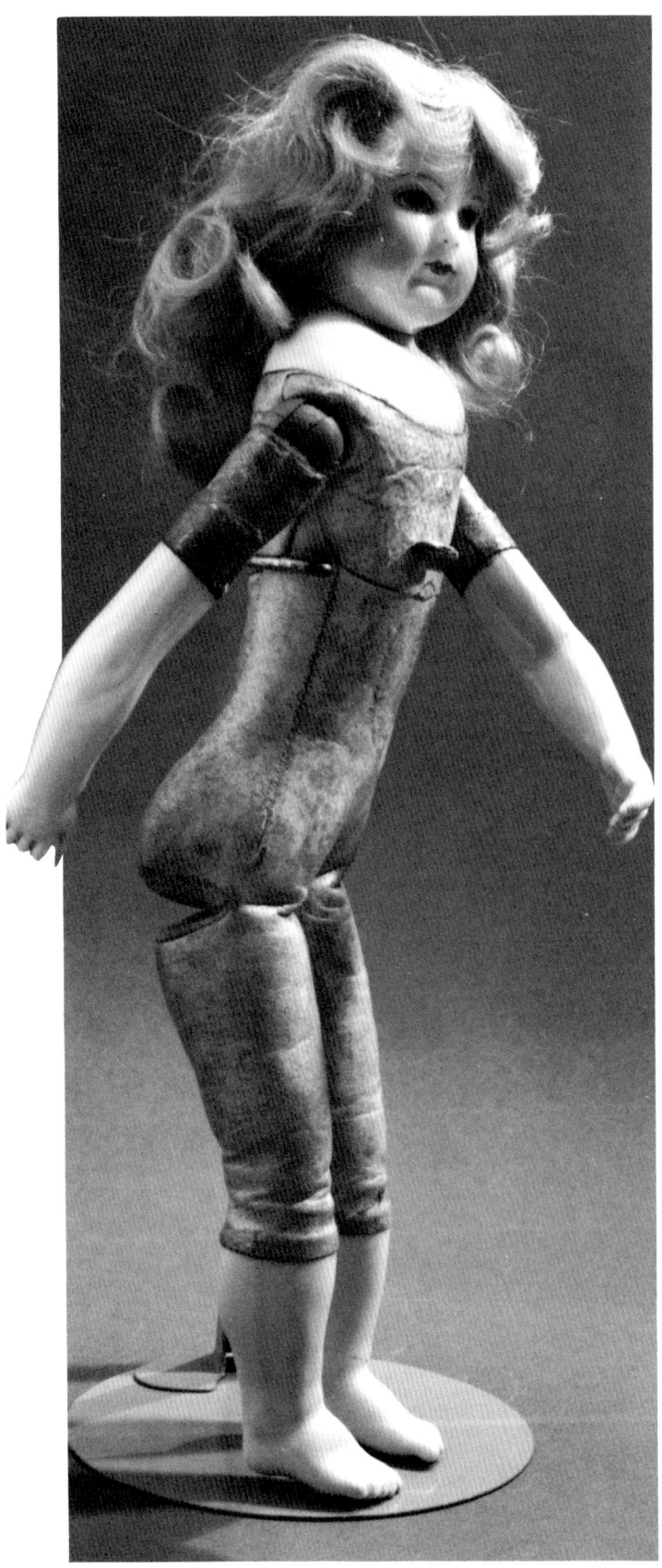

French china fashion with flat neck joint and bare-footed china legs, stamped with green oval trademark of Rohmer. Have you noticed by now that these dolls do not have highlights in their eyes? The same painting style once again, this time over a creamy complexion tone, matching bent china arms with delicate separated fingers, and lower legs; fingertips and toes are touched with extra pink. Upper arm is wood, covered with leather down to the china; the shoulder joint and the rigidity make retaining a position possible. Highly desirable features on such a small doll. She is 12⅜" tall.

circa 1850

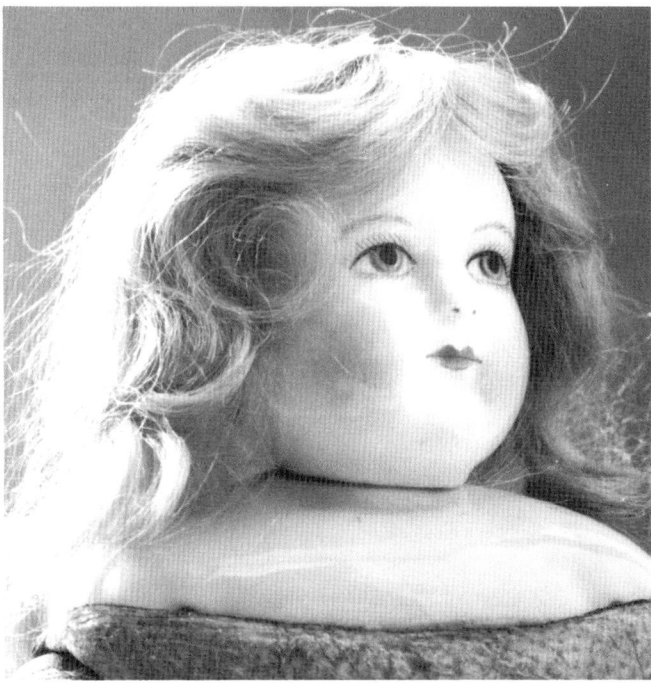

Many Rohmers of my acquaintance have this youthful look to the face and youthful shape to the body.

Youthful-appearing china fashion with molded, brown painted, brushstroked hair with a matte finish. This surface was probably an unexpected occurrence in the firing process of the paint and not a planned effect. Otherwise, the shoulder head is shiny; blue eyes, light brown eyebrows. Shoulder is round at the base. White leather, ungusseted fashion body. Shoulder head is 3½"; total height is 13¾".

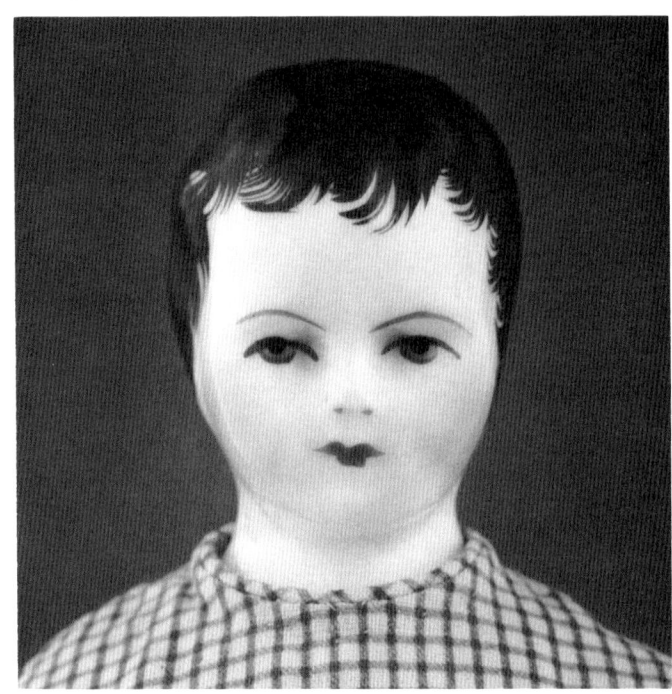

Glass-eyed china fashion doll; blue irises streaked with lighter blue lines; black pupils; this doll's eyes are installed with a very old-looking, hard opaque yellow-ochre substance. The holes cut out for eyes (eye cuts) are one-half inch across, large for size of face. Upper edges of eye cuts are painted brown; lower edges are painted grey. Upper and lower eyelashes are fine grey lines. There are fifteen very fine tan painted strokes in each eyebrow. Nostrils are bright coral dots; mouth is outlined in a lighter tone, and cheeks are still lighter. Overall complexion is a rich creamy color; inside of head is white, entirely glazed. This type china fashion has little sculpted detail — a smooth bump for a nose and large flat ears; but this doll is all eyes, and that is what counts in her appeal. Her leather body, once pink, has shapely, but stiff legs and no special joints. Shoulder head is 4½" and total height is 18⅝".

circa 1850

French china fashion with blue glass eyes, pink-toned shoulder head, stationary neck, cork pate and wig. A heavy stroke of brown outlines upper edge of eye cuts; she too has very fine grey lashes and tan feather-stroked brows. Shapely pink bisque lower arms; faded pink leather body, gusseted at seat. Incised E ı B on front shoulder under leather; 13½" tall; a slender, mature lady look.

Her tattered silk dress is backed with cotton and trimmed with half-inch-wide, hairpin-lace-edged silk ribbon; everything is pink and precisely handstitched; an example of the manner in which some of these lady dolls were dressed: with simplicity, but with fabric and trim of the time making all the difference in appearance.

circa 1860

ABUNDANT & PLAIN

Plain are the dolls that come to mind when any of these names is mentioned: Godey Lady, Civil War style, Flat-top, Highbrow and Common. Whatever name is used, they are the plain dolls, and they were a staple product for years. They had shining black curls beneath a smooth, center-parted hair style, similar to girl styles of the 1850s; scads of examples fit their basic description. Each one shown here has a slight variation, as though the manufacturers had their own versions. Do not regard the plain china doll lightly, as she did her job in the market for at least thirty years, and served little girls for several generations.

This area is where beginning collectors could find a vintage china doll with old-style workmanship and appeal at a reasonable price and expect quite a lot for their money. Why? Because these dolls are readily available. The choice is better; you can be politely picky about what you buy. The only sure way you will absorb what you are reading is to obtain a china doll to ponder and experience. It is best to take the first plunge at a price that does not stagger the mind. As one graduates to chinas not so readily available, the prices increase considerably.

The fact is, that though the plain ones may not win a prized ribbon at a doll competition, they are still a child's doll of breakable substance, made by craftsmen of another century — men, women and even children — and those remaining dolls are survivors!

Doll opposite also shown and described on page 94.

Note: Showing wear, the pattern framing photo opposite is reproduced from a child's dress of the period — actual dress, of brown-printed white cotton.

circa 1860

The dolls shown in this section are by no means identical, but this first description will basically apply to each example in the group. Usually these dolls have no brushmarks and seldom are pink-toned. Occasionally they are found with original body and complete attire. Bodies may be homemade all-cloth, precisely to crudely made; or commercial cloth with china arms and legs, or with leather arms and cloth legs. More often, only heads are found, and the rest is up to you. These dolls look appropriate in old cottons — plain or prints — made in simple style. Do not use modern blends; 100 percent cotton is available and should be used if possible. These are plain, pleasant ladies, and their appeal is an individual thing. Variations of this basic description will be noted.

This serene lady has molded, painted black hair with center white part, single curls at temples; ten vertical sausage curls surround head. Poured into mold; thick, heavy; extremely shiny. Bright blue eyes, slight highlight; black brows and lid outline. Eyelid crease line, small mouth with painted parted lips, and oval nostril indications all are red-orange. Her body is old, commercially made of cloth; clothes, old homemade cotton. She came described as needing repair, apparently because of pock marks — imperfections in the glaze. That is not a condition needing repair, but is often present, and, if not on tip of nose, is expected and acceptable in these dolls. Her shoulder head, incised with large 8 inside back, is 6¼" high; total height is 24".

circa 1860

A— thirteen sausage curls; whole doll is 22½".

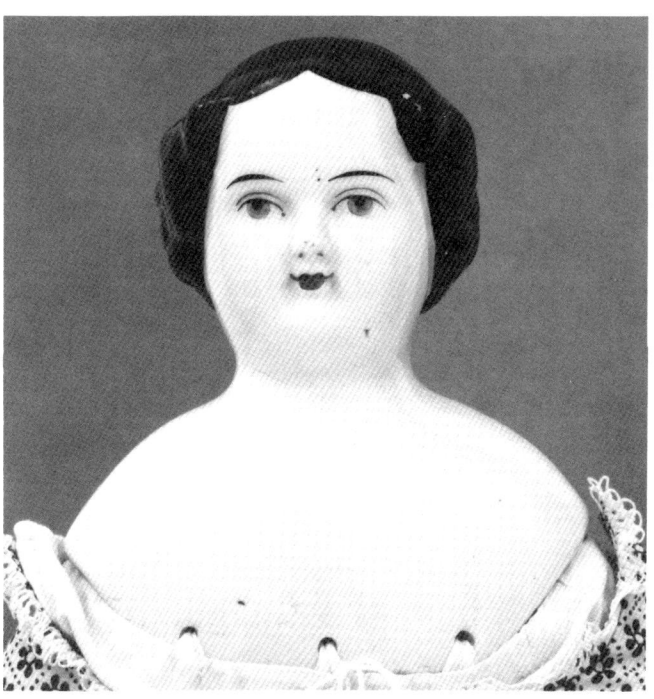

B— smooth, fat, vertical curls, pressed into mold; inside shoulder incised 7; 40 in lavender paint, 80 in black paint.

C— vertical curls starting high on head, adding extra width.

circa 1860

D— very wide neck; shoulders sloped, but narrow.

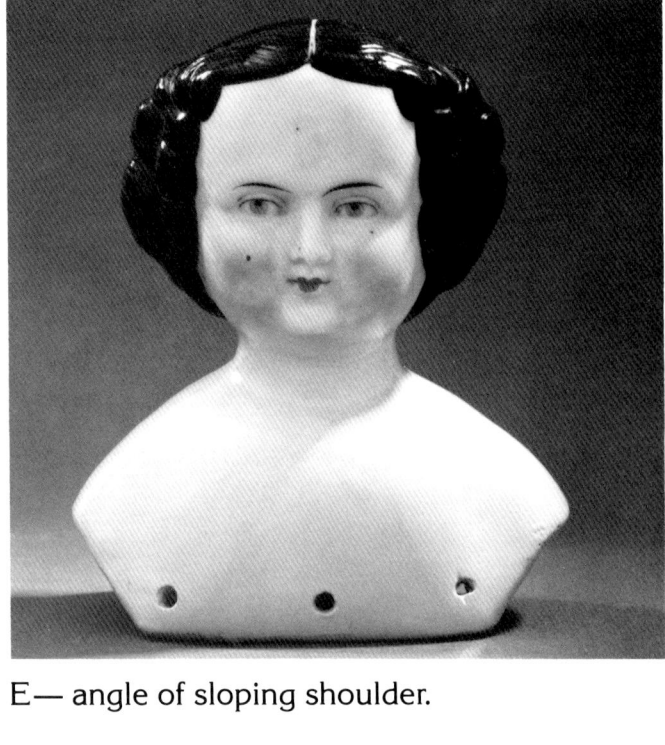

E— angle of sloping shoulder.

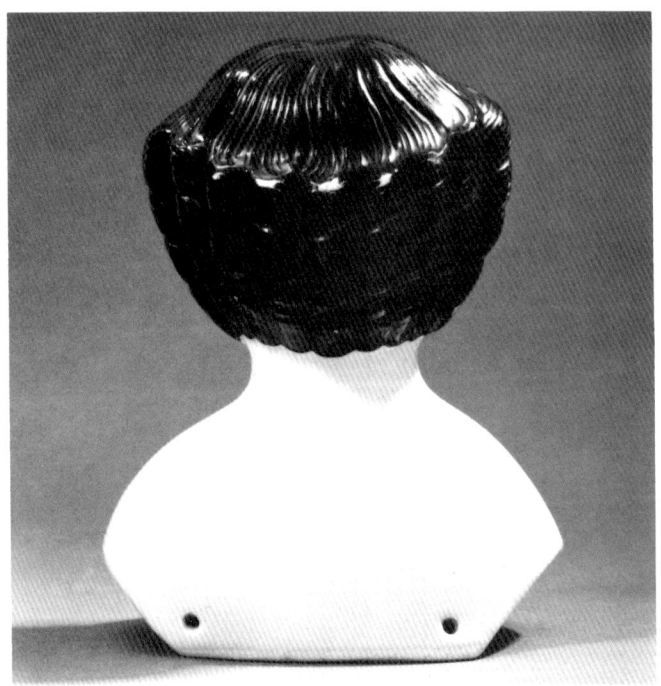

circa 1860

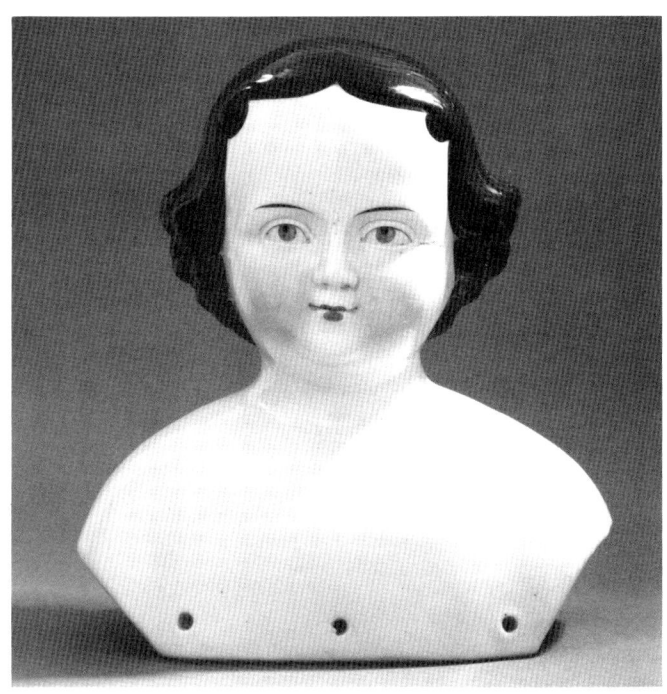

F— deep, molded eyelids; 7¼" tall; turquoise eyes.

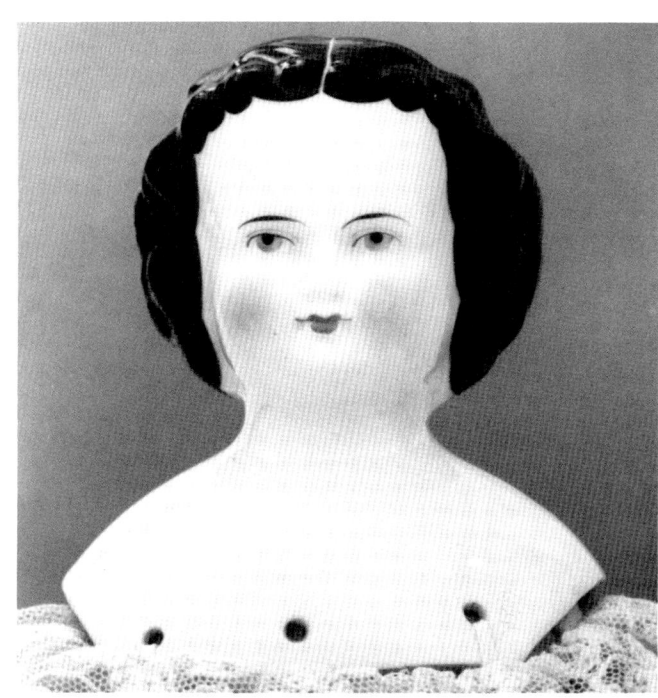

G— nice features, but hair painting stopped short of indicated molded area.

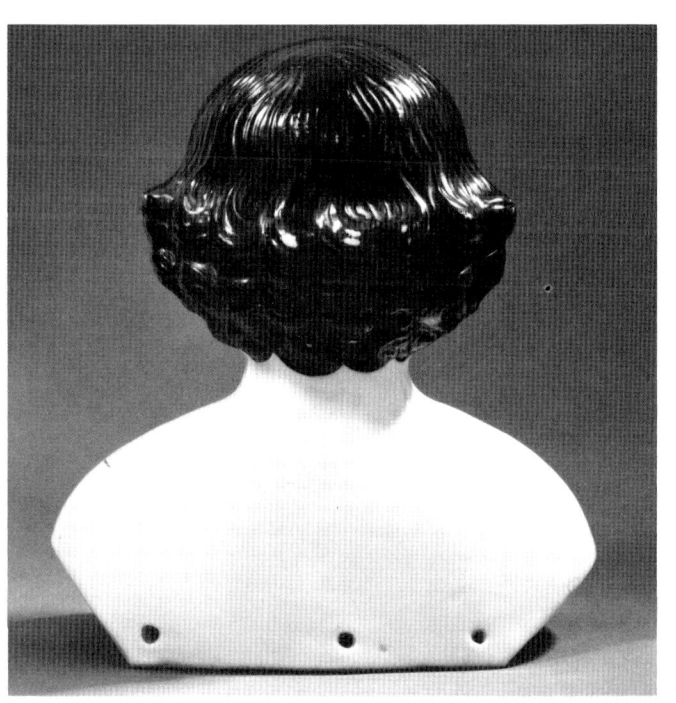

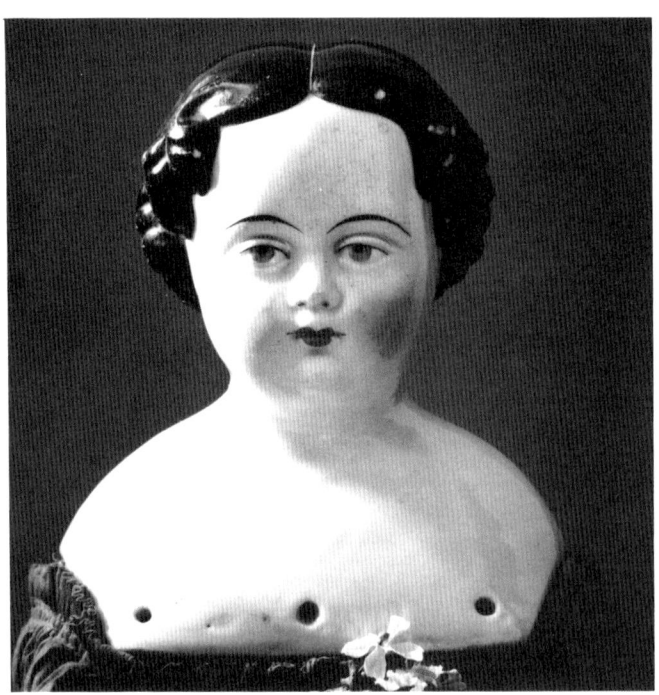

H— thick, heavy china, pressed into mold; incised with numeral VIII on outside, front shoulder.

I— brown painted eyes, ten curls; under shoulder, an incised 6; in brown paint matching eyes, a 23; in black paint, a 35; in red-orange, an X.

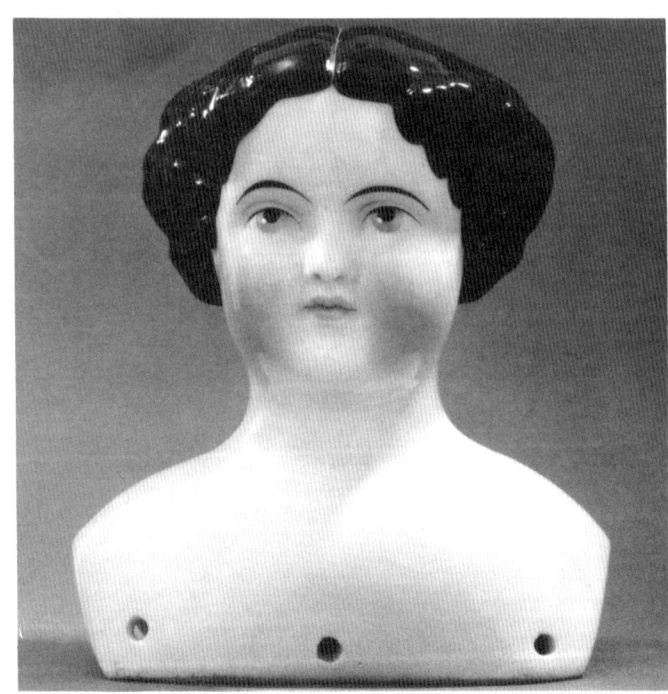

J— flesh-toned; shoulder is narrow and square; possibly made later when armhole fashion changed from drop shoulders to top-of-arm.

circa 1860

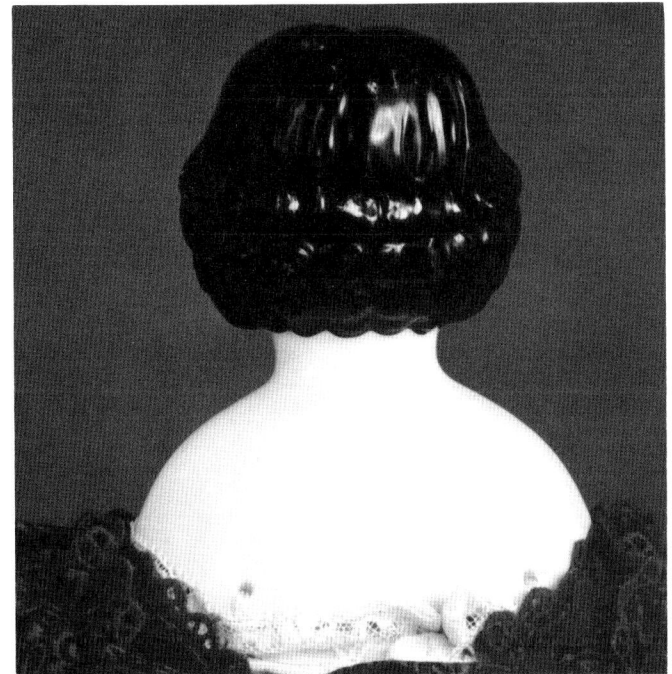

K— youthful appearance, brown painted eyes.

circa 1860

Other variations, not mentioned here, but used for making comparisons:
- style of and number of curls rounding head,
- number of sew holes,
- size of features compared to face,
- painted with or without parted lips,
- highlights in eyes, or not.

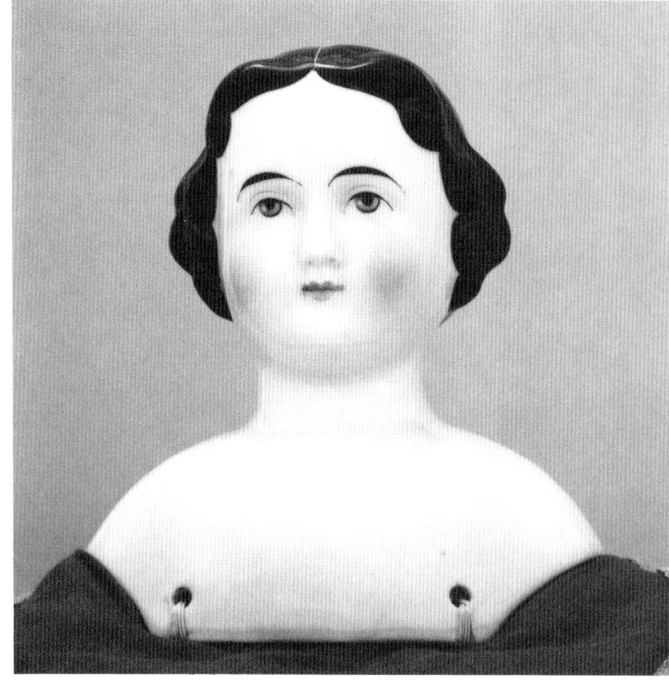

L— pink-toned, can also be found in bisque.

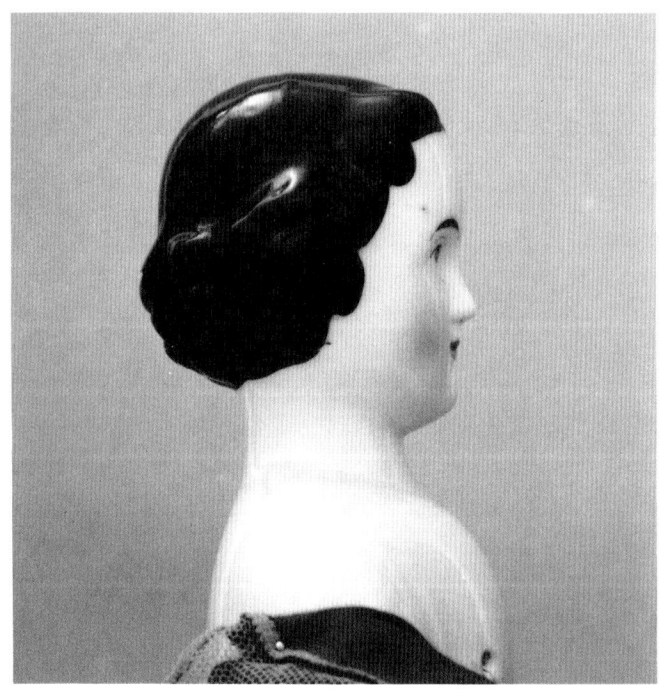

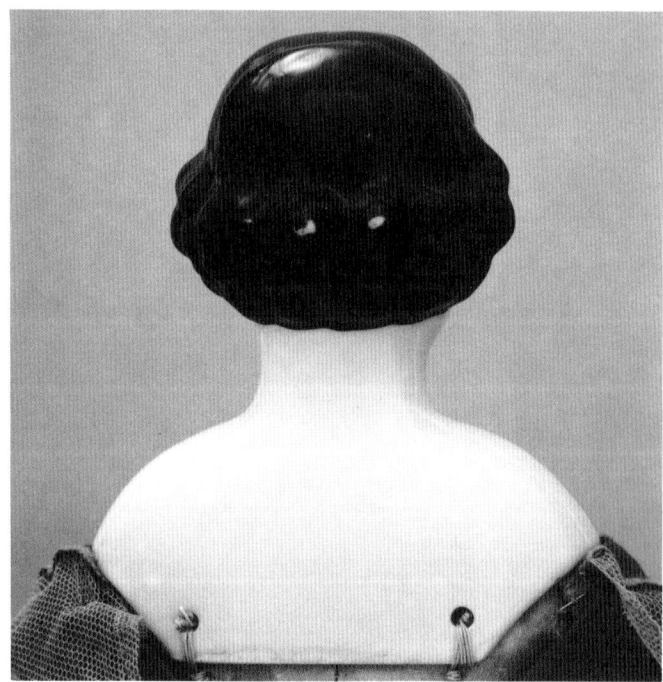

circa 1860

The man is clothed in: brown wool suit with vest, beaded watch chain, silk shirt, blue tie. Clothing is old. Head is 1⅛"; total height, 4⅛".

The lady is clothed in: gown of cream-colored ribbon, with delicate lace edging incorporated into its satin border, extra blue bows; petticoat and drawers; blue ribbons at knees. Legs have painted pink ribbons at knees, painted black ankle-high boots. Shoulder head, with single sew hole front and back, is 1⅛"; doll, 4⅛".

Hair style of man and woman is of the 1860s era, all proper painting detail, blue eyes; arms and legs not glazed. The child has black covered-wagon hair style and brown eyes, no part, single sew hole at front and back. Dress of dark red old cotton; petticoat, drawers. 1½" shoulder head; 3⅞" tall.

Shown in color photograph (5), page 22.

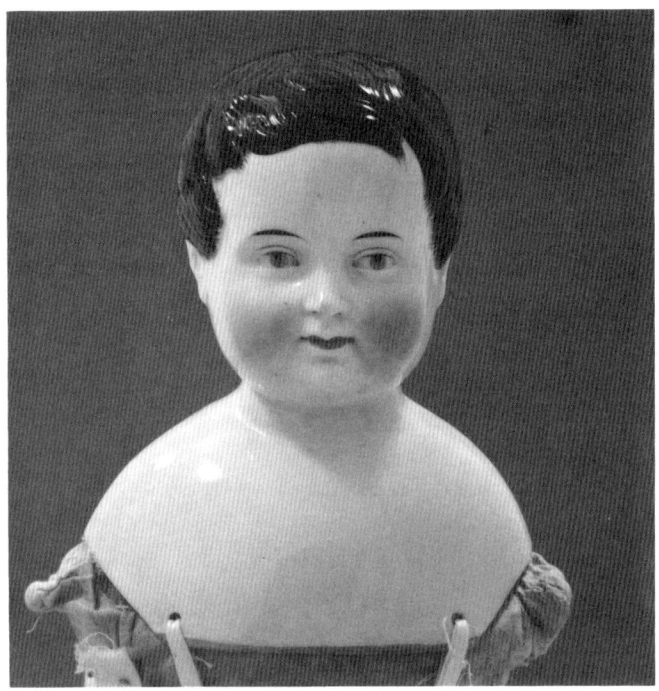

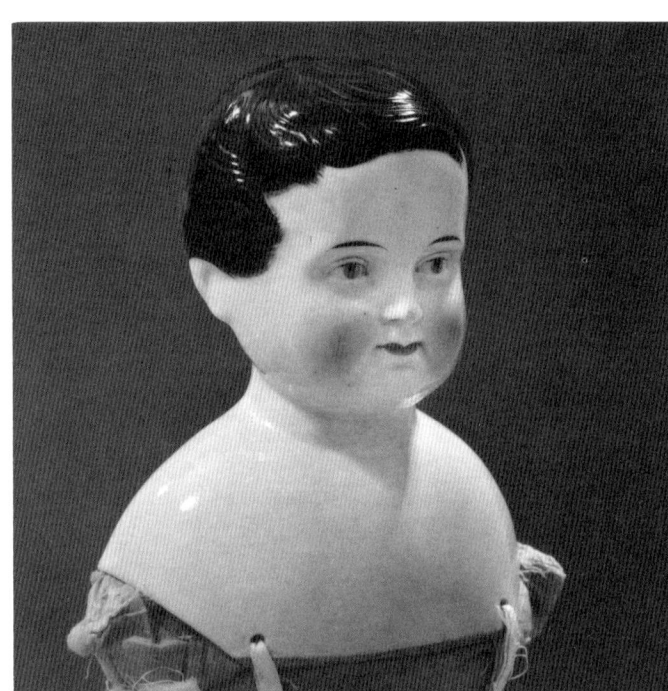

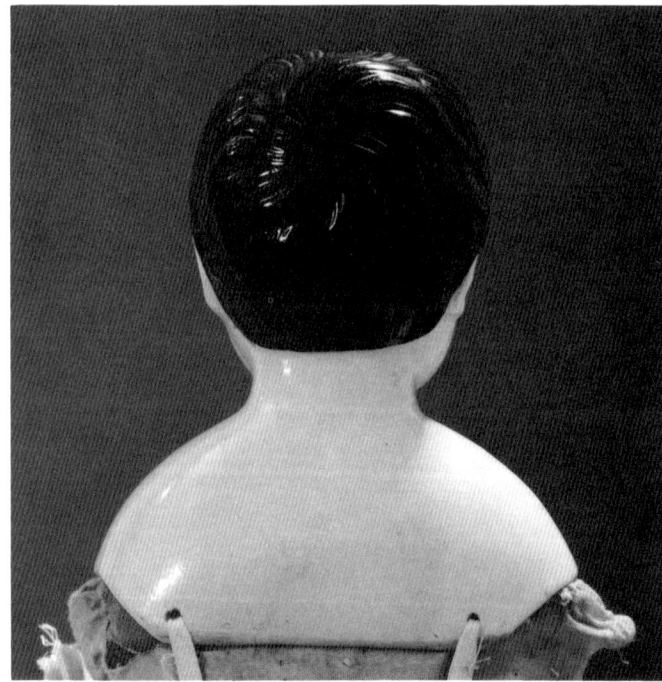

Men and boy chinas of this period are comparable to the lady dolls of this time, but are sought by fewer collectors. Are we more Victorian about this subject than the Victorians were? Or is it simply easier to dress lady dolls? When found, men and boy chinas are more likely to have original clothes than the ladies.

China boy or man with detailed black hair, waved from center-back to asymmetrical arrangement at face, as though combed across forehead. Black brow; blue eyes, no highlights; black then red-orange outline above eyes; nostrils, mouth and cheeks are red-orange. Entire head has good detail work in modeling; painting is casual, in comparison. China was poured and is very white; incised 10 inside, and 1 in red paint. Body is commercial cotton; long, narrow torso with flat, wide hips. He came dressed in a "made-recently" black wool jersey suit and white dickey. Head is 5" high; total doll is 20".

circa 1860

Peg-wooden china boy; black painted, side-parted hair. Full facial detail, bright blue eyes. On articulated wooden body, jointed at shoulders, elbows, hips and knees. Handstitched clothes look old: pink silk tunic with brown braid, ribbed white silk pantaloons — an appropriate costume for boys of middle 1800s. Lower legs painted grey with white buttons. His actual size is 3½".

Boy china doll with molded, black painted hair with brushstrokes at face; very pink in tone; blue eyes, tiny highlights; black outline at edge of blue irises, black eyelid lines; eyelid crease lines, open oval nostril indications and slightly parted lips all are red-orange. Well-shaped ears. The painting is precise; each stroke is exactly placed. Cloth body and leather arms; 4¼" shoulder head, whole doll is 17¾".

98
circa 1860

Original costume on china boy doll; hand-stitched, ungusseted leather body; overall well-defined modeling, especially of black painted hair. He is quite white; the eye painting lacks red at eyelids, and eye highlights are dots of white. The shoulder head is quite deep: 3¼" for a doll 11¾" tall. The notable thing about this small doll is the amount of handwork required to accomplish this costume. One assumes that it is correct in detail: the straps are leather, the emblems are metal, all the cloth is fine wool and his shoes have tiny ribbon bows. He does wear drawers. China dolls were often commercially dressed in regional costumes and should never be disturbed for any reason. This doll, whose shoulder head is average in interest, is special because he remains totally undisturbed. When he may have been manufactured is open to speculation and matters little.

circa 1860

Man doll of china, with decorated shoulder. The extra molding and painting on shoulder is: a pleated shirt front, including shoulder seams, a stand-up collar, single ruffle with generous bow tie. The plaid tie is painted blue, lavender and gold; the ruffle is stroked with lavender and edged in gold. He has painted black hair with side part, is well-molded and brushstroked around face. Very good detailed painting of face; an example of a doll made by a skilled company; a similar model came in tinted bisque. Many lady dolls have the same face. He is on cloth body with leather arms. No marks of any kind. The shoulder head is 6½"; the whole gentleman is 23½".

Feeling this doll to be special, I entered him in competition. He turned out to be one of three in the group, and in passing, a mid-Western friend announced she had a blonde version at home. A humbling experience. This is a case of dolls being scarce in one part of the country and readily available elsewhere. Nevertheless, his purchase was worthwhile, as it stimulated research into clothing for him and helped me acquire some understanding of men's clothing of that time — a neglected subject among doll collectors. Gentlemen wore quite colorful garments at home. The silk smoking jacket, circa 1870, on which this costume was based, was hand-embroidered and the lining was quilted; it had a matching cap with large tassel. So, though not rare, the gentleman doll is colorful, and I learned something.

circa 1860

FANCY & DECORATED

Elegant lady chinas with fancy hairdos were the other type of doll that was thought to have earned its way. These were produced by a number of companies, judging by the variety of facial styles, silhouettes and craftsmanship. Decorated chinas are within this grouping. The dolls were based on up-to-date hair styles of the time. The concept suggests that none would be made on a long-term basis. The style seems to have been an attempt by manufacturers to intrigue customers, retain interest in their products and compete with bisque and parian dolls. Collectors today will find that these dolls are fewer in number than those of the previous group, not so often available and definitely more expensive. Quietly elegant, sometimes lavished with gold lustre as a highlight to their ribbons, combs, bows and tassels, the dolls are a parade of the hair styles of fashionable women up to the 1880s. They are not usually marked; their molded hair styles serve as a guide for approximate dating and, being molded, remain undisturbed. Wigged dolls were often updated with new wigs or styling.

The word **decorated**, in doll terms, originally meant the painting done on a doll's head; that is, a doll's head was decorated, or painted; the words were synonymous. Within the china doll realm, the word **decorated** now also means the painting of bows, tassels, bands and other trim in a contrasting color to that of the hair. The doll on page 113, though interesting because of its many special features, is not considered decorated. The Grape Lady, and others in this group with contrasting color in addition to the basic hair color, would be considered decorated.

Dolls in numbered diagram of color photograph are also shown individually in black and white and fully described on pages indicated as follows:
(1) page 105, (2) page 107, (3) page 110, (4) page 111, (5) page 112.

circa 1860

Highly decorated lady china doll, called "Morning Glory." Behind left ear: one large orange and two smaller pink morning glories, all with yellow centers, and three large green leaves, shaded and veined with brown. Behind right ear: two large flowers, one coral and one blue, with white and yellow centers, one small orange flower, yellow-centered, and two leaves as before. The flowers were formed before the kiln firing, rather than applied afterward. The hair is pulled back to generous braided coil, with tendrils down nape onto shoulder. Unusual, too, is that at her hairline light brown is over-stroked with fine brushmarks of a darker brown, making a gradual transition into the dark brown of her hair. Eyebrows are two-toned; again dark brown over light brown. Blue painted eyes — no highlights; black pupils and eye outline; lid line, inner eye line, nostril indications and parted lips all are a soft red. White of eye left white. Long slender neck, slightly molded bosoms; three large sew holes, front and back. Poured into mold; quite thick at shoulder and glazed white inside and out, with pink tone applied over that. Shoulder head is 4⅜", and whole doll on handstitched leather body with well-molded china arms is 16¾" tall. This doll was placed among the decorated models — the obvious choice — but she has all the characteristics of the brown-haired group, as well. Inside left shoulder there is an incised *3*.

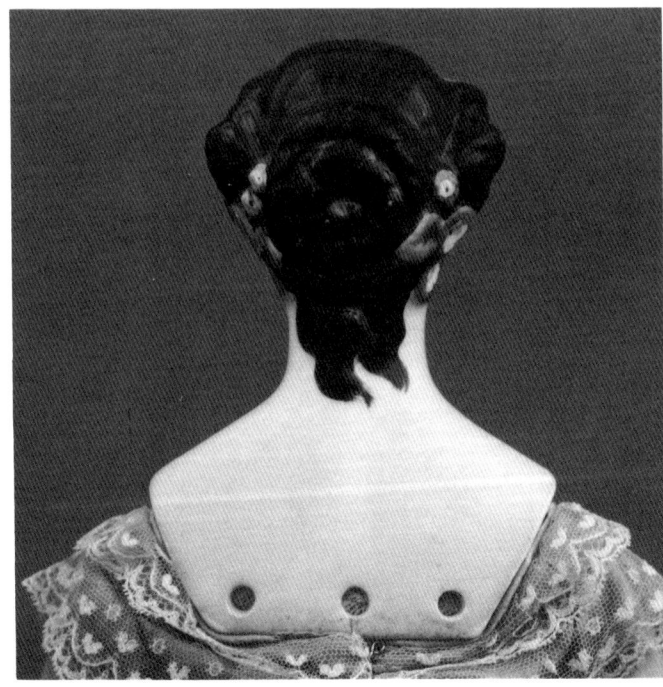

circa 1860

Lady doll with molded, black painted hair style; white center part, brushstrokes at temples; hair is fluffed out over ears, then gently pulled back into circular bun at center-back of head. Blue painted eyes, no highlights; black eyelid outlines; red-orange crease lines, inner eye dots, nostril dots and mouth. Eyelids are molded with depth. Heavy white china; a 7 is incised on front shoulder. Old cloth body with leather arms. Shoulder head is 5"; total doll is 20½". Whether or not it was intended as a portrait, this style is called "Jenny Lind."

Shown in color photograph (5), page 44.

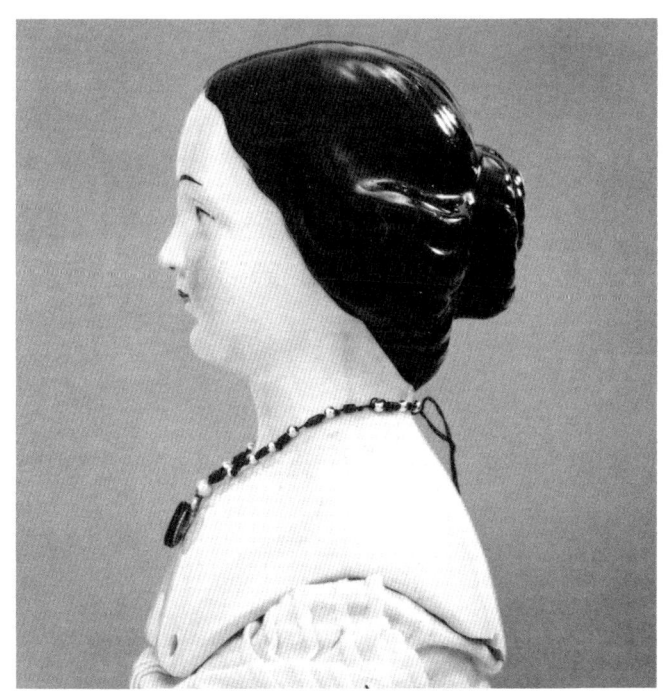
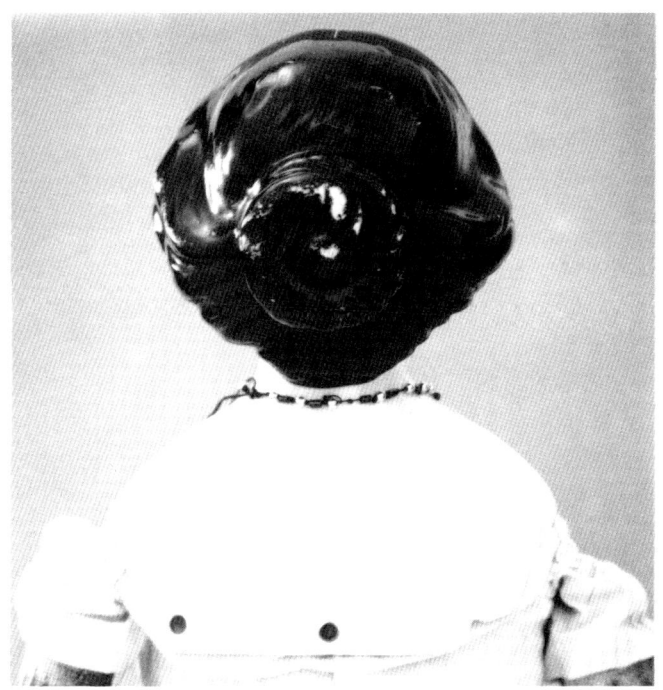

104
circa 1860

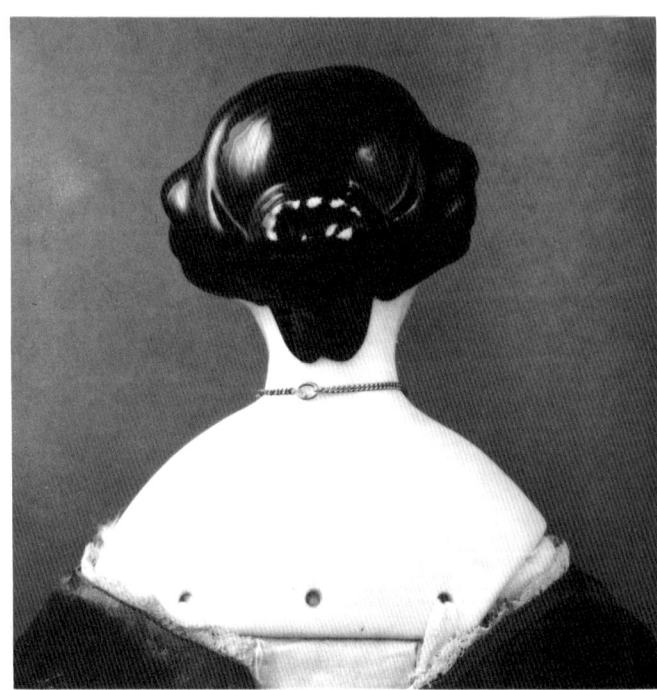

China lady whose apparently simple hairdo ends at the back with a surprising braided bun and bow, plus two dangling curls, as well as brushstrokes from eyebrow to mouth level. All proper painting present, and sought-after brown painted eyes with white highlights. Cloth body with old china legs, ankle-high painted black boots, blue bows at knees, newer china arms. Shoulder head is 4¼" high and whole doll is 17¾".

circa 1860

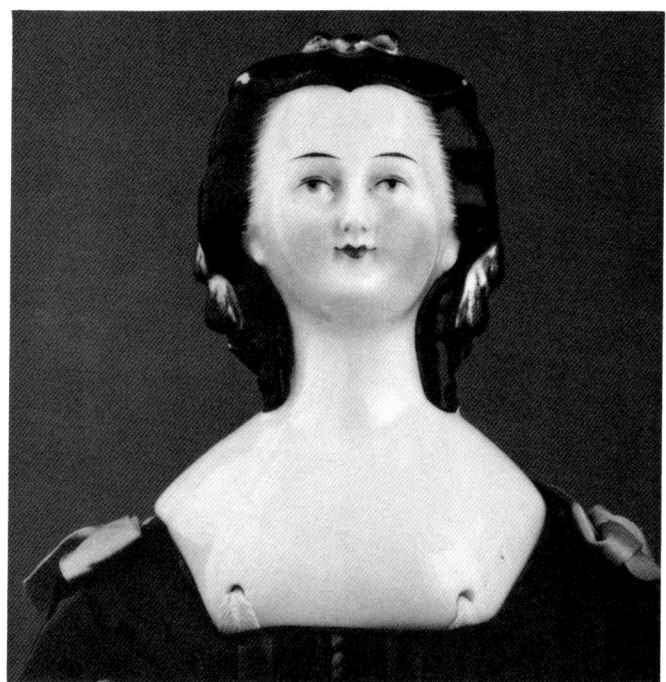

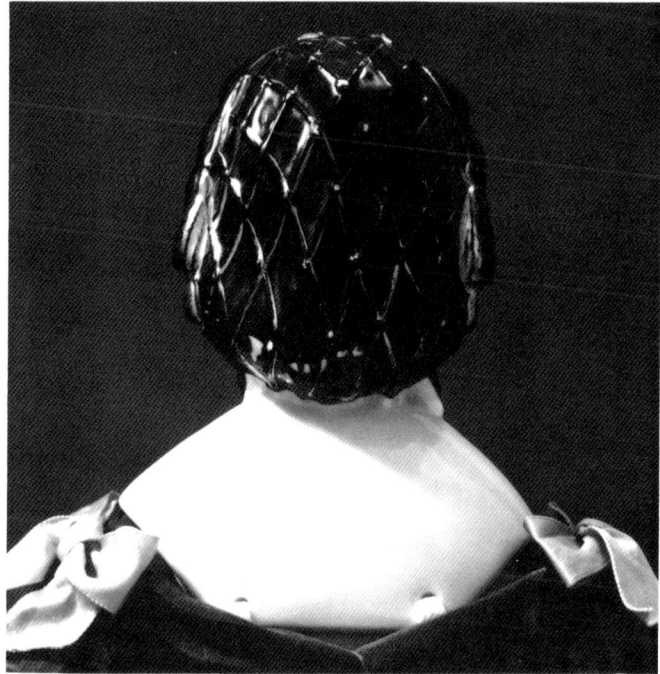

Shown in color photograph (1), page 100.

Gracefully elegant decorated china lady with painted gold snood, tassels and bow. Her black painted hair with widow's peak and no center part is generously brushmarked about the face, and ears are semi-exposed. The facial painting is delicate, simple, swiftly done and accurate in placement: blue irises, no highlights; black pupils, eye outline and eyebrows; red-orange eyelid crease lines, inner eye dots, nostril indications, mouth and cheeks. The snood detail includes two tassels by each ear and bow at center top; intersecting lines of snood are formed with a bead that is not touched with the gold paint — effect is that of a gold snood with black beads. Her neck is long, a hollow is at base of throat and shoulders are sloping; bosoms are gently rounded — not as pronounced as on some earlier dolls. The white china is smooth and attractive; shoulder head was not removed. Old cloth body and lower legs; old china arms, slender, with long fingers. This model is known to have been made in larger sizes, and its beauty makes it highly desirable. Head is 4¾" and total is 17⅞".

circa 1860

China head with detailed modeling of snood with band across top (sometimes referred to as an "Alice" band) and brushstroked forehead — all painted black, and showing scuffs. Note short neck and round face. A doll with snood similar to this one is pictured in a catalogue page from 1860 and was said to represent a child. This doll is 22" tall.

Inside shoulder head is a painted HE/60 and an incised 9.

circa 1860

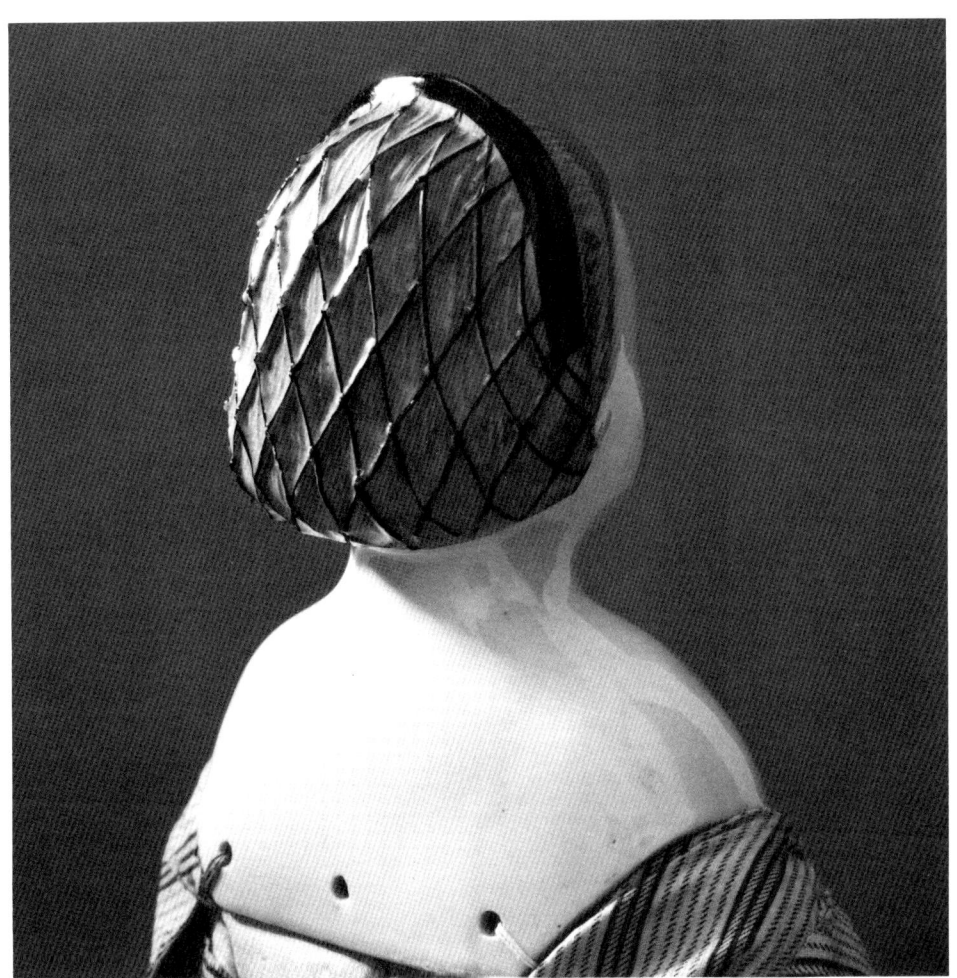

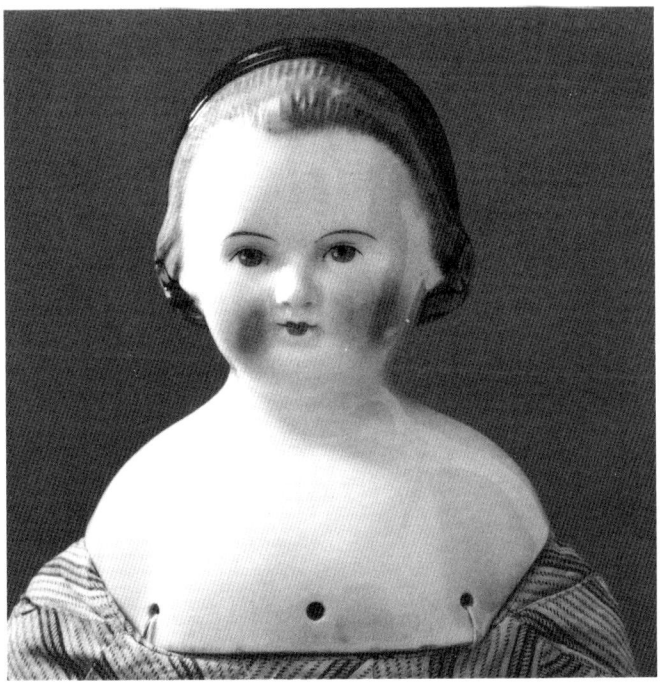

China head doll of same model as facing page; however, this one has taffy-colored hair, which gives her quite a different appearance. Black band and snood. Have you noticed there is a molded bead at each intersecting line of the snood? Neither doll has any skin tone; both are white. The painting on both is precise, giving them a sparkling, bright-eyed look. On homemade crude linen body; this one is 20½" tall.

Shown in color photograph (2), page 100.

108
circa 1860

China shoulder head with taffy-colored hair; black snood with flat pink band across top that ends with a bow at each temple. The snood has a black half-circle at center behind pink band, indicating a decorative comb, and a ⅛" black stripe from comb to base of neck. The white in photograph is where paint has worn away. A touch of gold remains on the pink. This shoulder head, though chubby and short at neck, has a mature look.
It measures 3⅝".

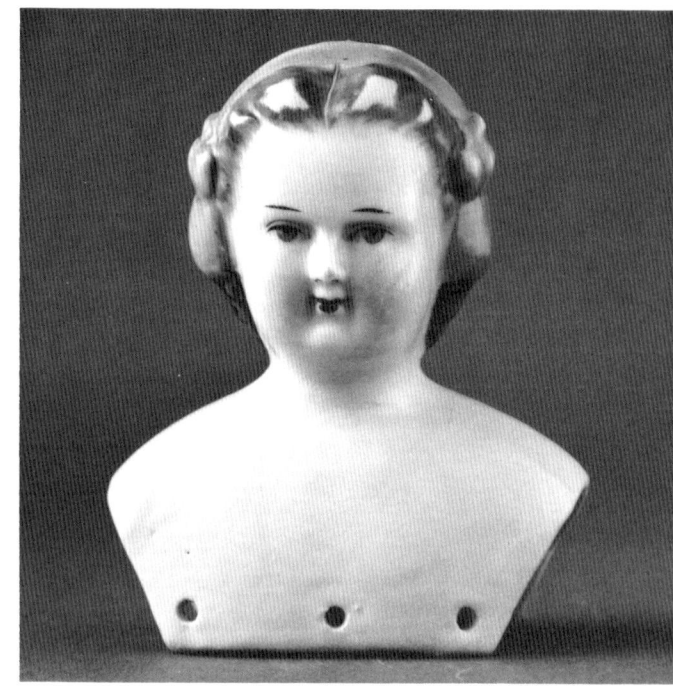

circa 1860

This taffy-haired snood lady of molded and painted china has a blue drapery across head, ending with plump tassels at each temple; the blue is highlighted with gold, snood lines are painted black. The shoulder head is part of an **autoperipatetikos** — a mechanical walking doll that operates by means of a key-wound clock mechanism; brass boots take one step and then another. No patent date here, but similar models have patent date of July 15, 1862 printed on disk at bottom of bell-shaped cardboard skirt that houses the mechanism. These toys were patented by Enoch Rice Morrison in England and America. China heads were sometimes used as part of such toys and others. This one still works; the shoulder head is 3" high, and the whole walking lady is 10".

circa 1860

China snood lady with molded, painted blue drapery across top and down past her right ear; left side has a pink feather. Snood strands are black. Taffy-colored hair gets lighter as it gets closer to face. Tan eyebrows, blue eyes (no highlights); eyelids are deeply molded and outlined in black; red-orange used for crease line in lids, inner eye dots, nostrils, cheeks and mouth. Narrow face and slender neck. Old cloth body, cloth lower legs and old china arms. Style is known as "Empress Eugénie"; several versions of this were made in a fine white bisque (unglazed porcelain) called parian. Shoulder repaired, no under-shoulder information available; measures 4½" and whole doll is 17½".

Shown in color photograph (3), page 100.

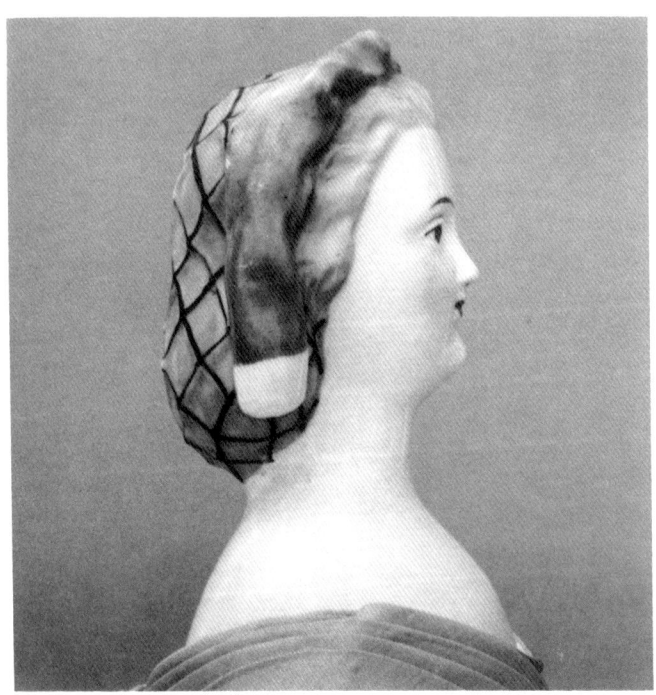
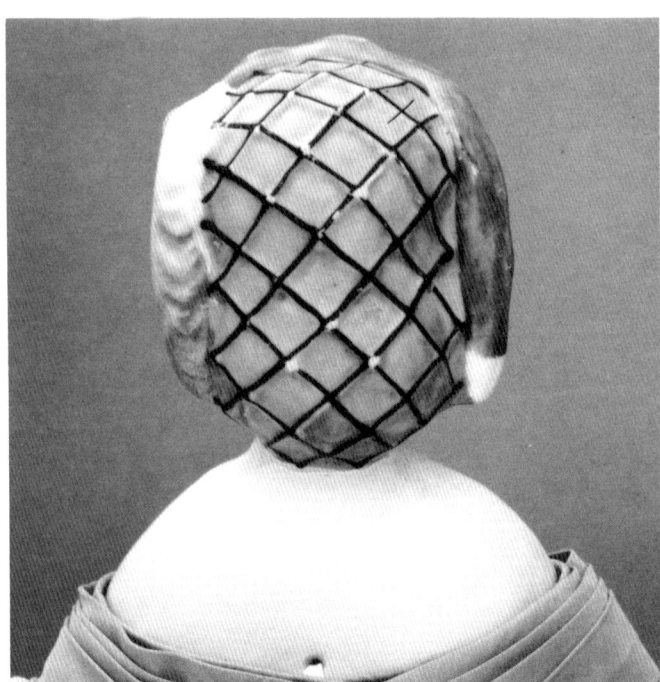

circa 1860

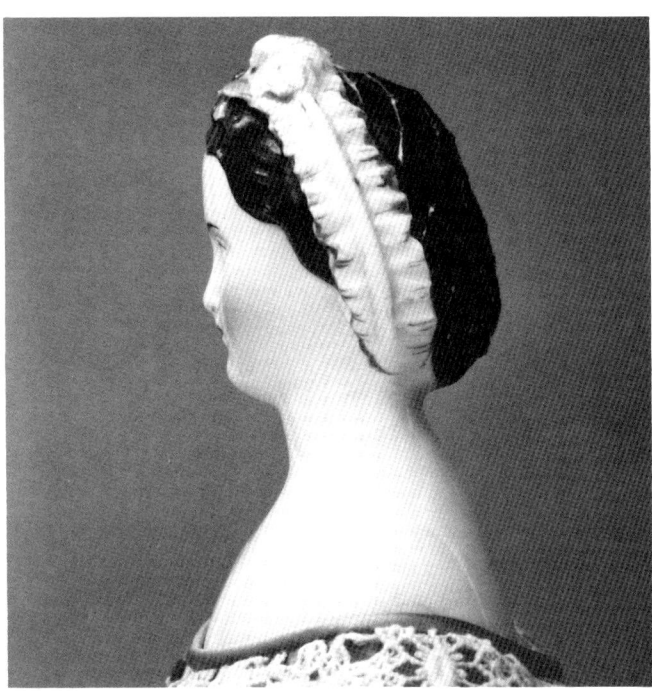

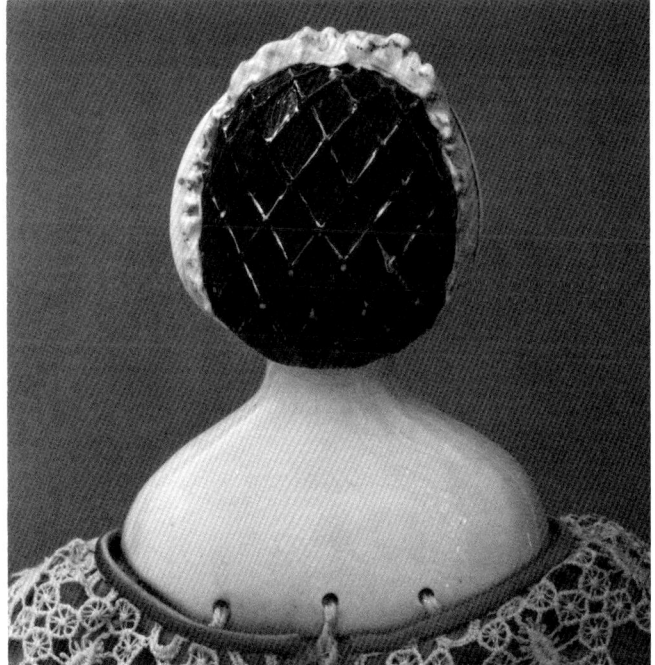

China head doll known as "Grape Lady"; black hair, no center part, waved in front down over ears and caught into gold lustre snood; molded white ruffle from beneath ears over top of head, centered with a cluster of bright blue grapes dabbed with gold, and several green leaves. The ruffle is edged with lavender lustre paint, as are lines depicting its folds. Blue painted, highlighted eyes; red-orange eyelid crease lines, inner eye dots, nostrils, cheeks and mouth. Graceful sloping shoulders, slight bosom shaping, three sew holes. Old cloth body, old china legs with blue painted shoes (above-ankle height and with heels), and orange painted bow under knees. The shoulder head is incised *6* inside and measures 4½"; total height of doll is 17¾".

A lesser known version of this china head doll is one that has pink fruit — strawberries, perhaps? — clustered at ruffle center, amid green leaves. It measures 6½", and because it is larger, there is more detail in the painting: face and shoulders have a slight pink tone, inner eye marks are half circles instead of dots, and nostrils are ovals instead of single lines.

Shown in color photograph (4), page 100.

112
circa 1860

Black-haired china head doll with gold snood and heavy gold lustre bows at ears; enough gold to give a mirror-like effect. The painting is crisp and well-done; blue eyes and the expected red-orange detail. This style of china doll has acquired the name of "Mary Todd Lincoln"; however, it is not known if it originally was intended to be a portrait of Mrs. Lincoln. On old cloth body with china arms and legs. Total height is 20".

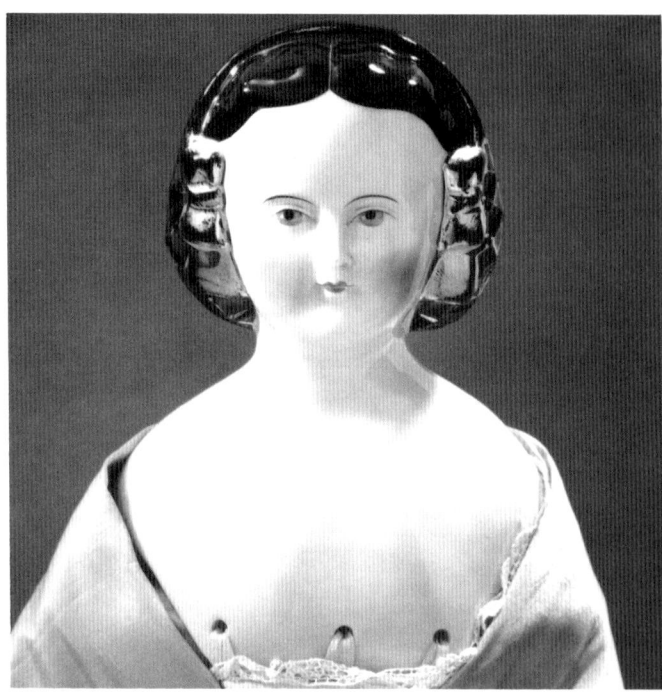

Shown in color photograph (5), page 100.

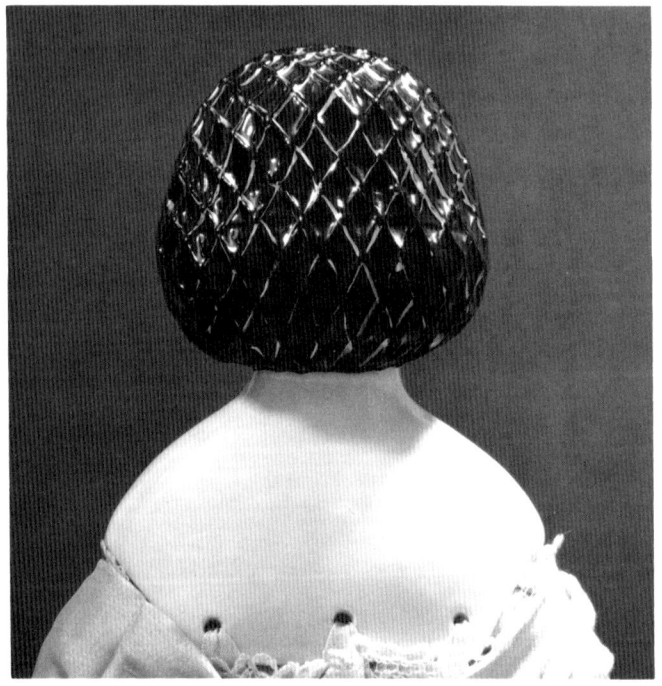

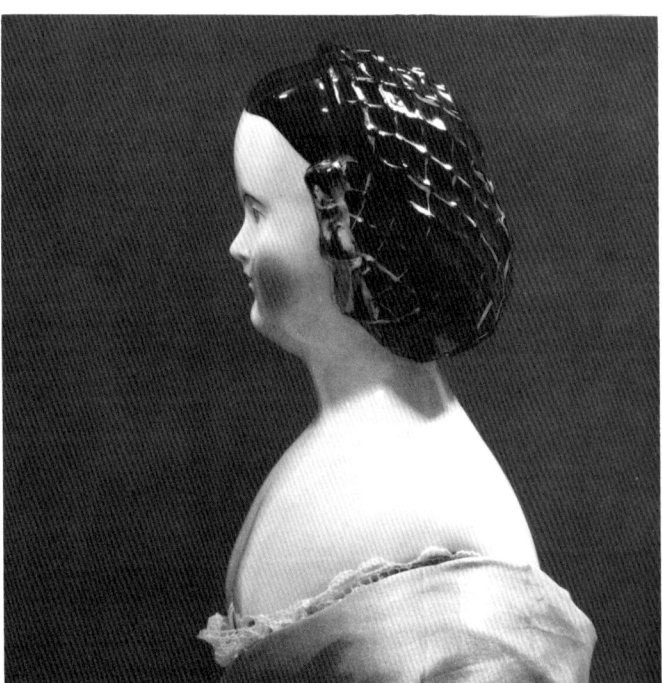

circa 1860

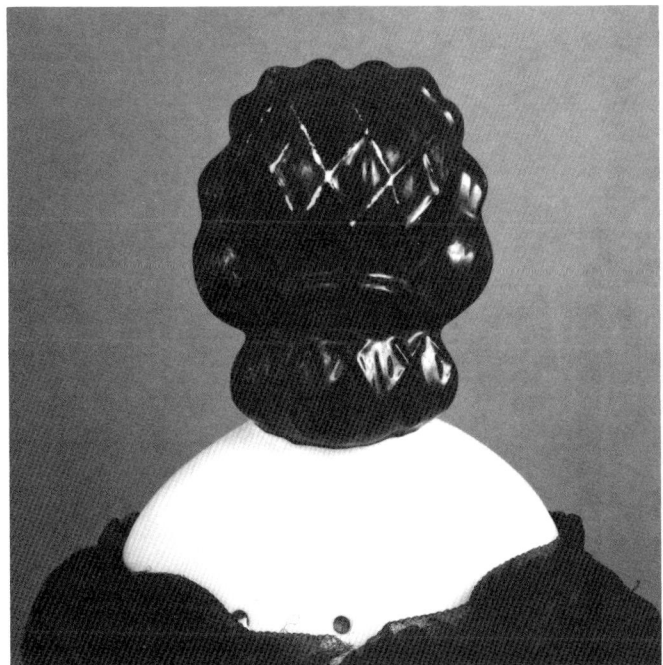

China lady with hair style of multiple features: white center part; six waves across top, ending in a long roll at each temple; hair brushstroked from temples to ears, puffed outward at sides; back reveals snood caught at nape of neck with wide comb and, beneath, a wide chignon onto shoulders. Smooth white well-made china. Hair, snood and comb are painted black; no additional color. The manufacturer appears to be the same as that of the Grape Lady. Sharp modeling at face and precise painting of features. On old cloth body; old straight, but chubby arms; china legs have molded, orange-painted, heeled shoes, fashioned with V shape at instep and blue lines to indicate ties; blue painted bows under knees. Shoulder head is 5" high; total doll height is 20".

114
circa 1860

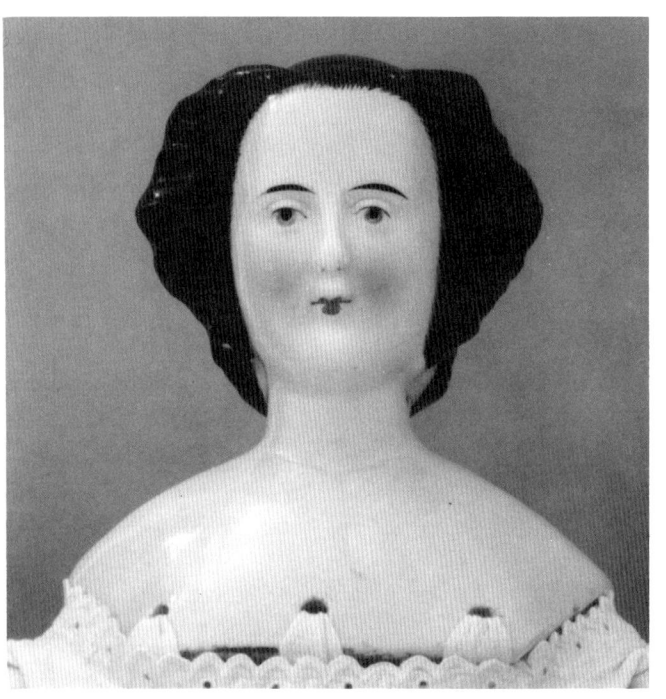

Lady china with molded, painted black hair: wide side wings, no part, brushstroked around entire face to chin line at each side; top is helmet-smooth; back hair flows from a twisted rope of hair — semicircular, with flat band or comb holding it at center — into a smooth, hard-edged fall. Doll is deep-flesh color and blue-eyed; fine line painting with expected detail, except eye highlights. Features are stern, lifelike, rather than doll-like; eyelids are heavily molded. Deep crease at base of throat down through center of chest. Pressed into mold. Old cloth body, china limbs. Shoulder head is 4⅜" and total height is 19".

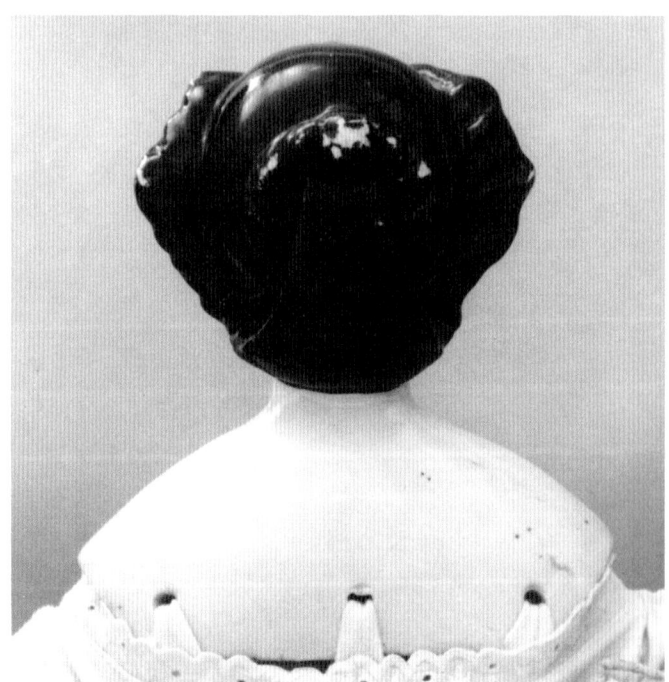

Shown in color photograph (6), page 44.

115
circa 1860

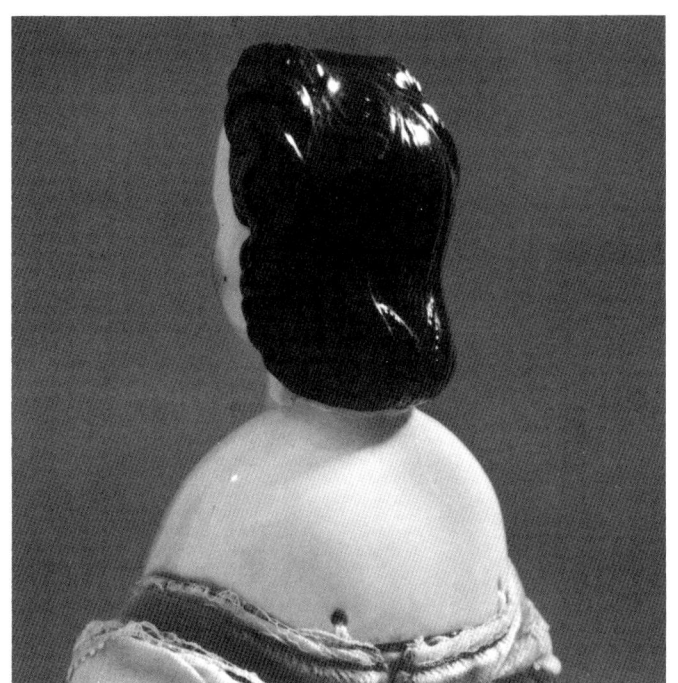

China lady with black molded hair pulled up and away from temples with brushstrokes at forehead; no part. Heavy braids at ears, tucked into back where hair is rolled under at shoulder; two more small braids inserted in V shape at center of under-roll. She is flesh-toned and blue-eyed, with no highlights. All details are well-painted; all modeling is sharply defined and noteworthy in a doll this small; particularly notice the beauty and sharpness of profile. (Comparing qualities of this doll and that on page 114, I feel these two examples may have come from same manufacturer.) Old cloth body, old china limbs; legs are painted with ankle-high black boots. Shoulder head is 3⅛" and total height is 12½".

116
circa 1860

Large china shoulder head with fancy hairdo; no part; black painted hair waved crosswise at forehead and pulled away at brushmarked temples; back hair restrained by fancy molded, but undecorated comb at nape of neck, with further rolls below. Heavy white china, unevenly pressed into mold; heavily molded eyelids. Proper painting; blue eyes with no highlights. Height, 8¼".

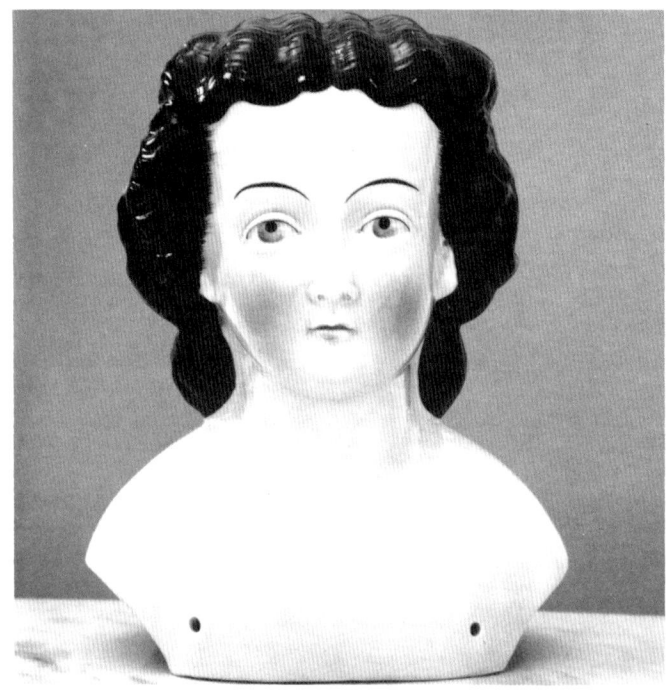

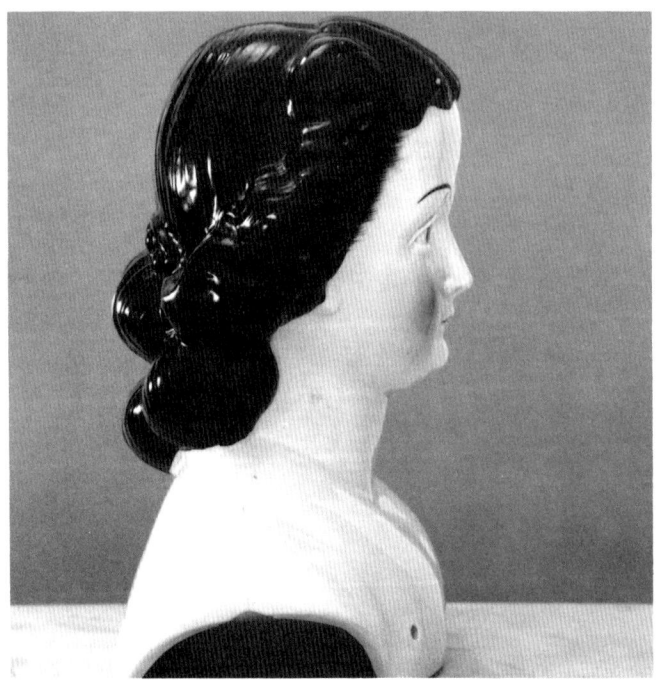

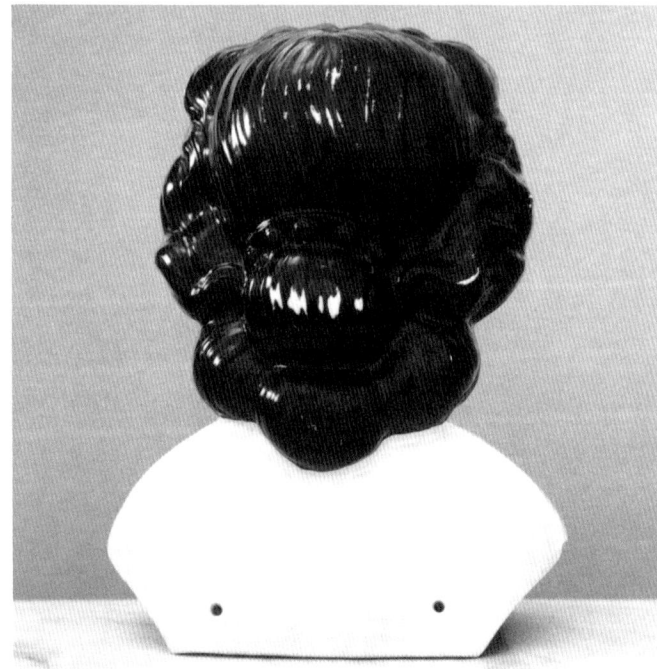

circa 1860

An aristocratic-looking lady of china, whose molded, black painted hair is gently waved around face and beneath two braids; braids encircle her head, ending in double bows at center back. She is of smooth white china, finely and simply painted, with light blue eyes, still no highlights. Old cloth body with old china arms and legs; legs painted with black shoes, ankle-high and small-heeled. Shoulder head is 5½" and whole doll is 20" tall.

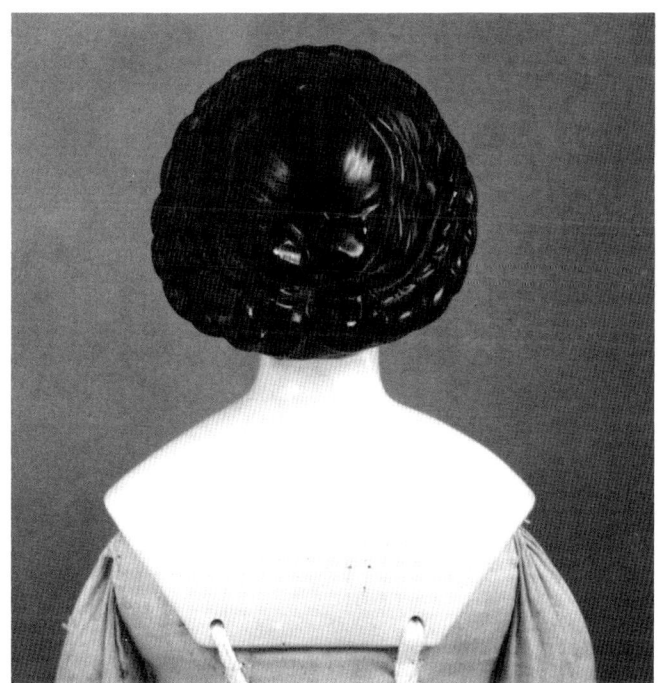
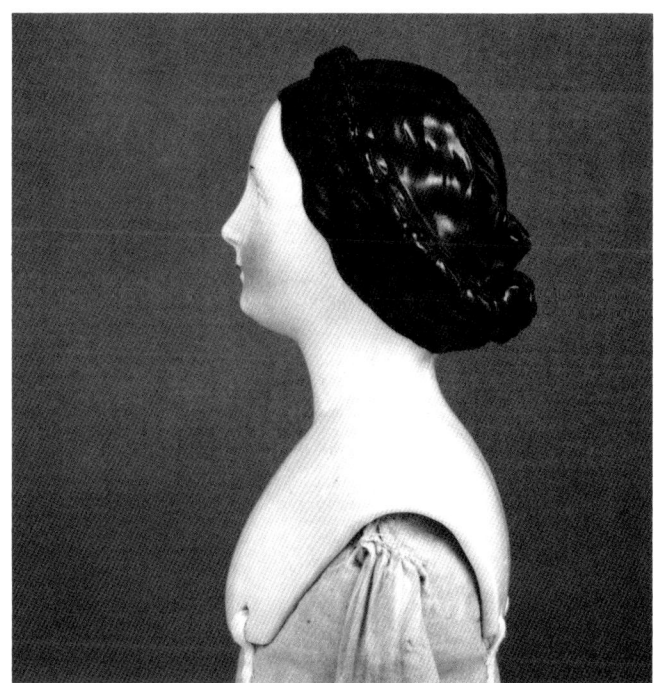

circa 1860

Decorated china lady with fancy molded hairdo: painted black hair pulled away from face with brushstrokes and reverse-roll into a band, which is painted with gold at each edge; many curls clustered at back; single long curl drapes onto shoulder from behind each exposed ear. Very white china; large bright blue eyes with minute highlights; red-orange features. Cloth body, china arms, and old china legs with slight heels on painted black shoes. Shoulder head is 4½" and total height is 17¼".

circa 1860

Decorated china lady with fancy molded hairdo and pierced ears. Her hair is painted the color of creamed butter and is accented with a painted bright-blue band. Hair is gently pulled away from face with brushstrokes; the long blonde curls cascade over back of head and down onto shoulder. White china with red-orange facial features; her blue glass earrings match the blue paint of her eyes. Old cloth body, china limbs. Her shoulder head height is 4½" and the overall measurement is 17½".

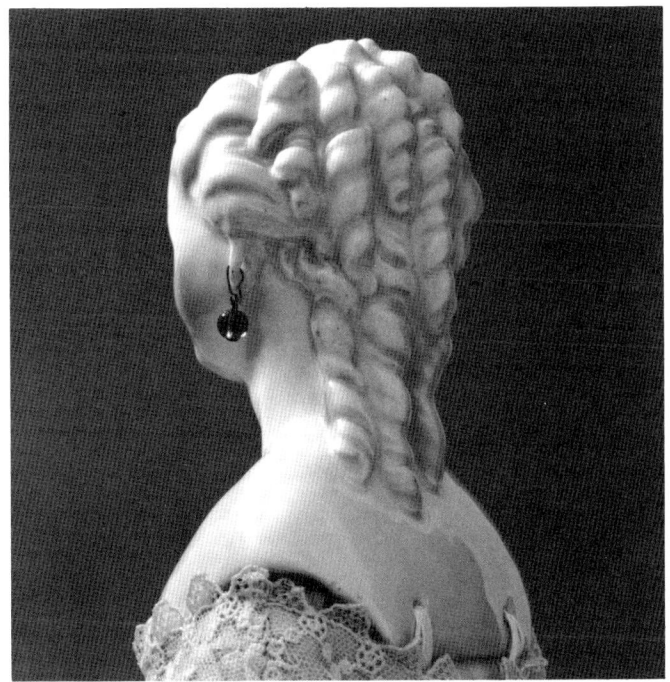

120
circa 1860

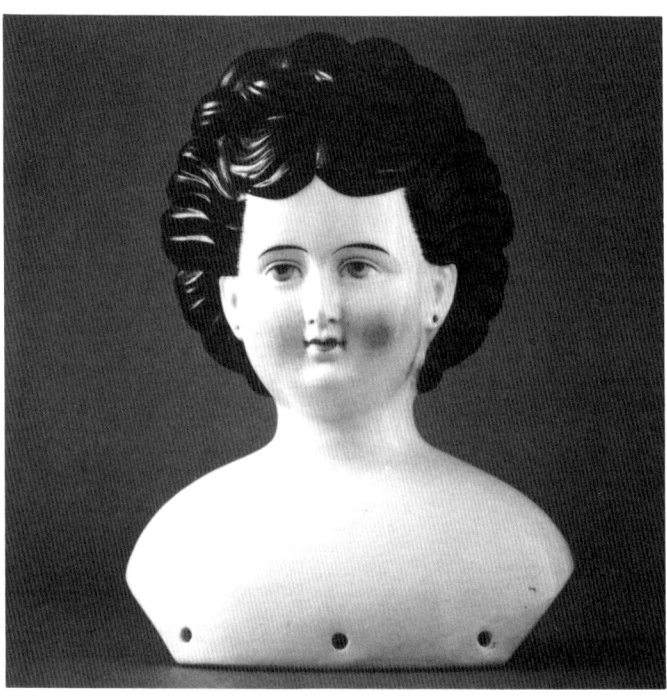

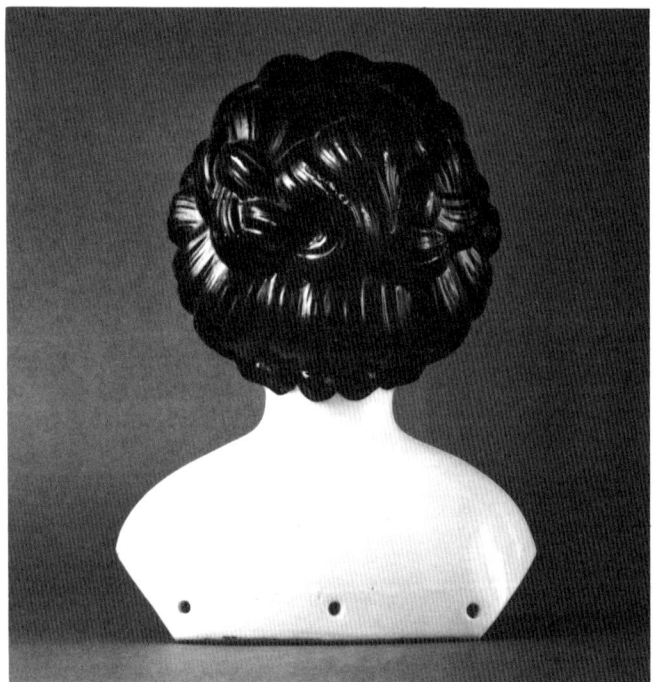

China lady doll with highly detailed modeling of elaborate hair style and pierced ears; hair painted black, waved from center, brush-stroked at temples, drawn back above ears into wide roll continuing across back, five small tight curls at nape, all topped by a heavy braid encircling crown of head. Pressed into mold, glazed inside and out, all white. This shoulder head is marked with a manufacturer's emblem. Doll has old cloth body with leather arms; shoulder head is 7", and entire doll is a large 25½" tall. Inside back shoulder is a shield with numbers below, impressed into moist clay before firing. The mark depicts a bent arm in a gauntlet, holding a dagger. A company known to have used a shield like this was **Conta & Boehme**, founded in 1790 at **Pössneck, Thuringia** (now East Germany).

impressed with dies
black paint

Research indicates they were "makers of luxury and fancy items." However, if that company made other dolls, "when" remains unknown.

121
circa 1860

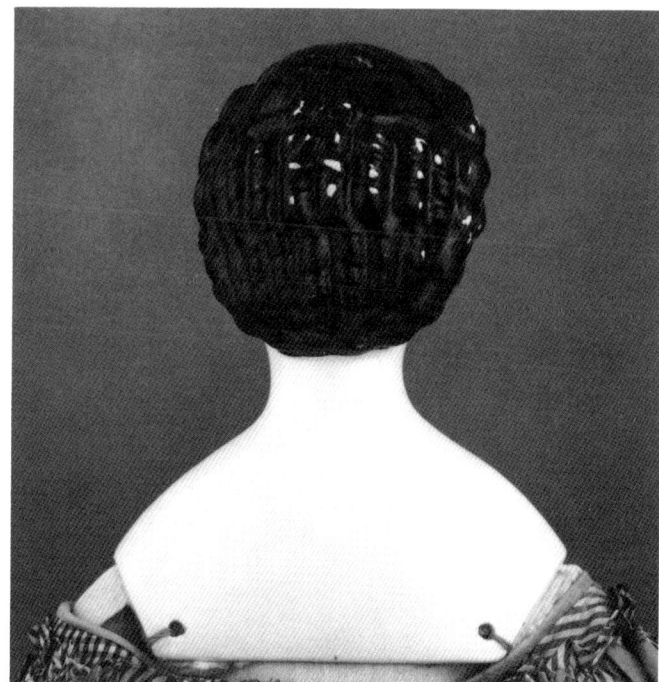

China lady, molded black hair with braids from center top down behind ears and tucked under low center back; smooth upper back hair down to two rows of slender sausage curls held by a molded band with neat, plain bow at center back. Hair painted in graceful curve around face to exposed ears; no center part, no brushstrokes. The neck is long and the chest gently molded to show bosoms. The face painting is delicate, fine-lined and pale; blue eyes, no highlights. Though an interesting hairdo, it lacks sharp detail, while the nose, chin, mouth and ears are most precise. On muslin body, replacement china arms and legs. Shoulder head is 6⅞" and overall height is 23¼". A *12* is incised at center back shoulder.

122
circa 1860

China lady with molded black combination hair style that includes: six curls on forehead, brushstrokes at temples, long extended curls behind fully exposed ears; also flat ledge across top, then smooth down to flat band, which restrains row of irregular, heavy sausage curls. The hair style seems to be an experimental one, perhaps an attempt to combine ideas not yet thoroughly worked out; though not beautiful, shoulder head shows the signs of striving, creative craftsmen at work. A bright, vital face; eyes painted blue — no highlights — but proper red-orange line detail. The china was pressed into the mold, glazed inside and out; inside is a red-orange ✗, probably the sign of the painter using that color, and an impressed VI on outside right front shoulder. On a cloth body with leather arms. The shoulder head measures 5" and whole doll is 20½".

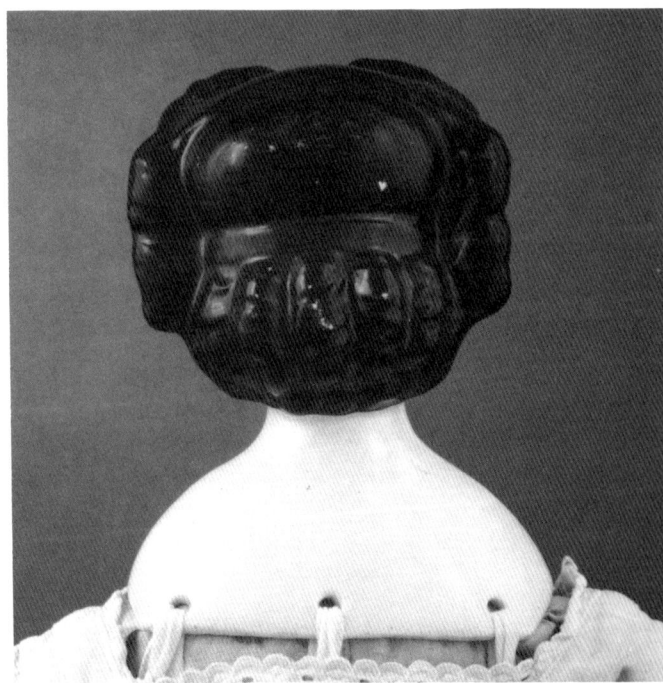

123
circa 1860

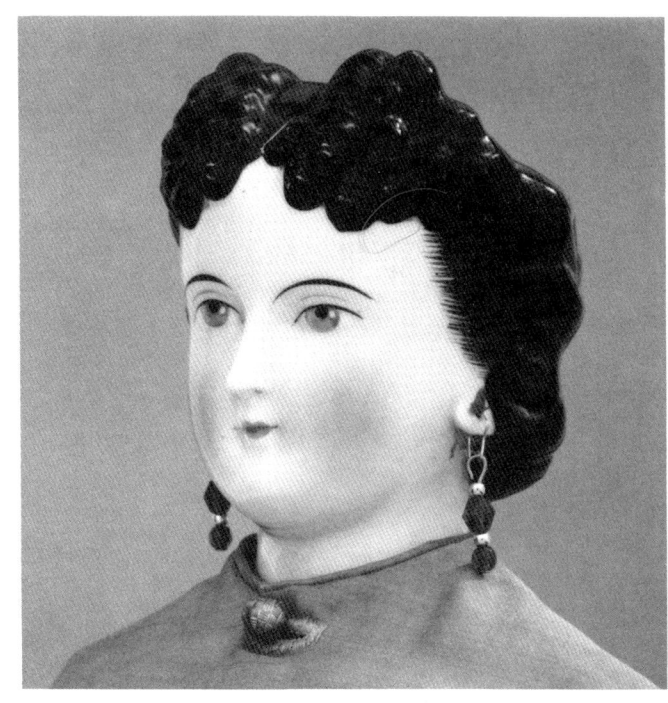

China lady doll, molded hairdo painted all black; curls onto forehead and pulled back at temples with brushstrokes, flat molded band across center white part, puffs and two rolls at center back; extended ears, pierced with earrings. Large blue eyes with highlights; red-orange paint for other details. Smoothly poured high-gloss china, skillfully painted. Three sew holes, front and back; shoulder partly repaired. Old cloth body and china arms and legs. Shoulder head measures 5⅛" and whole lady is 19½".

A smaller matching lady's shoulder head is 4¾" high and has two sew holes in front and back; total height is 18¾". Same maker, same skilled work, but molding of hair not as well defined. No marks of any kind on either doll.

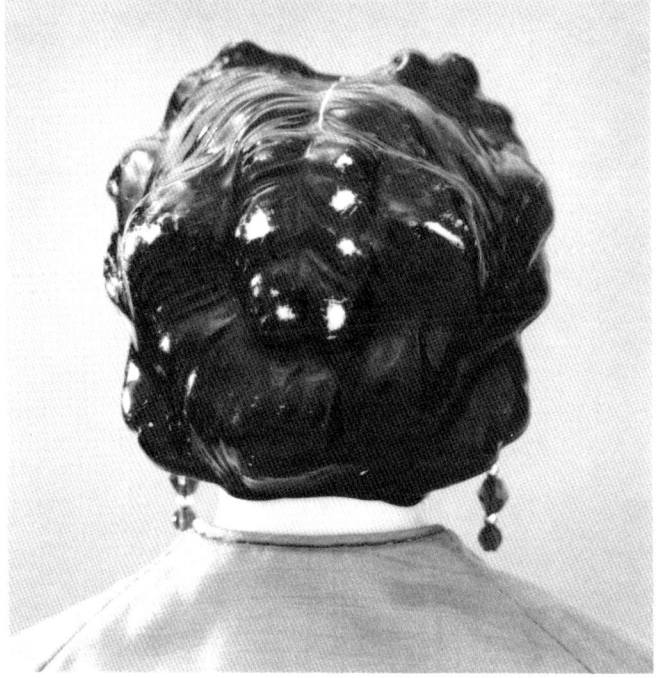

circa 1860

China lady again with curls at forehead and temples; rows of waves in back end with small irregular curls at nape, no brushstrokes. Hair is black, eyes, blue; red-orange facial detail. **Extended ears, pierced** — means that ears are enlarged and stand out from the head, thus holes for earrings can be made straight through the lobe. (Flatter molded ears require holes for earrings to be made straight into head.) Smooth white high-gloss china. Old cloth body, china arms and legs. Shoulder head is 5½" and whole doll is 21".

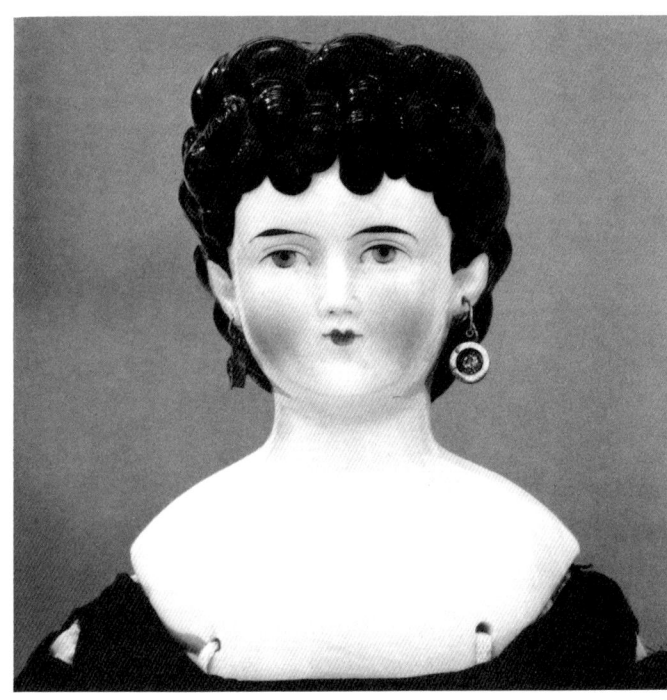

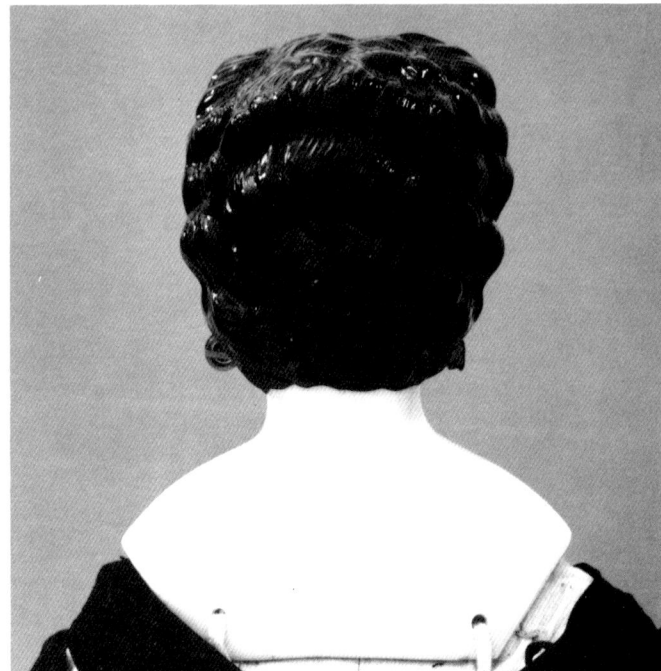

125
circa 1860

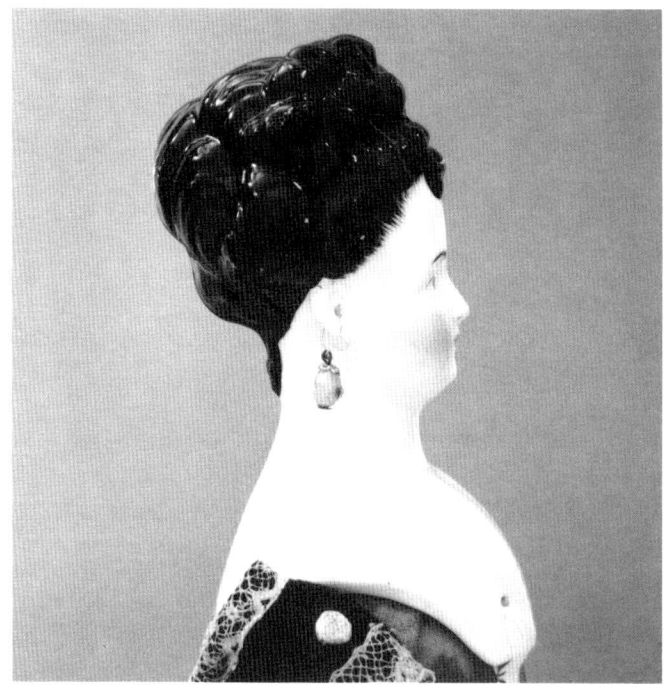

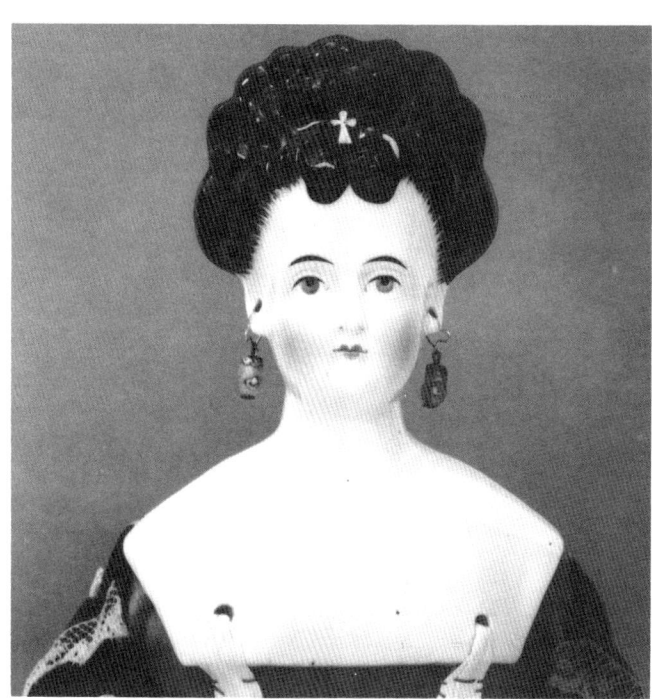

China lady, molded black hair with cross nestled between two curls on forehead; remainder of hair is pulled up high above ears and forehead into rows of curls; swirls in back end at nape with two curls onto neck. She has deep brushstrokes at face; extended, pierced ears. The cross, temporarily painted white for photo, is actually black and you have to look closely to see it. Bright blue painted eyes, no highlights; simple red-orange details at eyes, nostrils, mouth and cheeks. Heavy white china, pressed into mold. Old cloth body, china arms and legs. The shoulder head measures 5¼", including inch-high curls; her total height is 19¾". Outside of back shoulder at right is an impressed **20**.

circa 1860-70

THAT BEAUTIFUL FACE

Once again, it is as if one company set out to make an entire line of highly desirable china head dolls and they did so by using just one face and shoulder design. Variations were made by changing the molded hair styles and the coloring, and by adding a few unusual features. The dolls opposite, and the remaining examples within this section, are of this group. They represent two concepts — their hair styles ranging from plain and simple to fancy and decorated — but seem to be of a later period. The only 1860 style that was not included by the manufacturer of this group was that of the snood ladies, and because of that, I feel they may have been made at least a decade later. There is nothing crude about these dolls; they are smooth and well-made. They were poured into their molds, and their painting, in both color and line work, is superior. However, there is, as yet, no way to know exactly when they were manufactured. Only one doll in this group of nine has an impressed marking on its back — a single letter, revealing no information at all.

The color variation here is the use of pink for facial detail, in place of the expected red-orange. Of the dolls in this selection, two still have the red-orange detailing, but are like the others in face and shoulder modeling.

Another known doll that fits into this group and needs to be mentioned is a lady with the same modeling and pink painted features, and a simple ringlet hair style with flowers at the side of her molded, black painted hair. She has another feature of distinction: the head and shoulder are separate units, joined by a socket head arrangement that enables the doll's head to swivel and to tip in all directions. The example studied was approximately 15" tall. The doll is a rarity, seldom seen, less often available for purchase.

For an additional member of this group, refer to the doll on page 50, a bald head glazed china.

The fine ladies and their young gentleman friend shown here have shoulder heads of the same height, but overall height varies, due to the use of different body sizes. I have not seen these particular heads in larger sizes, though they may exist; some smaller ones can be found.

Dolls in numbered diagram of color photograph are also shown individually in black and white and fully described on pages indicated as follows:
(1) page 128, (2) page 132, (3) page 134, (4) page 136, (5) page 137.

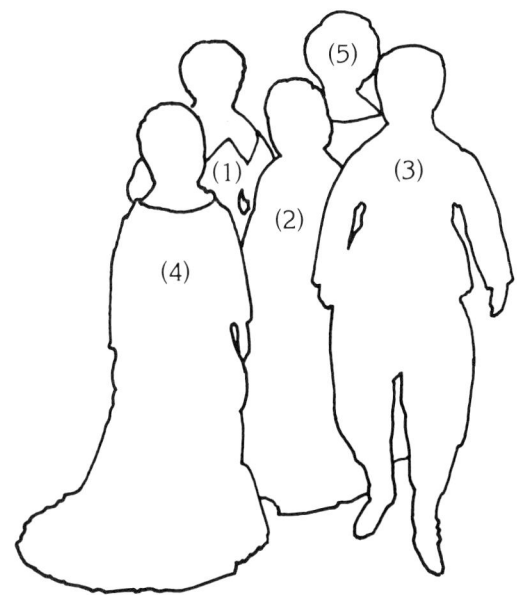

128
circa 1860–70

Simple hair style, painted black; molded with twenty-two ringlets, small at temples, circling to deeper curls at back; center white part. This china lady has pale blue painted eyes, right side of irises edged with darker blue, white paint spot for eye highlight, black lid line and eyebrows. Now a difference in color: eyelid crease line, inner eye dots, oval nostrils, mouth and cheeks are painted pink. This attractive color, which probably was called rose, replaces the red-orange of other chinas. The painted lines are fine and delicate. Her bosom is molded, and her shoulders are broad and sloping, with a smooth inward curve at outside edge. The painting of features is the same for all in this group, except as noted. A simple, well-made shoulder head on homemade cloth body with china arms and legs. At bottom center back of shoulder, there is an N impressed with a die — hard to see, as it is filled with glaze. The shoulder head is 5⅞" and overall height is 22½".

Shown in color photograph (1), page 126.

129
circa 1860-70

This china head lady has twenty-four ringlets molded in style of doll on page 128. The manner of line painting is the same also, but the color is red-orange, not pink. Well-painted, simple, yet she has an added attraction — a necklace made as part of the mold, then painted. Dark beads of painted cobalt blue alternate with white beads outlined in gold; between them shows a "string" painted red-orange. The necklace qualifies her as a decorated china. The shoulders are shaped as previously described; three sew holes and no marking; height is 5⅞". Whole doll, with old cloth body and leather arms, is 21½" tall.

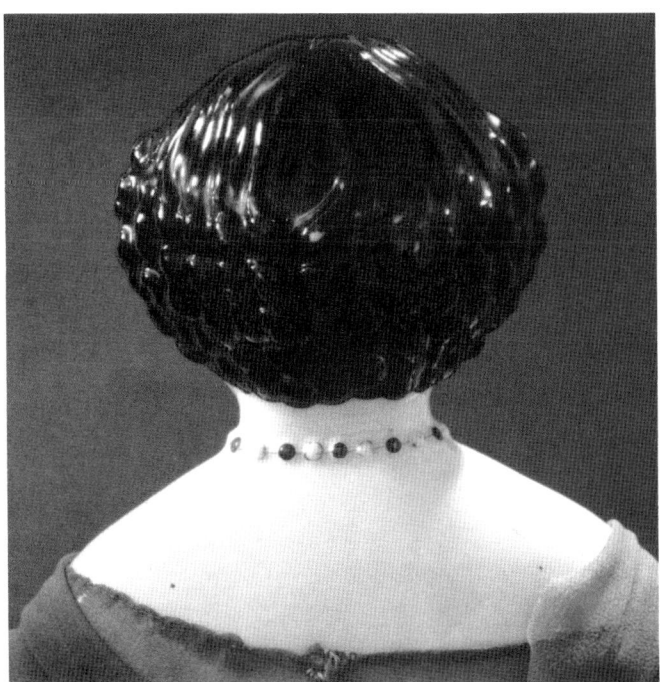

circa 1860-70

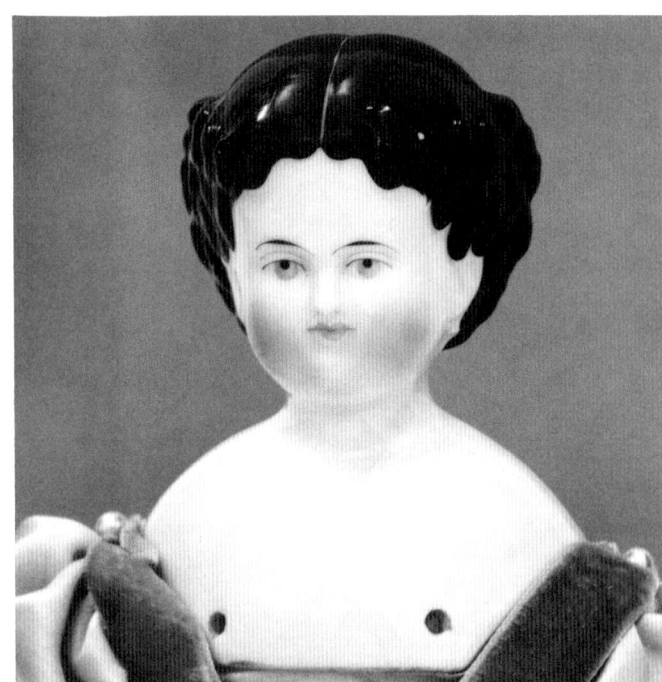
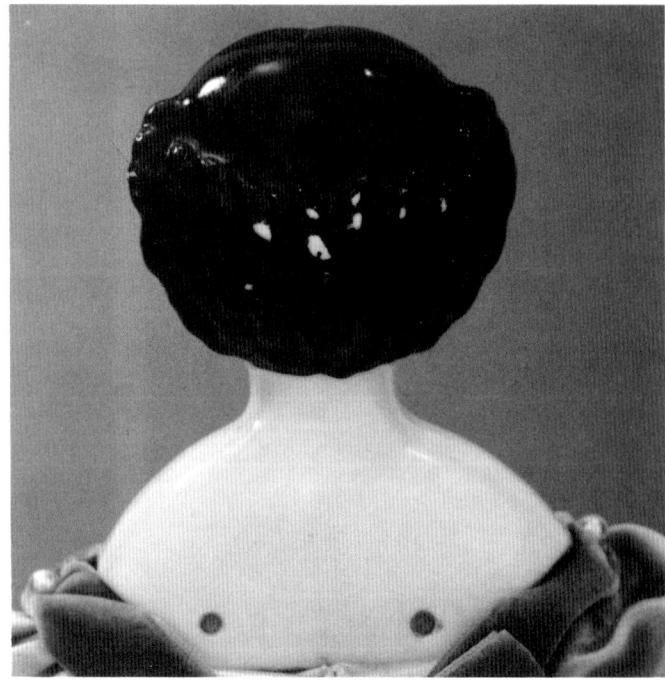

Smaller china lady, black painted hair style, mold is slightly changed from previous doll; barely touched with brushstrokes at temples, ears left exposed. She is well-painted, with very pale blue eyes and pink facial detailing; these colors against the white china have a soft pastel look. A shoulder head of this size will often have lost precise detail of molding. On a cloth body with china arms and legs, she is 14½" tall. Whatever the reason, this version is sometimes called "Mrs. Bumblebottom," a character name unknown to me.

131
circa 1860–70

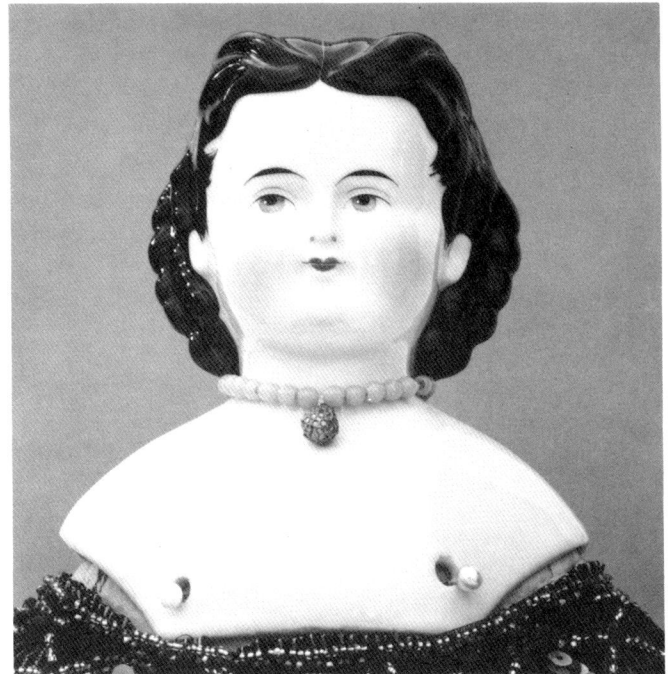

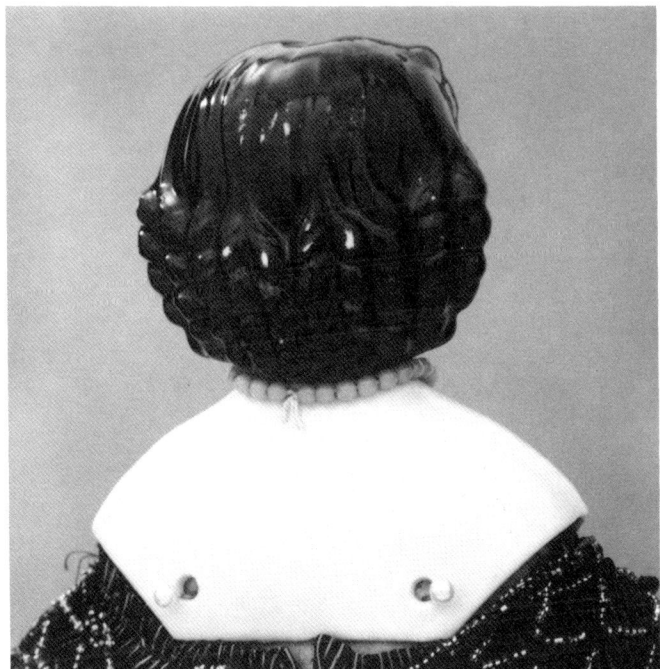

China doll with black painted hair gently pulled up and away from center part, leaving wide forehead expanse, lightly brushstroked at temples, semi-exposed ears, ringlets across back ending a bit deeper on back of neck. The same face shaping still present, but red-orange detail at face, and bright blue eyes. On cloth body, china arms and legs; her overall height is 19". Sometimes called "Adeline Patti."

circa 1860–70

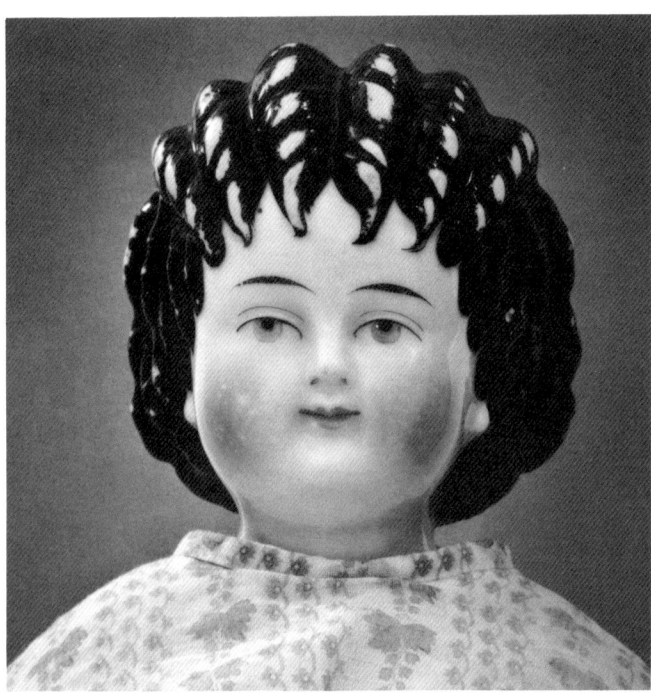

China head doll with hair style called "curlytop"; black with many worn-away rubs accenting all the hair detail. She is well-painted, with pale blue eyes highlighted with white painted spots; pink facial details, including a darker pink curved stroke through center of mouth, and pink-tinted cheeks, all on pure white. Appealing and acceptable to me, as her face is so nice, but condition is not recommended to all. On cloth body with china arms. Shoulder head, repaired, 5⅞" high, overall height is 21¾".

Shown in color photograph (2), page 126.

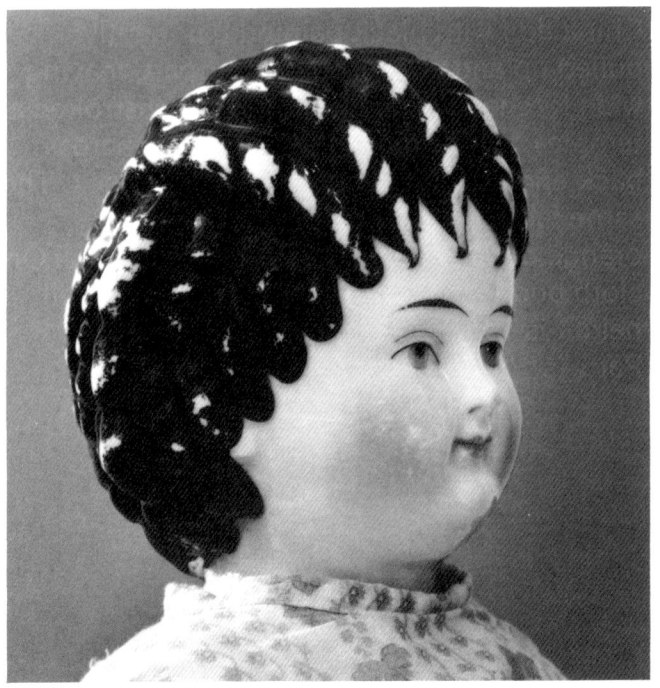

133
circa 1860-70

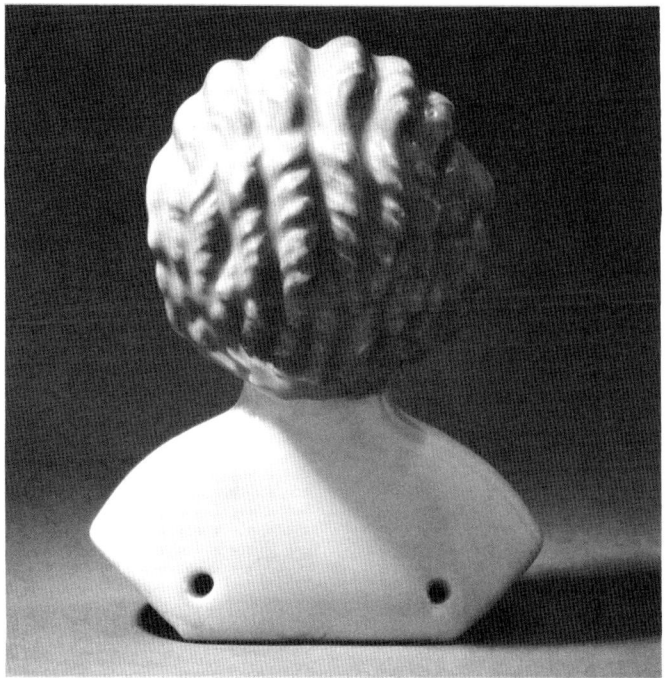

China doll with curlytop hair style; brushstrokes from four center curls onto forehead; the color is called **café au lait** — meaning coffee with half milk. Descriptive and accurate. Pink-line facial detail, bright blue highlighted eyes; her eyebrows are darker tone of hair color. A very appealing color combination. She has old cloth body with china arms and legs. Photograph shows the inward curve of shoulder to side of sew holes. Shoulder head is 4¼"; and whole doll is 16½".

134
circa 1860–70

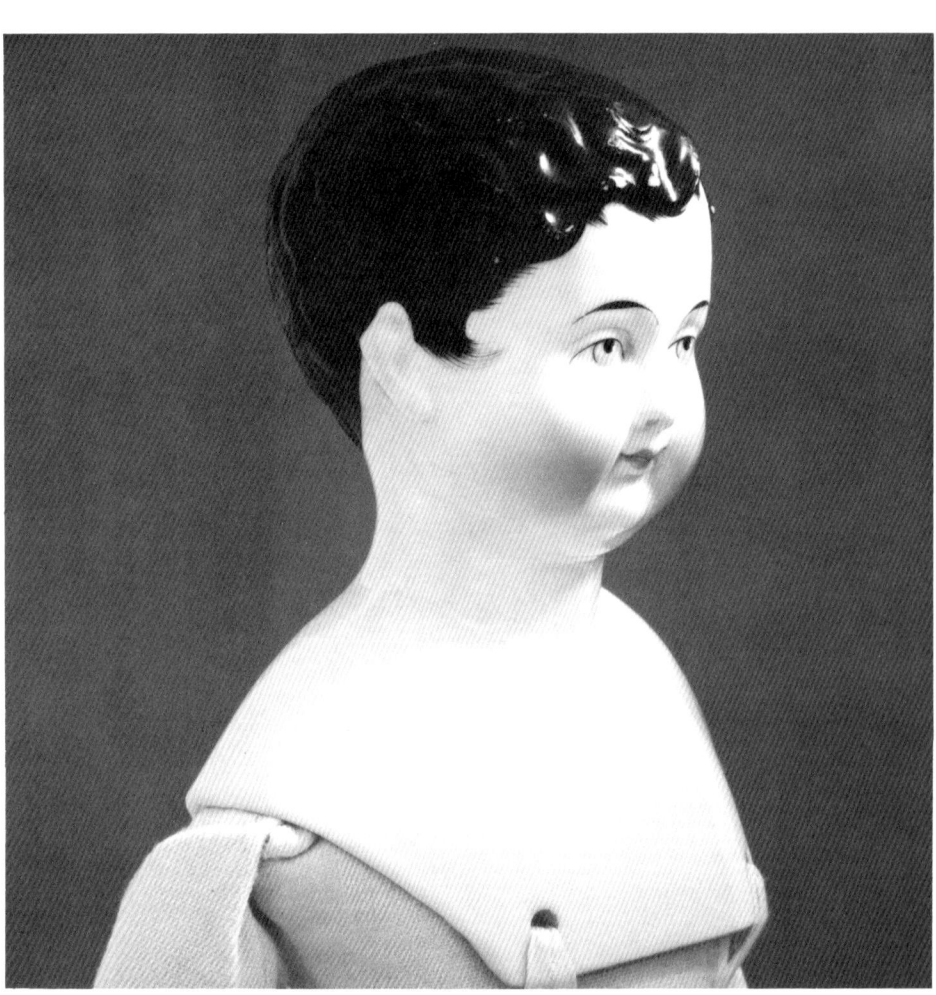

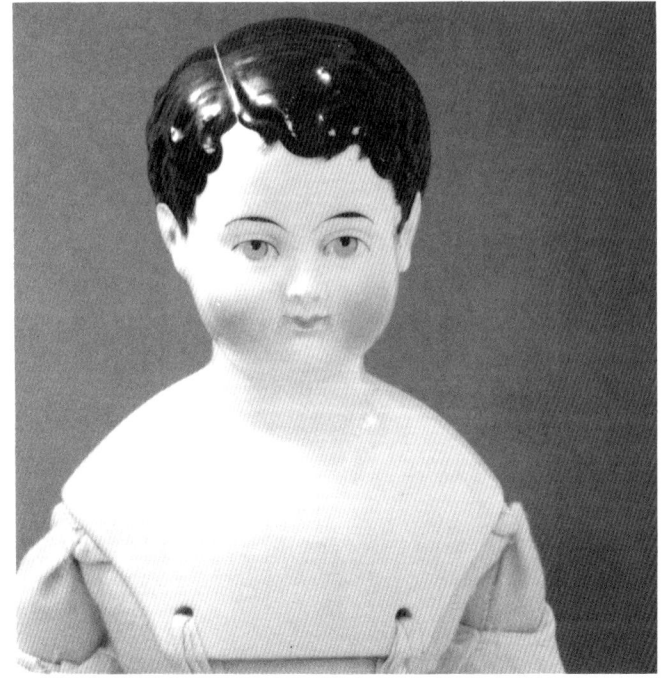

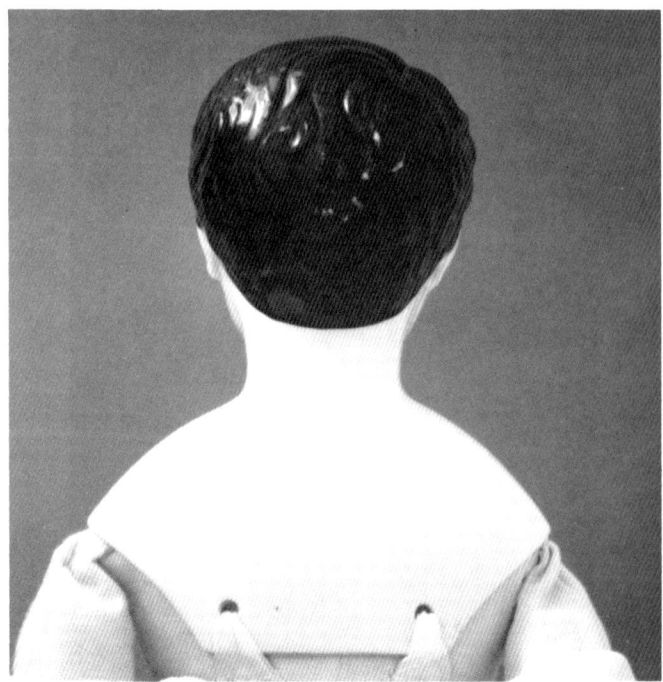

135
circa 1860–70

Young gentleman china doll with painted black wavy hair; side-parted with random brushstrokes at sideburns, temples and forehead; shapely ears. This size shows best molding — especially around nose, mouth and double chin — of the same face that dolls in this group all have. His color details are pale blue eyes and pink line work on white china.

His old frail clothing consists of: lined black wool twill jacket, trimmed with flat silk braid and buttons, separate lapped closure at neck, braid applied to sleeve, curving up to elbow, two buttons, side vents at back with three buttons and silk trim; lined trousers reach calf, silk braid on side seams and two buttons, waistband is V-shaped at front, closed with one button at each side. White shirt of fancy piqué has six half-inch tucks across front, inverted toward center; closed with small white pearl shirt buttons; collar is curved to exactly follow his neck shape; no undies; brown stockings; black leather high-top shoes, flapped to side, closed with three round gold buttons.

His body is cotton twill, his hands are molded, painted metal. Shoulder head is 6" high; whole doll height is 22".

Shown in color photograph (3), page 126.

136
circa 1860–70

China head doll with café àu lait painted hair: ringlets across forehead, brushstroked temples, molded hair band, ringlets turned front to back over remainder of head and ending on shoulder. The only black painting is on hair band and eye outline; white china; eyebrows a tone darker than hair; pale blue eyes; pink inner eye dots, eyelid crease lines, nostril dots, cheeks and mouth — accented with darker tone in shape of double arch. Delicate painting prevails. Commercial cloth body marked 5 on seat; narrow-waisted, wide-hipped; legs, homemade, ending in leather or oilcloth sewn-on boots extending to knees; replacement china arms. There is also a black-haired version of this hair style; both are called "spillcurl." Shoulder head is 5¾"; entire doll is 20½".

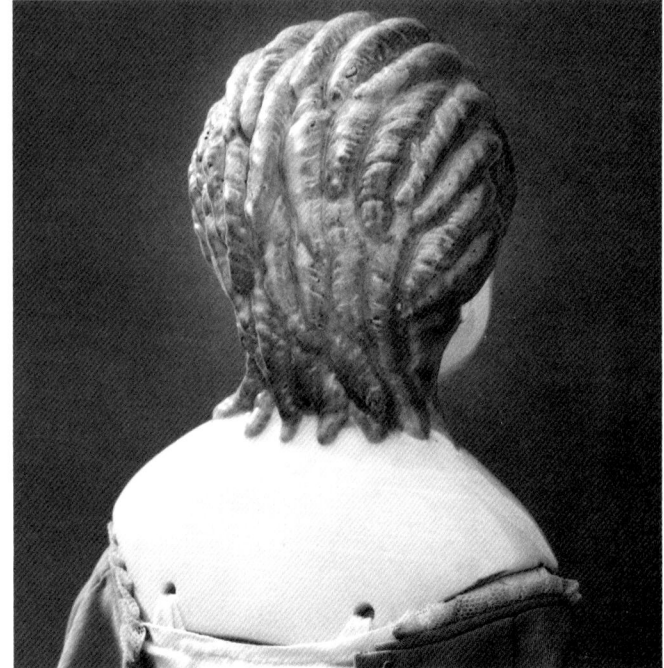

Shown in color photograph (4), page 126.

137
circa 1860–70

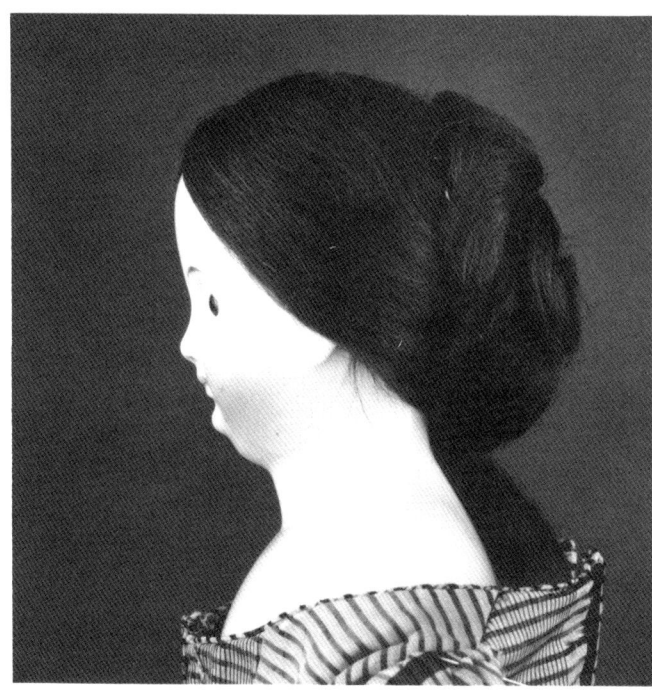

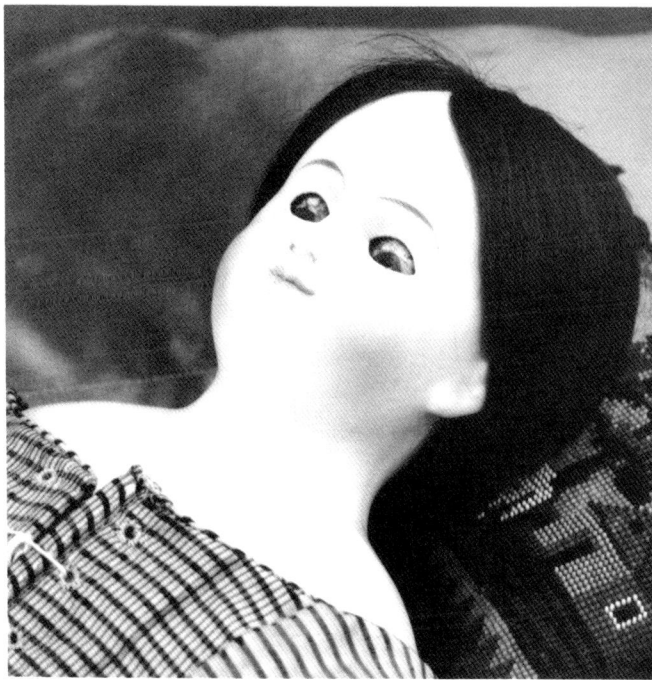

This doll has blue glass eyes that open and close, called "sleep-eyed" — a rarity in chinas, and she belongs in this group. The same molding, but with complete ears; the same colors, but eye painting limited to pink inner eye dots (when closed, eyes do not have outlines or crease lines). The sleep-eye feature made possible because the cut-off pate gave access to inside of head so that eye mechanism could be installed. The painted facial features are: pink single-stroke nostrils, pink cheeks and darker pink line curving through mouth; eyebrows are light brown. Cork pate and wig. The shoulder head is 5⅞"; the whole doll on old cloth body with leather arms is 23". Unmarked.

Shown in color photograph (5), page 126.

circa 1880

BLONDE & BLACK-HAIRED CHILDREN

China head dolls with black painted hair had been the expected product for forty years; during that time, a blonde or fair-haired doll would have been an oddity. While the styling of the past was no doubt continued by some manufacturers, a new style became evident around this time: tousled-haired children, many of them blonde. With these dolls, the overall shape has been changed; shoulders are narrower in proportion to the head, and are formed with chubby curves and an indentation at the underarms. The cheeks are more rounded, features enlarged, eyes are more generous and emphasized by a lively manner of painting. The numbers incised on the backs of some of these dolls are thought to indicate style and size — as though from a series — or they may be merely the manufacturer's method of keeping track of things. The shoulders of lady dolls are now less pronounced, lacking bosom molding and long necks; while the shoulders of children have become more shapely. A bold and definite eye painting, outlining the irises with black paint, benefits all. The change is welcome, and these bright, shining round-faced blonde and black-haired children, and some ladies, are hard to resist.

Dolls in numbered diagram of color photograph are also shown individually in black and white and fully described on pages indicated as follows:
(1) page 140, (2) page 141, (3) page 142,
(4) page 147, (5) page 148, (6) page 150,
(7) page 154.

140
circa 1880

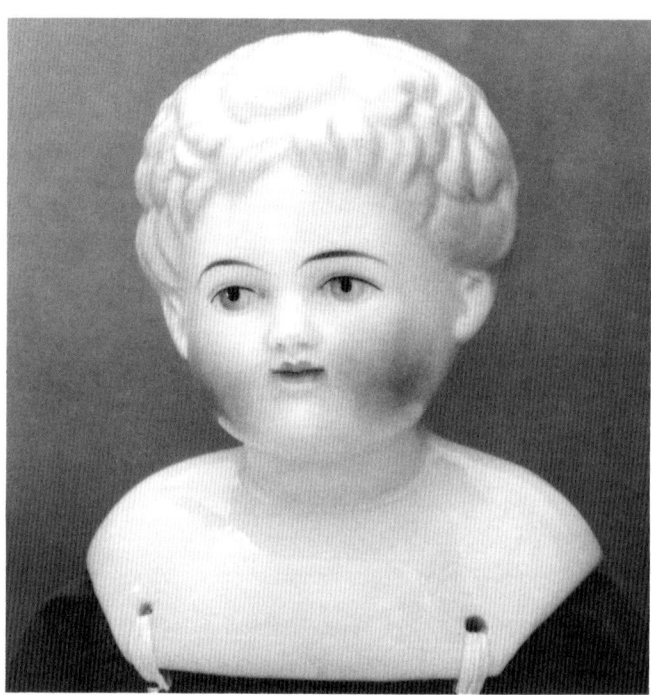

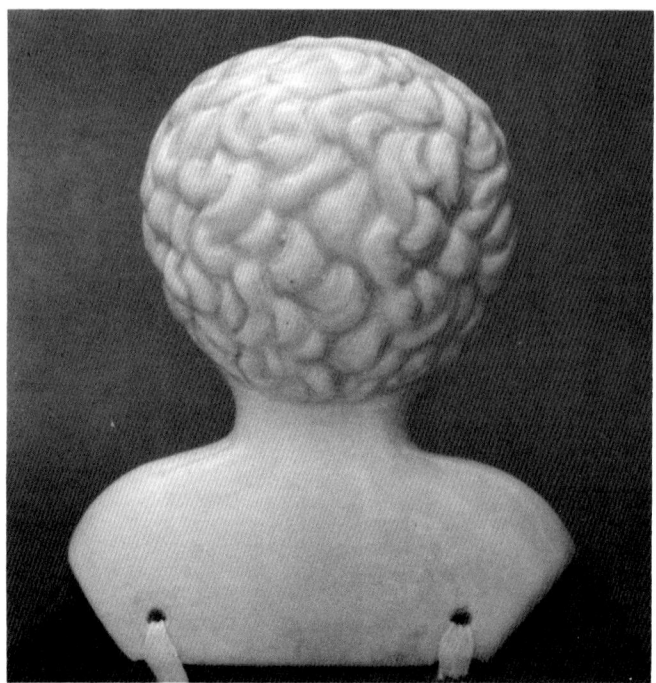

Boy china doll with short tousled blonde hair; exposed ears, short neck. Pale blue painted eyes, applied white highlights, light brown eyebrows, black only on eye outlines and pupils. Soft rose at eyelid crease, inner eye dots, nostrils, cheeks and mouth. Cloth body, old china arms, replacement china legs. Shoulder head is 4" and he totals 17" high.

Shown in color photograph (1), page 138.

141
circa 1880

Blonde child with casual ringlets surrounding head; hair somewhat smooth at crown but protruding in back; curls clustered in middle of forehead. Shoulders are narrow for head size, and formed with short neck and childlike chubbiness. Face painted like boy doll described on page 140; in addition, the eyes are outlined with a firm black stroke and irises are outlined in black. Head is severely cracked and crudely repaired, but face has a clear, bright, crisp look — how could anyone resist it? Cloth body, china arms. Shoulder head is 5" and whole doll is 23". Impressed at left of center back sew hole is number 890 and to right, number 9.

Shown in color photograph (2), page 138.

142
circa 1880

China head child doll with blonde, curly molded hair: small ringlets arranged casually and full lifted straight bangs. Dark brown eyebrows, blue eyes; other expected facial details present. The shoulder is narrow and quite rounded, with a hollow indicating a backbone. She is 18⅜" tall. This type child doll, also made with black hair, is called "Highland Mary." Impressed on back shoulder , filled in with glaze.

Shown in color photograph (3), page 138.

circa 1880

China child doll with blonde, wavy hair. Painted blue eyes, black eye outline and soft rose eyelid crease line, nostril dots, mouth and cheeks. Paint delicately applied. Tan eyebrows. The china was poured; white and translucent. Doll is 15" high. Two other examples of this type are shown: page 144 at top, and page 145. They vary in appearance, due to size and color.

This doll on cloth body, thought original: two rows of machine stitching down center of torso, curvy china arms, and legs that are slender through foot, rising to chubby calves — with black painted, heeled high boots. Doll wears old knee-length chemise; drawers just cover top of china legs; petticoat — flat in front with gathers held to back — just covers painted blue bow at china knees. All garments of matching cotton fabric, machine-stitched, lace-edged, tucked twice and hemmed, and they fit like a glove.

circa 1880

Child china doll with blonde molded hair, short and wavy, one curl onto right forehead, exposed ears. She has tan eyebrows; blue eyes; black pupils, iris outlines and eye outlines; other details soft red-orange. Photograph shows the curve of the shoulder prevalent during this era. This doll most detailed example of this type shown, due to its larger size. Shoulder head alone is 6⅝" high.

Blonde china head child, often used as boy or girl and sometimes man or lady. Brown eyebrows; red-orange eyelid line, dot at inner eye (on left eye only) and nostril dots. Only pupils and upper outline of eyes are black. Blue eyes with tiny white dot for highlight. Ears partially exposed. On cloth body with china arms and legs. Shoulder head is 4¾" and whole doll is 19".

circa 1880

Child china doll with black molded hair, short and wavy, one curl onto right forehead, exposed ears. Eyebrows are black and eyes are grey-blue; red-orange eyelid lines, inner eye dots, nostril dots, cheeks and mouth. The black hair has a matte surface; the white complexion shines. Old cloth body with leather arms; lower legs have red-striped white cotton for stockings and black leather high boots with heels, sewn altogether in one seam. This forms lower leg, stocking and boot in one step, called "made-in-one" — originally a factory sewing method, adopted later by home-sewers. Shoulder head is 4½"; whole doll is 20".

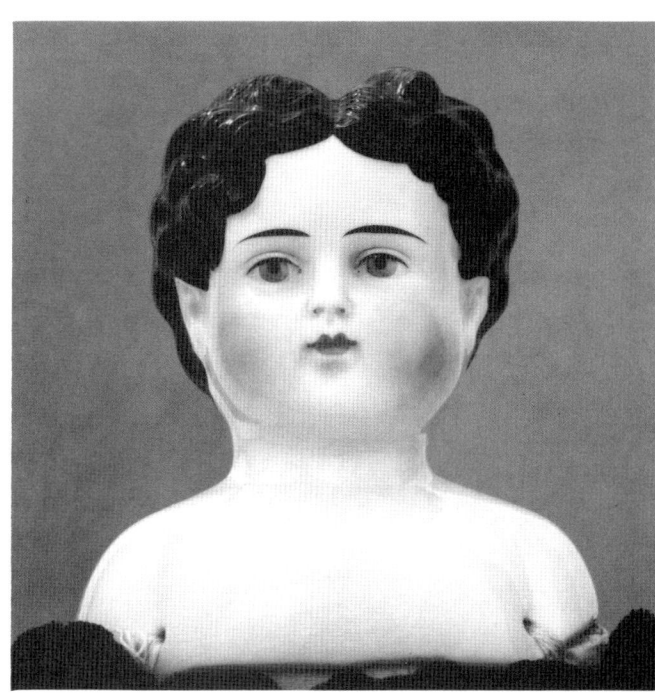

Doll below of similar mold, but neck is wider, shoulders are narrower; also note the outline of irises and line in mouth. Shoulder head is 5" and is incised on back 784 8.

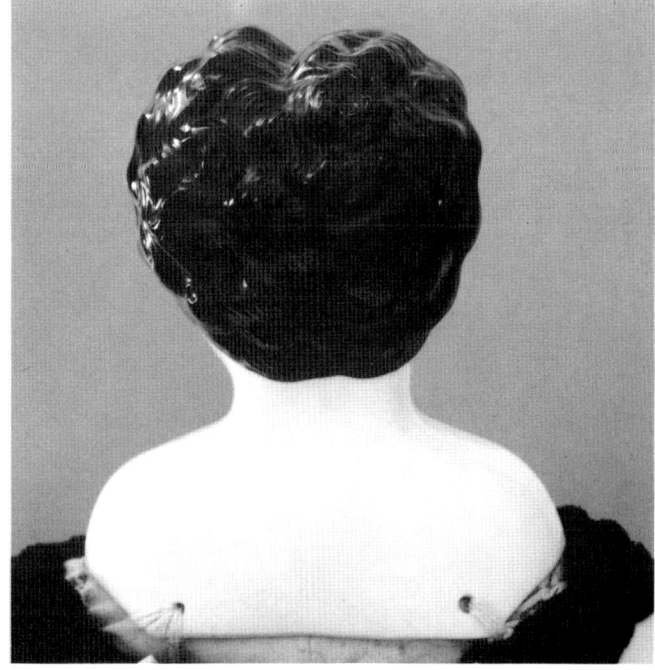

circa 1880

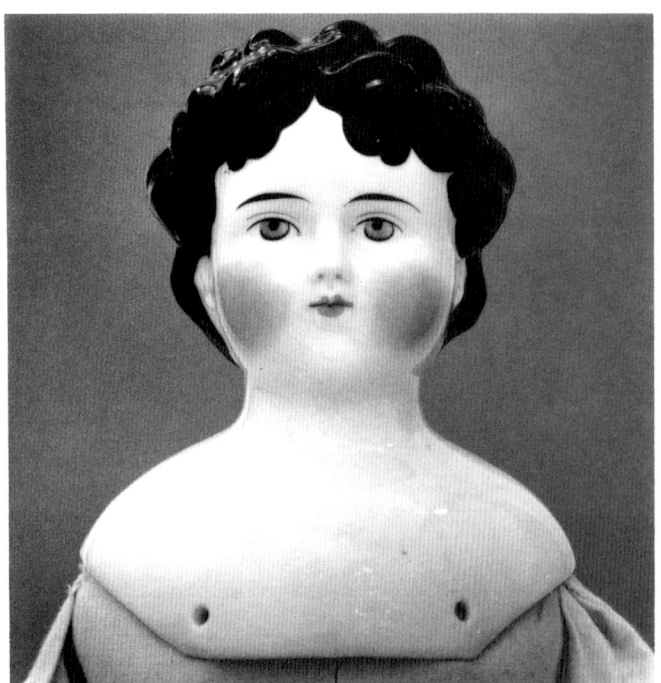
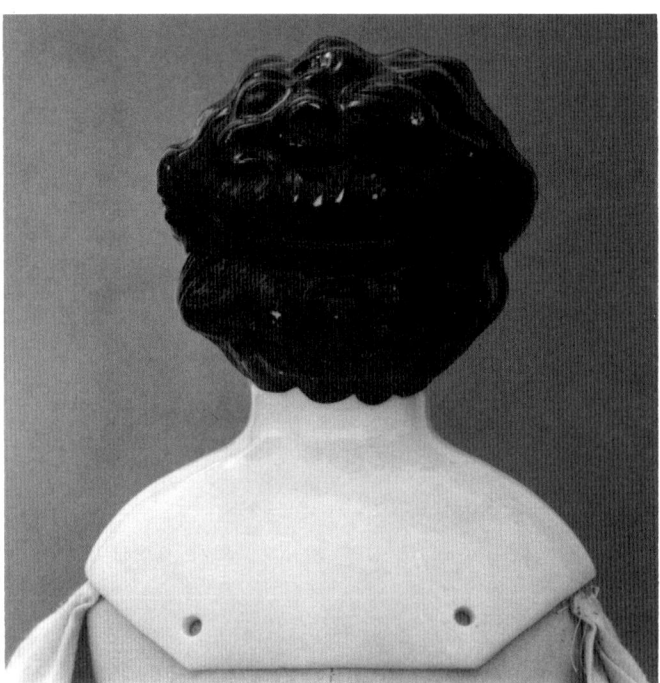

China head doll with black molded hair: two separate clusters of curls onto forehead, with molded band and bow across top, showing again at back; wavy hair above band, curls below. Band is same black as hair. Ears are semi-exposed; average neck length and smooth adult shoulders. Painted blue eyes; irises and eyes outlined with black; black eyebrows; other feature detail is red-orange. This type has been known as "Dolly Madison" for many years. Doll is 22" tall.

China doll with two curls centered on forehead; molded bow and band, painted black. The face is flat and wide with intense red-orange facial details and painted blue eyes. Another company's variation of previous style. Old cloth body with china arms and legs. The shoulder head is 5" high and whole doll is 19½" tall.

147
circa 1880

China head doll with dark blonde molded hair: two separate clusters of curls onto forehead; molded, painted black band with bow across top, showing again at back; wavy hair above band and curls below. Ears are half exposed; smooth adult shoulders, average length neck. The style is the same as shown on page 146 (at top), but doll differs in size and color; the color used for this blonde lady could be described as butterscotch — unusual, attractive and shows off the molded detail; the eyebrows are dark tan and the painted eyes, grey-blue. Old cloth body, machine-stitched leather arms; entire doll is 20¾" tall.

Shown in color photograph (4), page 138.

circa 1880

China child with black painted, molded hair; highly detailed; three separate ringlets onto forehead and tousled ringlets over entire head. Childlike shoulders and short neck. Detail of hair molding more evident in this large head. Painted blue eyes and expected red-orange and black lines of features. On cloth body. Impressed on back shoulder: *1008 11* Shoulder head is 6¼" and the overall height is 25½".

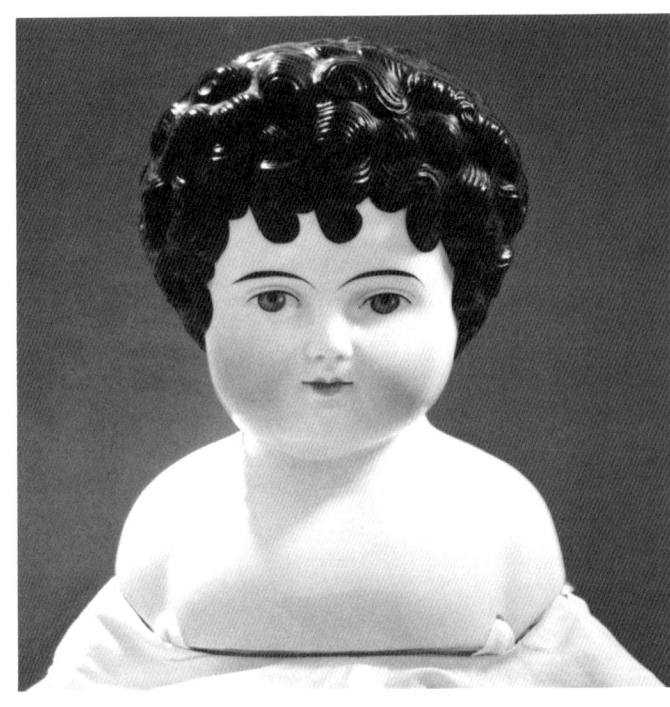

Shown in color photograph (5), page 138.

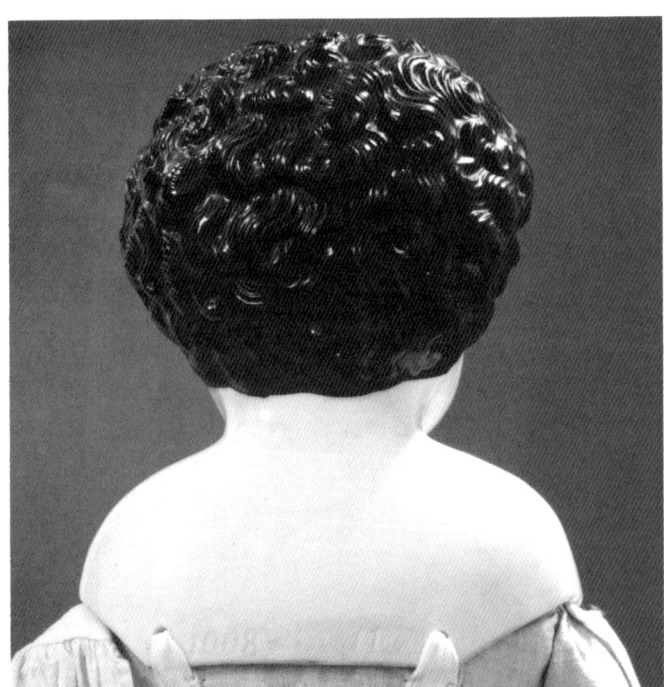

circa 1880

China child with molded, painted black hair; styled short and wavy, separated at forehead into curls, and waved down to semi-exposed ears. Blue eyes; black outline to eye and irises; red-orange line work, cheeks and mouth. Short neck, chubby curved shoulders; the young child look. Replacement cloth body with china arms and legs. Impressed on back shoulder *1046*. The shoulder head is 5¾" high.

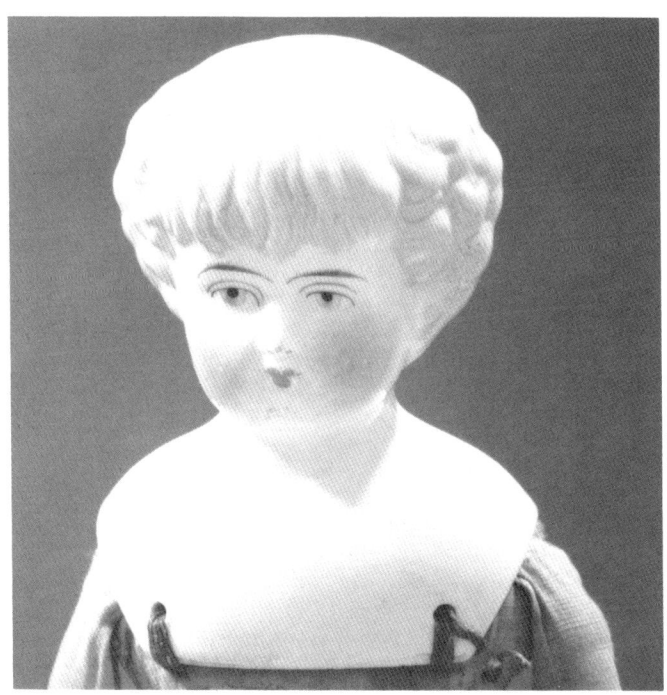

December 7, 1880 is the date of a patent registered to Charles T. Dotter of Brooklyn, New York, for a shoulder head type doll on a cloth body that featured a printed corset. The patent drawings, showing front and back views, do not indicate the shoulder heads themselves were marked; but china heads looking like the drawings are found incised with "Pat. Dec. 7/80." Also to be found are cloth bodies printed with blue or red corsets on the front only and the patent date printed across the back. Representing a lady, the products were made with black or blonde hair; though not exciting in workmanship, they are informative. For once a certainty in time, company and doll, though we don't know how long they were produced. When purchasing, exercise restraint, as these dolls are not comparable to early marked dolls and should sell for only a moderate sum.

circa 1880

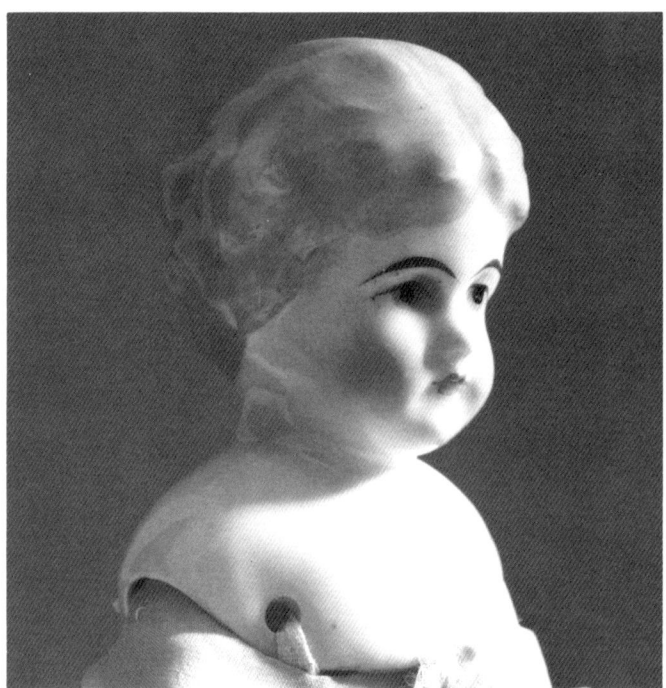

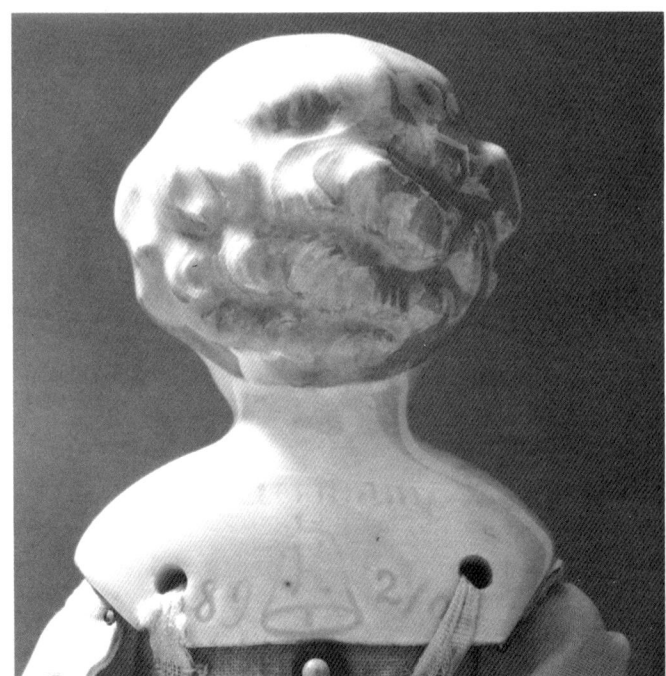

Blonde china head doll with no part and fluffy curls, and detailed modeling at back. Flesh-toned; painted blue eyes with large black pupils; heavy black eyebrows; red-orange mouth and cheeks. No eyelid lines, inner eye dots or nostril dots. Old cloth body; lower legs have made-in-one red cloth stockings and brown cloth boots; replacement china arms. Shoulder head is 2⅞" and whole doll is 10". The mark of Kling and Co., a K in a bell, is incised on shoulder at center:

Some dolls appearing to be Kling-like are found unmarked; they may be flesh- or pink-toned and colorful, or may have white complexions.

Shown in color photograph (6), page 138.

151
circa 1880

Painted with fine lines, but lacking some details. Molded, painted black hair; no center part. Doll has blue eyes, red-orange cheeks and mouth. The droopy, full cheeks give a childlike appearance. On replacement cloth body with china arms and legs. Though hair style is of earlier period, doll is placed here because of lack of facial detail; had doll been made earlier, there might have been more detail, even though doll is small. Height of shoulder head is 2⅞", overall height, 9¾".

circa 1880

A small china head doll with black bow centered at forehead amid all-over curls; bow is easy to miss. Hair is styled short enough to leave lower ears exposed. Painted blue eyes, red-orange mouth. No extra details. The shoulder head is 3¼" high.

China legs in shapes found on dolls, circa 1880.

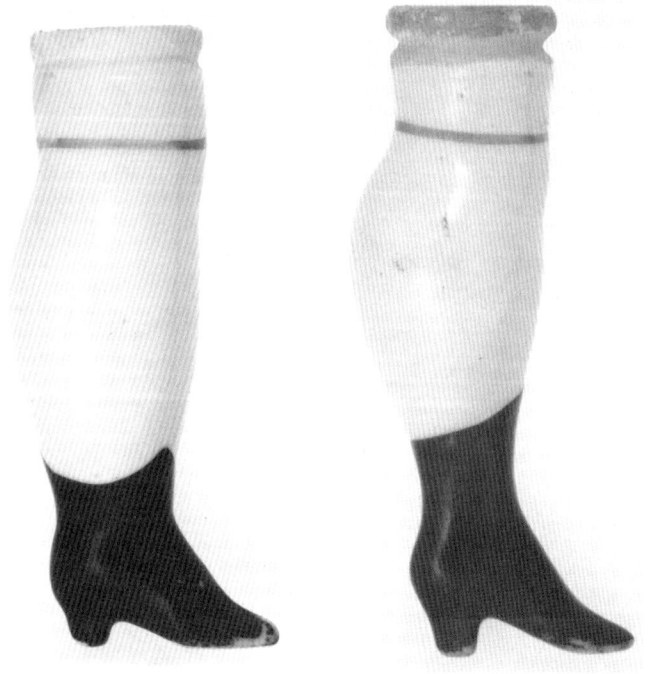 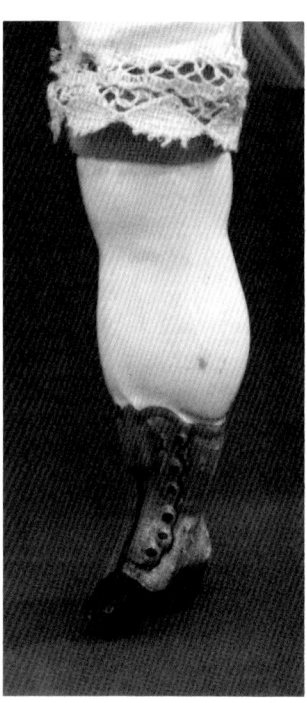 

circa 1890

Little girl china head with wind-tossed curls, all molded and painted black. A swirl of hair at center top tumbles onto forehead, forming bangs; wide, triple-layered curls cover ears; waves across back end in row of small curls at back of neck. Though bangs were popular at this time, this arrangement is not often seen. Simple painting includes only necessities: black eyebrows and eye outline, blue eyes, red-orange mouth. The shoulder head measures 3½" and may be the only size that was made; it also is known in blonde. Style is interesting; quality is lacking (note irregular sew hole placement). Incised GERMANY on back shoulder.

China legs and arms in shapes found on dolls of 1890–1900, each piece considerably shortened and bulbous.

 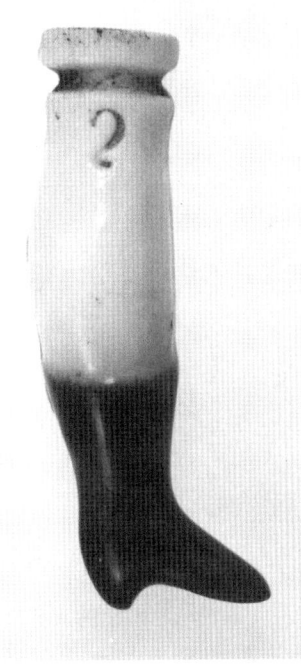 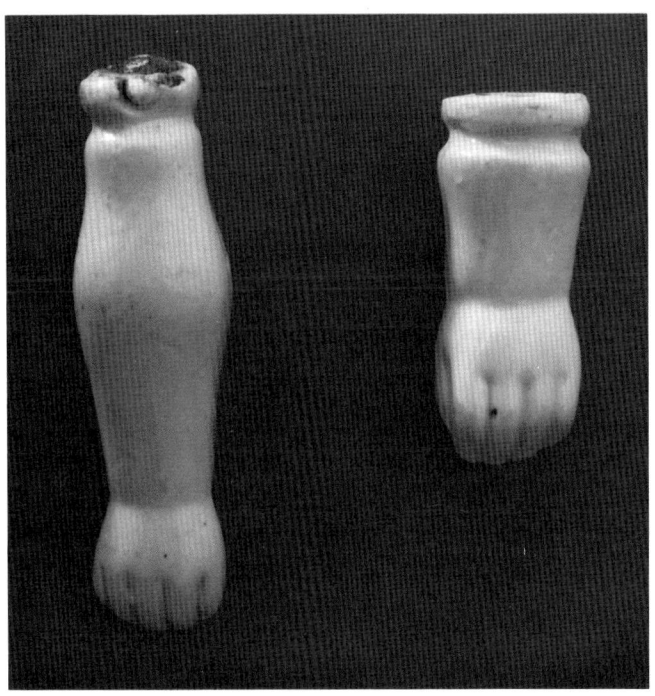

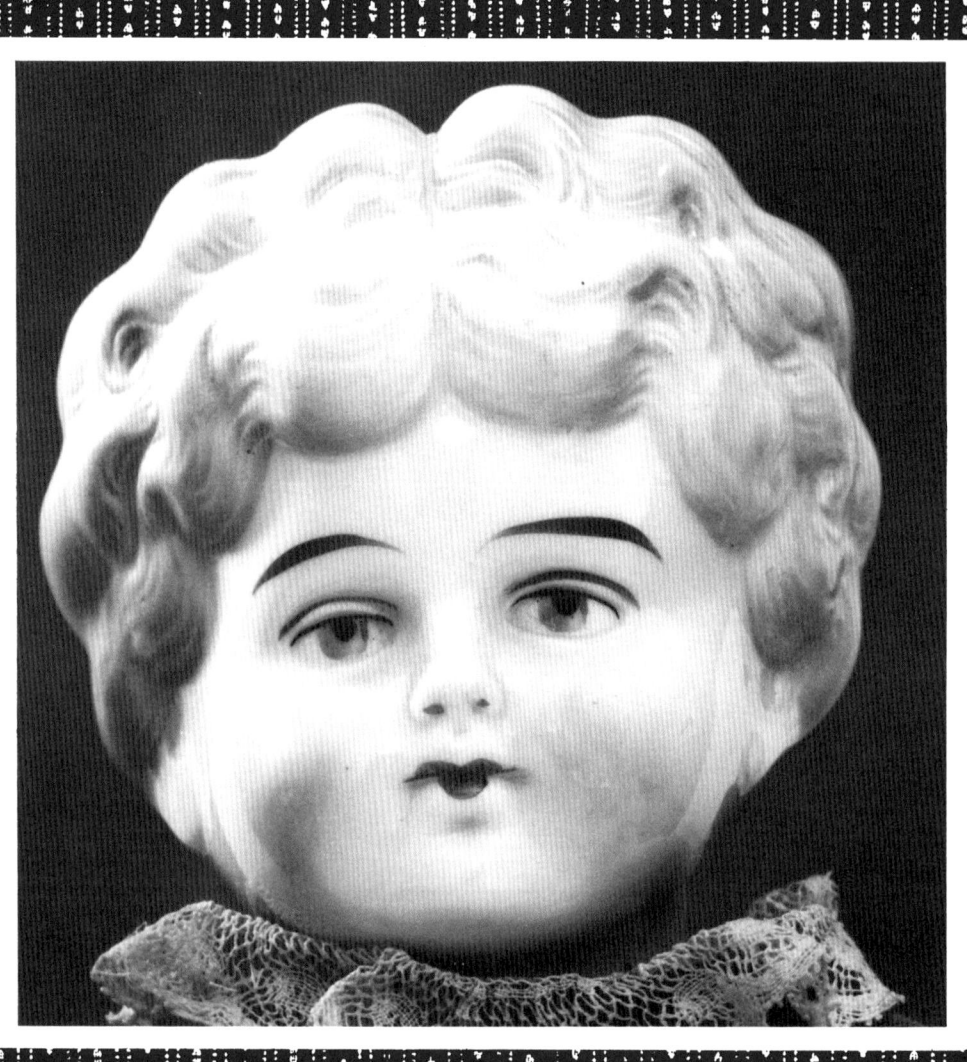

circa 1890

IN CONCLUSION

China head dolls had been in existence for fifty years. Here, they are nearing the end of their time. Waning interest of consumers had changed the focus of manufacturers, who allowed the quality of the dolls to deteriorate.

Traditional china head lady dolls were still being made, and their hair styles were modeled to suit the period. China arms and legs were reduced in length in proportion to the rest of the body, so dolls of this era appear to have very short limbs for their height. Arms and legs were now made as a right and a left; a single shape, called "universal," was made for each limb and used in pairs. Shoulders are narrower on many of these dolls. All these changes were means to keep china head dolls competitive in the marketplace.

The traditional china shoulder head also was made in several other versions: Pet Name dolls; Jeweled dolls; Educational dolls, whose bodies were printed with flags and their origin or flowers and their names; and U.S. Emblem dolls, with a fine eagle and the names of states. The Pet Name dolls had a collar and a lady's name molded on the front; the collar was touched with gold paint, and the name was painted in gold. These dolls came in various sizes with names such as Dorothy, Edith and Pauline — twelve names in all are thought to be from one company. As the hair is styled to nearly cover the forehead, dolls with this hairdo and others that are similar have acquired the unflattering name, "low-brow." Dolls of this time may or may not be incised with country of origin on back shoulder. These were still dolls meant for little girls.

China dolls made into decorative accessories for ladies — such as pincushions and tea cosies — already were being produced, often designed to look like people of the 18th century. The last photograph in this section is of that type, called "pincushion figure," and is not considered a doll.

The heyday of the china head doll as a plaything for a child was long past; by the early 1900s, chinas had nearly conceded to other dolls made for a brand new century.

The style of this molded, painted blonde lady doll was prevalent during the 1890s and into the 1900s. It was made with black or blonde hair in a range of sizes and many levels of quality, from china with a good smooth, pleasant feel to it, that was well-painted, to pitted, rough china, poorly glazed and painted. The example shown here was well-molded and has attractive coloring; the features are placed properly and painted by a skilled hand. The shoulder head may have been a replacement for a child's doll, as the old cambric body was wrapped with a strip of fabric to extend her girth so that her orange cotton dress would fit. The shoulder is undecorated and unmarked, and the total height is 19".

Note: Pattern framing photo opposite reproduced from a child's dress of the period — actual dress, of indigo-printed white cotton, shows wear.

156
circa 1890

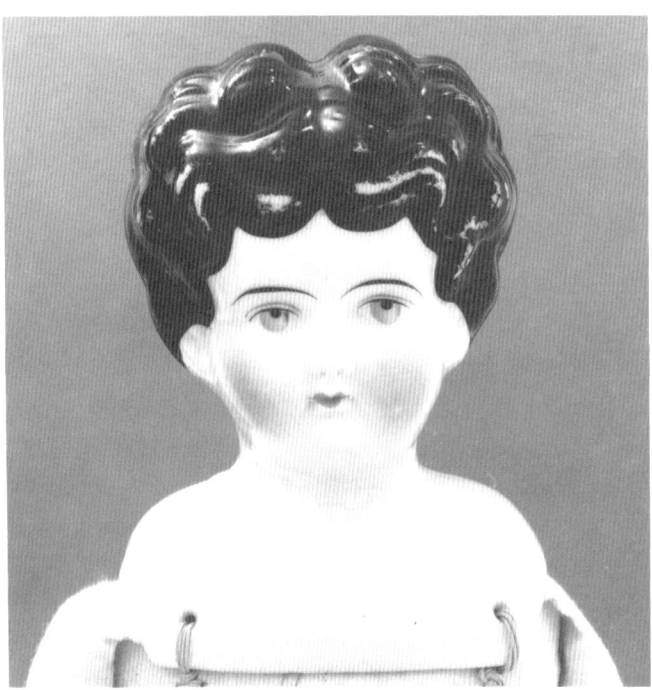

Black-haired china doll with hair style called "low-brow." There is no part in hair and forehead is nearly covered. Lower ears are exposed. Blue painted eyes, red-orange eyelid lines and nostril dots. Prominent chin and then double chin. Number *3* incised on center back shoulder; doll is 4" high.

U.S. Emblem cotton body of the type to be used appropriately with head shown here. The china arms and legs are short in proportion to the rest of the body — that is the appearance of dolls manufactured during this era. The knee bows are painted blue, the shoes, brown. The design is printed in colorful yellow, red and black. The length of this body is 10".

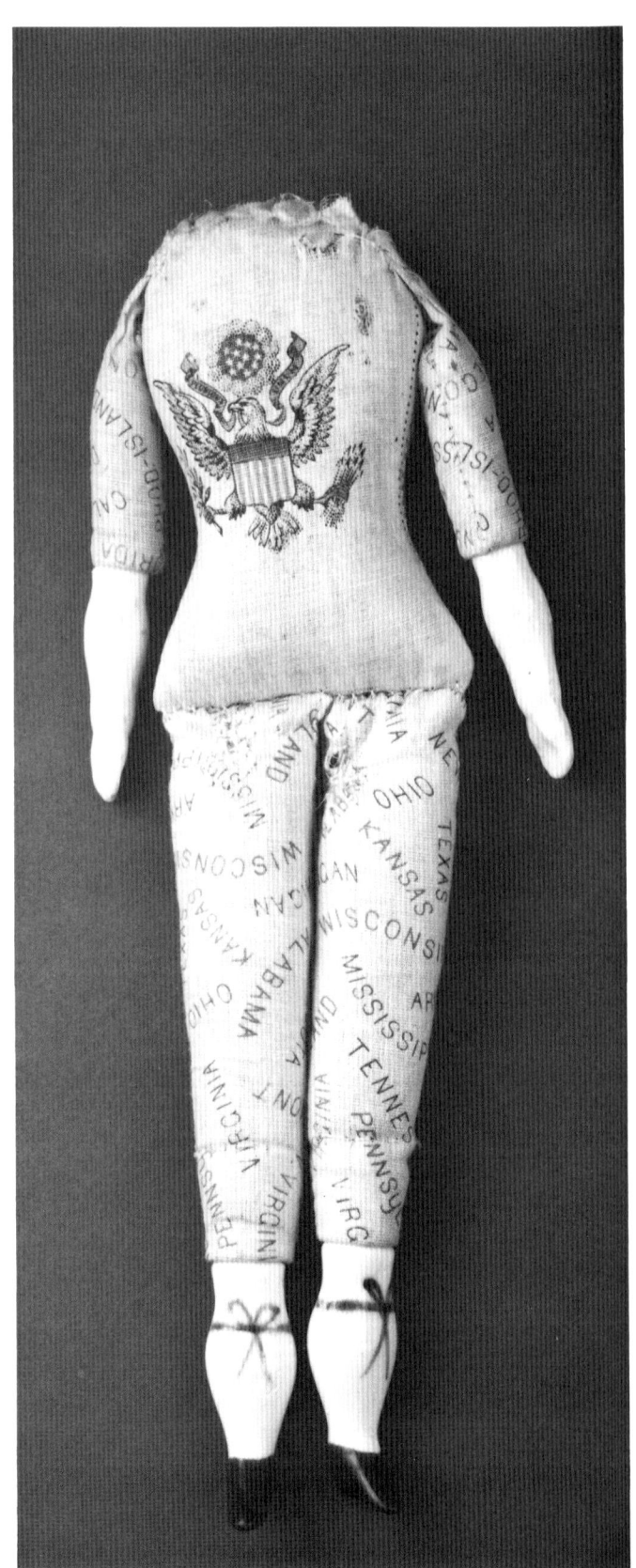

157
circa 1890

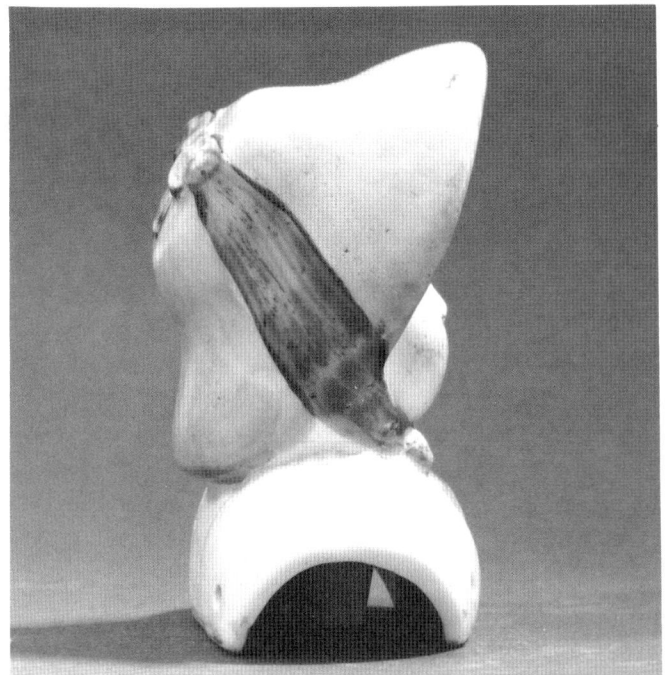

Hatted shoulder head of molded, painted china. The hat is orange; blue bow at crown ends in tie under chin; white ruffle beneath brim. Bangs are pale blonde; eyebrows are tan; eye outlines are black; other line detail of face is red-orange. This style is often seen, but it and other hatted models of this era lack the quality of earlier hatted chinas. The early ones are rare. This little girl shoulder head measures 3⅜" high.

circa 1890

In my part of the country, specifically northern California, these dolls are thought to be of Japanese origin and to date from the 1920s. In other areas, they also are thought to be from Japan, but from the 1970s. And at least one similar blonde china lady doll is known to have the word BELGIUM printed on her back in gold — that doll has a decorated shoulder and beads in her molded hair. Here, the blonde shoulder head is 3¼" high. The black-haired version's total height is 12".

The confusion over the origin of these two dolls is no more surprising than other information about china head dolls. Much of it is misinformation. Much is repeated rumor; no chicanery intended. Caring and curious people may eventually discover many facts about the doll field that now are a mystery — but only if collecting persists and collectors insist.

Decorative Accessory

This well-made china shoulder head lady is placed at the end of this era to show that it was still possible to manufacture quality chinas. Though interest in china for dolls had faded, there was interest in china (or porcelain) objects as decorative accessories for the home. The example on this page is an exception to my rule of collecting only "china-dolls-as-dolls." There is no clue to when, where or by whom this shoulder head was manufactured; no numbers, no marks, nothing incised. The hair is pale blonde, the molded bow is black; eyes are concave and irises are grey-green, as are the upper eye outlines. The lower eye rim and eyelid crease lines are pale flesh color; the mouth is a darker shade, and the cheeks, a lighter tint. Otherwise totally white; it is poured into the mold and glazed inside and out. There is a turned-under rim at all the edges of the shoulder. It was on a padded, wired armature, complete to waist only; delicate arms with slender hands and tapered fingers.

She may have been a tea cosy. Because of the shape of shoulder and bosom, I feel that she may be from around 1910. Beautifully sculpted with extremely fine detailed features, the shoulder head measures $4\frac{5}{8}$".

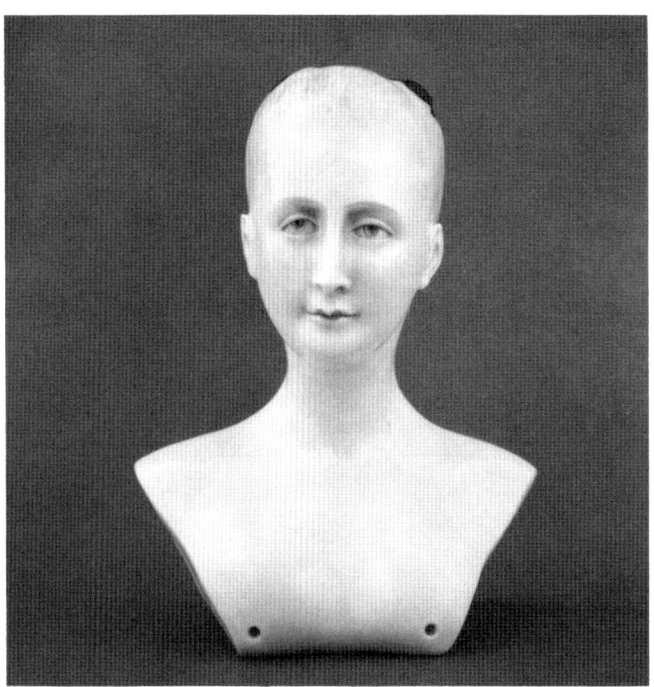

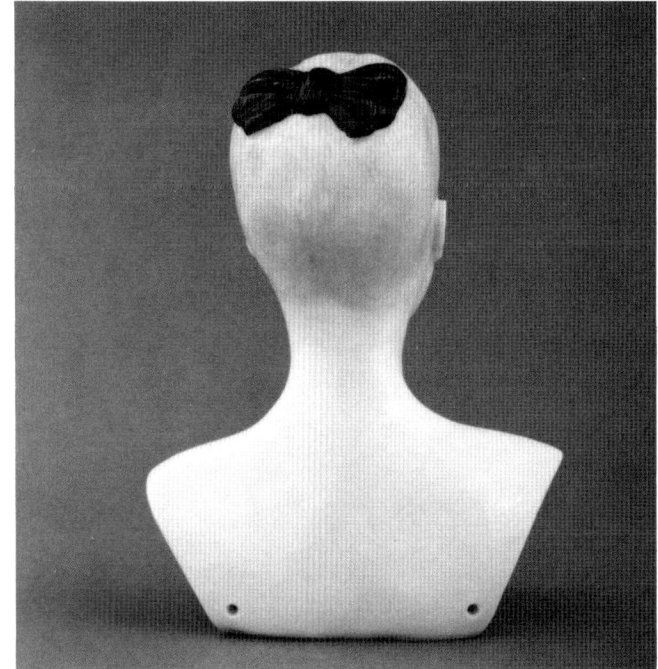

THANK YOU

Why people find themselves collecting dolls is personal to them, but reasons range from pure sentiment to pure finance, with many in-between stages. The intrigue can be sudden, swift and nearly overwhelming, but once begun may lead to unexpected benefits and pleasures. Among them can be: the mutually interested new friends around the country that you find in your search for information; the discovery that you may have untapped, unexpressed talents; the participation in activities that can keep you occupied beyond belief; and, most of all, the opening of yourself to a doll world that is eagerly trying to learn and to teach. One unexpected and extremely fortunate benefit for me has been that this is a shared interest with my husband, Ken; there are not enough words to explain how this has enriched our lives.

I cannot think of another memento from another century that could be more personal than a doll — probably selected by a grandmother, mother or close, loving friend and outfitted with hours of handwork, great care and precious fabrics, perhaps saved from the past. Then the special gift was bestowed on a child who may have loved it enough to save it for her child. Can you think of another object holding more personal expression?

Dolls, and to me that means old ones, can truly be an educational toy beyond one's original expectations. Evidence of that is this book, an endeavor that has been encouraged by a handful of caring people; I know who they are, they know who they are, and I thank all of them.